THE AGING MIND

No-one approaches aging with enthusiasm. Activities we accomplish easily in our 20s and 30s become more difficult as we grow old. But, though change is inevitable, recognising and understanding precisely what is happening to our bodies and minds allows us to continue to manage and enjoy our lives.

Patrick Rabbitt is a cognitive gerontologist who has researched physical and mental aging for over fifty years. He can therefore interpret his personal daily experiences of the aging process through a comprehensive understanding of what gerontological research has revealed about how our bodies and brains age, and how these changes affect our everyday experiences and lives.

Engagingly written, Professor Rabbitt's book is a fascinating account of why our sensory and cognitive experiences change as we get older, and what these developments mean for our overall physical and emotional wellbeing. Describing the latest research, the book covers the mental changes that affect our daily lives such as those in memory, intelligence, attention, sleep, sensory perception, anxiety, depression and perception of time passing. It also discusses how far we can keep and develop the skills we have mastered over our lifetimes. The book debunks unhelpful myths about the aging process and offers guidance on how we can age better.

This is an absorbing account of the aging process from one of the most eminent gerontologists working today. Its warmth and candour make it an engaging and helpful guide for those interested in understanding their own, or their relatives', aging. Its rigour and comprehensiveness make it ideal for students seeking an accessible alternative to standard textbooks on aging and for health professionals working with older people.

Patrick Rabbitt is Emeritus Professor at the University of Manchester, UK, and remains an active researcher affiliated to both the University of Oxford, UK, and the University of Western Australia, Australia. He is also Honorary Fellow of the British Psychological Society and of the British Gerontological society and a Member of the Academy of Europe.

THE AGING MIND

An owner's manual

Patrick Rabbitt

Routledge
Taylor & Francis Group

LONDON AND NEW YORK

First published 2015
by Routledge
27 Church Road, Hove, East Sussex BN3 2FA

and by Routledge
711 Third Avenue, New York, NY 10017

Routledge is an imprint of the Taylor & Francis Group, an informa business

British Library Cataloguing in Publication Data
A catalogue record for this book is available from the British Library

Library of Congress Cataloging in Publication Data
Rabbitt, Patrick.
The aging mind : an owner's manual / Patrick Rabbitt. – 1st
Edition.
pages cm
1. Cognition–Age factors. 2. Ability, Influence of age on. 3.
Developmental psychology. I. Title.
BF724.55.C63R33 2015
155.67'13–dc23
2014024363

ISBN: 978-1-138-81237-6 (hbk)
ISBN: 978-1-138-81238-3 (pbk)
ISBN: 978-1-315-74344-8 (ebk)

Typeset in Bembo
by Swales & Willis Ltd, Exeter, Devon, UK

To Dorothy, for everything

CONTENTS

ACKNOWLEDGEMENTS

Much of the work described in this book depended on data provided by 6506 delightful, warm-hearted and generous citizens of Newcastle-upon-Tyne and Greater Manchester who, for 20 years, not only put up with our boring experiments but tried to cheer us up if they felt we were getting despondent. Vicki Abson, Nuala Bent, Maureen Jones, Lynn McInnes and Pippa Brown managed these people and studies and, tactfully, kept me more or less on track with what was going on. More post-doctoral and research students than I can here record contributed brilliant ideas and valuable criticisms and also much happiness and support. These people continue to make notable contributions. Some, like Lynn McInnes, Elizabeth Maylor, Louise Phillips, Tim Perfect and Ian Stuart Hamilton are now senior academics and distinguished Professors and internationally known for their continued work in cognitive gerontology. Others, like Brian Stollery, Mark Forshaw and Steve Jones now make excellent contributions to other areas of psychology or, like Sal Connolly and Belinda Winder have found different, and possibly more effective, routes to increase human knowledge and well-being. All are remembered with great gratitude and affection. For tolerance and correction of my ineptitude in production of this book I am grateful to Libby Volke. My interface with Taylor and Francis has been Russell George, to whom I am grateful for several pleasant conversations, three coffees and two paninis and for useful insights into how publishing works.

Introduction

1

TALKING ABOUT OLD AGE

I began to study aging in 1969, when I was 25, and have happily carried on for the next 54 years. Since then, I have probably thought about aging every day. In Cambridge and then in Oxford I made many small experiments to find out how and why older people become slow at making simple decisions. Then, in Manchester and Newcastle my colleagues and I spent 20 years following over 6500 remarkable volunteers who, when we first saw them, were aged from 52 to 92. This taught us about how age affects people's brains, and so their minds. Now I am older than most of these kind and gallant people were when I first met them and it is amusing to recognise the changes that my colleagues and I detected in them appearing in my own everyday life and lapses. It was always thrilling when new tables of data from volunteers gave us fresh insight into how our minds and bodies change as we become old. Nowadays it is an even greater entertainment to see how these changes shape my daily experience of life and my idea of who I am and what I am capable of as I still trundle about. There is also contentment in finding that the work that my colleagues and I have done is useful, not because it shows that there are things that we can no longer do as well as we once did but because it highlights things that we can still be quite good at, and confirms that we can still learn to do better. We all know that, in general, our mental abilities change in old age in ways that we deeply resent, and so do not like to think about. This means that any account of these changes may be misinterpreted as a scary list of the diversity of dooms that will surely befall us. This is not the case. The more closely we study age changes the better we recognise how slight they are, how very gradually they progress and how they can be slowed and ameliorated and what are the best steps that we can take to cope with them.

In this respect, the message of cognitive gerontology is the same as that of all other sciences. The universe that we live in is the only one we can know. It is irrelevant whether we like it or not, and it is only by doing our best to understand just what is going on that we can hope to change bits of it enough to make the only life that we have more comfortable. What we find out is not always comforting, but there is always interest, excitement and dignity in understanding our situation as clearly as we possibly can.

Age changes are inevitable and most of them are not what we would most wish to happen. Many people seem to need to avoid thinking about the details of these changes. My profession has not allowed me to do this. This is fine by me, because I have always found aging an enthralling topic and it is now just as much fun to apply what I have learned to understand what is happening to me and so to improve my personal condition, if only slightly. I have been very lucky to find many others who share these pleasures and who are as dubious as I am about our reasons for doing so. Of these, one of the most valued was Mike Horan, Professor of Geriatric Medicine in Manchester, who continually self-deprecates by saying that he took up his line of work because he has always been fascinated by how things go wrong with bodies and minds. I share his enthusiasms, and my family and many of my colleagues have had to become patient with this. Warm relationships can only be maintained by allowing each other space to trot even unattractive hobbyhorses through the pleasant pastures of our conversations.

Among strangers, such as most readers of this book, communication must work differently. Many young people do not truly believe that they will grow old and switch talk away from this grey area to anything more congenial. Because it is likely that young readers will be undergraduates, graduate students and health professionals who need a course-book in cognitive gerontology, chapters are referenced to allow them to explore topics further for academic or professional reasons. Since they will read this book for these practical purposes, I need not apologise to them for providing more detail than they may need but I must beg pardon for how I have set this out. I have tried my best to be as accurate and comprehensive as I ought to be, but I found that I simply could not bear to write yet another textbook. So I have tried to describe not only what we know about all aspects of mental aging but how we found all this out and, more importantly, to give people a glimpse of the excitement and the everyday fun and comradeship that makes scientific research the happiest career that I can imagine. I also needed to give myself as much fun as possible while writing. Hence, the (mainly lame) jokes. I am sorry if they do not work for you but they made my task much easier.

Middle-aged people may read this book for different reasons. In their uneasy time of life, many of them desperately want to be told something encouraging: ideal news would be that theirs is the first generation of humans for whom aging and mortality have been indefinitely postponed or, at least, that they personally will be spared the particular changes that they most fear. Of course most are, quite rightly, far too savvy for such breathless optimism. My first offer to them is that I can, after all, offer some good news: the changes to come are far smaller and more gradual than they probably imagine and there are very simple ways to slow them and to reduce their effects on our lives. Although most of the changes I describe are hardly detectable in middle age, it does help, at this point in life, to have a map of the territory ahead and to plan the journey to come. Middle age is also a time of life when parents and older family and friends become an issue. To be the most help to them that we possibly can, we must try to understand what they are experiencing and, in particular, to grasp that most of their problems have many different, and some unexpected causes and consequences. Better comprehension of what is happening really does calm irritation and worry, allow more insightful and so more affectionate relationships and encourage more effective and compassionate care. I have never understood why many people mistake attempts at scientific objectivity for cold indifference. This is certainly not true of medics or of cognitive gerontologists who do care very much indeed, and want to do the best they can to help, but realise that they have no chance of being any use unless they can find out, and explain, the way things are.

The readers I feel most easy about are people in their sixties, seventies and eighties. With these people, I find conversations a joy. We do not have to worry that we don't understand each other. We do not want to talk about grand panaceas for our condition because we have long lost any belief that these exist. People of my age are sharply knowledgeable observers of their own difficulties and those of their partners and friends and do not flinch from recognising the changes that they are experiencing just because they are unwelcome. They are happy to talk about their problems in detail, but in neutral, practical terms. Since I have become old, some of the best and most illuminating conversations I have had are with my age-peers about the big and small things that happen to us and how we can best take the edge off them or put up with them by understanding them better. These chats have probably taught me more about how our minds change as we grow old than any of the laboratory experiments that I so carefully planned.

So, this book is a try at a conversation with my generation about the changes that we must all share, how and why these things happen to us and what we can do about them. I hope to show that research over the last 50 years has done something much more useful than confirm that aging is an inevitable series of disasters escalating to a bitter end. What research actually shows is that although most changes are not for the better they are much slower and less drastic than most of us imagine and fear and that, as with all our problems at any stage of life, the only effective way to cope is to understand what is happening to us as accurately as we possibly can. It is superstitious to hope that changes will not affect us if we succeed in ignoring them. It does help to recognise what these changes are, how they come about, how they affect our lives and how we can minimise their effects and even become happily amused by many of them. I shall be very content if writing this book, helps others to do this, even a little. Chapter 2 begins with an account of why aging happens to all of us or, as Oliver Hardy might have put it, how evolution got us into the fine mess that we are in.

PART I
What is Aging?

2

WHY WE AGE

We feel that our built-in obsolescence is a design flaw that unnecessarily adds to human misery. If we must die, surely our bodies and brains could continue functioning, perfectly fit and merry until everything falls apart so fast that we hardly have time to notice. What went so badly wrong?

When biologists find a feature that is almost universal to all living things their first assumption is that it must be selected by evolution because it brings survival advantages. For death by aging, this seems a tough case to argue. How can degeneration of every member of a species increase chances of survival? As individuals we are dying continuously and piecemeal. Each cell in our bodies has a limited lifespan. Some, such as the neurones in our nervous systems, have quite long lives. Most of our brain cells are dwindling survivors of those we were born with. Most of our other cells reproduce and replace themselves, but can do this only from 40 to 120 times before reliably accurate replication becomes impossible. This maximum is named "The Hayflick Limit" after Leonard Hayflick, who discovered that cell cultures were not, as had been thought, potentially immortal [1]. Copying errors of instructions to make new cells increase until fatal errors occur. The potential of chromosomes to accurately copy themselves is marked by the length and integrity of their telomeres; structures that can be thought of as "caps" that prevent them unravelling [2]. There is now a growth industry in measuring the telomere length of cells harvested from individual's bodies to estimate the extent of their cell aging and thus how much time the person may have left. I find it easier to think of unfortunate uses for this information than of its practical value for most of us.

A good effect of the Hayflick limit is that it restricts the development of genetic instabilities of individual cells that might result in cancers but, in the longer run, it limits their lives and so our own. Exceptional human bodies like that of the witty[1] and gallant French Centenarian, Marie Calman, have survived for over 11 decades.

They managed to do this by replacing themselves almost in their entirety until their self-reproductive limit was reached. Throughout all our lifetimes we are patterns in a time-stream of changing matter like eddies and ripples in brooks that seem solid but are always braids of new water.

An exception to this continual churn of death and replacement is that even in our old age most cells that make up our brains and nervous systems are still the ones that we were born with. Their numbers slowly diminish but, since we start out with many billions, with luck enough will survive to keep us active, competent and amused to the end. This is a sensible design feature. To lose and renew all of our brain cells every 10 years might seem a good way to keep a competent young brain but our nerve cells, and the connections between them, store everything that we have ever learned. Continuous substitutions would erode our memories of all we know about the world, ourselves and each other.

It matters less if the other cells in our bodies replace themselves and die because they do not have to hold all that we have ever learned. Apart from the continually diminishing viability of their components, our bodies are always liable to damage, whether from accidents or from the accumulating burdens of all the illnesses and damage that we experience. We try our best to survive in an ocean of frantically and indefatigably reproducing viruses, bacteria and microorganisms with which we continually compete. Over millions of years, we have made alliances with hundreds of families of these creatures and now could not live without these treaties. As things are, most of our body-mass is made up of cells of quite different species to our own indigenous "human" cells. These were once humble economic migrants from less affluent lifestyles to our succulent swamps of flesh and fluids. They have become assimilated citizens usefully contributing to our body-economy. Throughout our lives, viruses and bacteria continually challenge our defences and the declining efficiency of cell-replacement reduces the effectiveness with which we can resist them and repair damage. During our first years, we improve rather than wear out and for decades after this all goes pretty well, but in the long run the energy and resources to defend and repair ourselves become increasingly hard to find.

Why we could not live for ever

Staying permanently and perfectly self-replicating would not solve the death problem. Accidents would inevitably occur. Witty mathematical models, devised for practical reasons such as budgeting for the replacement of crockery and wineglasses in restaurants, accurately predict the diminishing survival chances of brittle objects in a risky world. Inevitable accidents and chance erosions mean that all objects have limited life expectancies and, even without the Hayflick limit, so would we. Exceptionally lucky individuals might survive the disaster lottery for millennia but damage will accumulate and chance will get us all in the end.

Not all for each but each for all

Unlike wineglasses, we can reproduce ourselves and our individual deaths do not end our species. Some animals have settled for a simple scheme in which the tasks of keeping their bodies alive by replacing failing cells and fabricating entire new organisms are combined. Bacteria simply split and carry on as pairs of new entities and so are, at least potentially, immortal, though they change from generation to generation. Some simple many-celled creatures do a little better. A tiny animal, called a "hydra" because it resembles a bush of serpents sprouting from a single trunk, occasionally indulges in its own dull form of sex and buds off entire new entities. A single severed hydra limb can also re-grow an entire new body. This seems a real but unexciting form of immortality. If my severed arm grows a new body and brain how far could this new entity still be the continuous trajectory of the "me" that I experience? What could it retain of the information and skills I have acquired during my separate life?[2] We do not believe that hydras have minds to worry about such things, but more complicated creatures like dogs, monkeys and us remember their lives and so have a sense of continuity of experience that each feels is uniquely its own. We might not feel that this is a more attractive form of personal immortality than we already achieve by the alternative method of deputing some of our (sex) cells to detach themselves from the rest of us so that they can get together with other people's (sex) cells to construct different independent beings. However we may now feel about this, the evolutionary dice were cast millions of years ago and we have to accept the only deal in the known universe: as individuals we each die but our species can live on, though, also, in gradually changing forms. Like individuals, species are also patterns in time, deceptively constant at brief inspection but in longer perspectives constantly changing to keep alive in the world.

Besides dutifully carrying on our species, could we not also survive as individuals as long as chance allows? Surely the indefinite survival of individuals could also be a good idea for a species because it would perpetuate valuable knowledge of how to survive in the world?

An early idea was that the indefinite survival of individuals would be counterproductive because they compete with each other for exactly the same food and other resources. This seems convincing as we watch a pullulating human population gobble the resources of the entire vast planet. Our current population explosion is driven as much by longer survival of individuals as by increasing numbers of successful births. The technologies that enable this are unique to us but, in the wild, many factors combine to cull species. As the number of individuals in a species increases, so do the numbers of its increasingly well-fed predators and the odds of epidemics of infectious diseases. Many studies of animal populations find that diminished resources and overcrowding not only increase the risk of mortality for individuals but also reduce fertility and slow down reproduction. Slowing down reproduction limits the speed with which a species can adapt to a changing environment. New and slightly modified generations are key to species survival.

Sexual reproduction combines genes from different individuals and so makes each birth a new experiment in survival. Darwin's big idea was that if altered genetic legacies (mutations) are unhelpful they lower the odds that the particular animals that carry them will live long enough to pass them forward along the species time-line. Carriers of helpful mutations are more likely to survive to breed and so make their individual novel inheritances a common legacy. Without mutations, a species would remain fixed over time. Stasis would be an option for a species perfectly adapted to an everlastingly unchanging world but no paradise is future-proof. The world changes endlessly and drastically and species that cannot meet new threats or seize new advantages are locked in ruts they may cosily inhabit for millennia but in which they will perish when dire changes inevitably occur.

This is the core of the story but there are a few twists in the plot, mainly involving sex and violence, the staple plots of the natural history films that we all enjoy so much. Tom Kirkwood, an early observer of this scenario, claims to have had, in his bath, an Archimedean moment in which he realised that mutations are most useful if they are passed on early in life because losses to predators, illnesses and accidents will ensure that, as time passes, fewer and fewer individuals survive [2]. Even in a species in which all animals could indefinitely keep their youthful resilience and capacity to find mates and reproduce, longer-lived individuals would become increasingly rare so that the young would always monopolise breeding opportunities. Mutations that increase chances of youthful survival and successful early breeding will gradually be passed on more often than those that maintain and repair older bodies. Because most animals are destined to have short lives, "live fast/die young" has become the strategy of choice in the great game of species survival.

Even if the survival odds for each individual did not steadily fall as its lifetime extends, a live fast/die young game plan would come to dominate species development. Animals not only compete for food, but also to have successful sex. Individual members of a species compete with other members of their own species to find, gain the attention of and mate with partners whose characteristics offer the best chances of survival for their resulting offspring. Especially for male animals, competition for the best mates can be very expensive in terms of energy and other survival resources [3]. High costs of sexual competition further reduce the odds of living long enough to achieve late-life mating that might allow long-surviving individuals to pass on their golden-years genes.

High costs of sex

In his "Letters to His Son" Lord Chesterfield warned against careless sex: "The pleasure is momentary, the position is ridiculous and the expense is damnable." Males of most species pay heavily for sex because they compete for female attention in diverse and strenuous ways: extreme bellowing, head-butting, prancing, chasing and biting, neck-wrestling (giraffes), ceaseless singing (songbirds), huge energy-expensive and mobility-limiting ornamental tails (peacocks, birds of paradise) and even time- and energy-consuming home-improvement with laboriously assembled collections of shiny and colourful objects (bower birds). It would not increase the odds of long-term survival of a species if, in each generation, many males killed each other leaving exhausted survivors to mate if they could. Competitive encounters between rival males are usually just strenuous enough to establish which would be the most likely to win a battle to the death if things went too far. Even non-lethal sexual competition is harrowing and things sometimes do go too far. Stags and mountain goats sometimes cripple each other permanently but, apart from the accumulating stress and damage of rutting encounters, there is also a background of accidental damage and slow biological deterioration which makes success in competitive jousts less likely and further reduces the odds of passing on genes that might promote survival in late life [4]. Strenuously competitive encounters are especially dangerous in beetles and other insects that have external parts that cannot heal after damage. This risk is avoided by craftier animals like male field crickets who, although they become skinnier and increasingly fragile as they age, continue to chirp at the same rate, just lowering the frequency so that their alluringly gruff chirring tells females that they are successful survivors and so good bets as mates. Some credentials of maturity can be humble, peaceful and thrifty of energy and resources [5].

Even when physical damage is minimal, encounters run up heavy costs. The Norwegian Government sponsors thorough surveys of their elk population and have found that as the mating season progresses, older stags become starved and exhausted with accompanying severe lowering of their sperm counts and so of their mating success. Younger stags who have been less exhaustingly rampant, noisy, and belligerent, and have occasionally paused to feed rather than maintaining weeks of famished vigilance and aggression are then in better condition to sneak in and pass on their live-fast genes [6]. Male houbara bustards, birds given to spectacularly energetic sexual displays, are an instructive case. Those young males who are particularly persistent in frantic and prolonged displays tend to lose their fertility earlier and rapidly become incapable as they age. Houbara hubris makes it more likely that the most energetic males will pass on genes for a gilded youth rather than for a golden sunset.

In the survival struggle, infancy is a dangerous time and genes that promote the survival chances of newly born animals are therefore good candidates for selection. An example is the survival struggle of wild mice. For baby mice, the greatest survival risk is cold, and only 10 per cent survive to sexual maturity. Late survival genes would be of little help to the mouse population. Because of accidents and predation, the number of survivors also falls as age increases. Even if elderly animals could be as successful at winning mating jousts and reproduced as successfully as the young, few of them are around to do this. The selection force for older survival becomes so weak that it cannot overwhelm other trends. Harmful mutations that delayed their effects until old age do not affect youthful survival and silently accumulate, un-culled. Because destructive mutations are not culled they are also very diverse, affecting all aspects of viability, from joint wear and muscle wastage that reduce physical agility to losses of immune system resistance that increase vulnerability to illnesses. This is why, in most animals, aging has come to be a falling apart of many different but interlocking systems rather than the collapse of any single critical function.

Some advantages of reproducing later in life

In the Great Species Survival Game, mating when young has risks as well as advantages. Animals just entering sexual maturity have not been rigorously tested by their worlds. A fully grown adult is a seasoned survivor and so a better bet as a carrier of desirable genes. In the natural world, the advantages of maturity over untried adolescence are perpetuated in many different ways. Slowly acquired body and muscle bulk gives dominance in seeing off rivals. Other ostentatious signals of the long survival needed to achieve them are huge antlers, tusks and teeth; staying power in sexual flaunting and noisy and prolonged mating calls; and energy-expensive accessories such as big bright tail feathers and crests. The typical pattern has come to be that the odds of successful mating increase until maturity is reached and then plateau. Continuous culling by accidents, predators and diseases gradually reduce the odds of long survival, and older animals become increasingly rare and make diminishing contributions to the next generations. Selection pressure is weaker both for very long survival genes and for very early peak genes, modifying the strategy to "live (quite) fast/die (quite) young". This is as good a recommendation for the uneasy condition of early middle age as I have been able to discover.

Advantages of married life

The high cost of sexual competition makes monogamy a desirable option even for beasts and birds. As Mrs Patrick Campbell put it: "The deep, deep peace of the marriage bed after the hurly burly of the chaise longue." A single successful competition for a mate can be followed by lifetime retirement from pre-mating frenzies. Energy no longer wasted in exhausting competitions can be spent rearing offspring. This also benefits females by sharing burdens of feeding and caring for offspring with their partners.[3] So it is unsurprising that monogamous animals tend to live longer than those that must struggle through debilitating mating seasons. The enhanced later-life mating opportunities of monogamy also results in better odds of selection for "late life enhancing genes" and encourage a live slower/die later strategy for the species [3].

Why women live longer

A different question is why male and female humans age at different rates. The longer survival of human females is not general across all animals. In some, such as chimps, macaques and toothed whales, males live longer. One explanation for longer female survival in humans has been that high-risk live fast/die young strategies are more appropriate for males whose lives are shortened by the stresses of sexual competition. In the earliest human hunter/gatherer groups, this might also have happened because male hunting is more dangerous and strenuous than female gathering. Other explanations have been related to the characteristically human phenomenon of menopause: women lose fertility many years before they age and die while men continue fertile (though gradually less so) until the ends of their lives. Menopause may have species survival advantages for humans because child-birth is risky and the end of fertility allows time and energy for successful rearing of children already born. Another suggestion has been that post-menopausal women benefit species survival by helping to rear their own grandchildren and the children of genetic relatives such as brothers, sisters and cousins. This idea has also been linked to a suggestion that, in simple societies, women of all ages, even the elderly, make a greater contribution to the group food supply than men do. Rebecca Sear and Ruth Mace [7] found that, in some South American tribes and for the Hadze in Tanzania, agriculture and gathering, which were mainly carried out by women, contributed most of the calories that a village consumed. This seems evidence for the continued value of even middle-aged and elderly women in these particular societies, but it does not resolve the question because women remain more durable even in societies such as the Inuit, where male hunting is almost the sole source of nutrition. Sear and Mace's additional analyses modify the idea that the longer survival of individual relatives is always beneficial for their extended families. They found that the death of a mother always greatly increases the risk of death for her children but, in contrast, the death of a father usually has little, and often no effect. In most of the tribes that they studied, children with older relatives were better nourished but the idea that grand-parenting is especially beneficial did not stand up across the board. Differences between children who had and who did not have living grandparents were small, only slightly greater than between children with and without fathers. Maternal grandparents seemed to help more than paternal grandparents. The presence or absence of uncles and aunts seemed not to be of much consequence, although having an outstandingly prosperous uncle was an advantage. The survival of older brothers and sisters, potential helpers in the nest, seemed an ambiguous benefit. There was some evidence for a survival advantage but there was also evidence for rivalry and so greater risk. In general, although there were advantages from family support these seemed to differ widely with the patterns of relationships found in different societies and were not as great as anthro-pologists had first thought.

It is interesting to speculate how these trends may translate to modern, urban societies but changes from the simple life have been so many, diverse, swift and unpredictable that this is still only an intellectual game. We might imagine how the increase in economic independence of women might change mating patterns. We can also think how the opportunities for dating advertisements in the digital age bring new opportunities for less florid or strenuous sexual competition and reveal changing trends in mate/age selection. Elizabeth Jagger examined lonely-hearts advertisements by people of all ages and found that these were mainly placed by older, but still fertile women and by young men [8]. This is hardly a surprise for evolutionary theory. Older women may feel that they are paced by their biological clocks and young men are not only more likely to be more attractive and potent than the limp middle-aged but also to be unattached. On the other hand, advances in geriatric medicine and the direct relationship of age to affluence in rich societies can run counter to the evolutionary push. Conspicuously affluent and powerful older men can attract desirable and fertile young women. It may also be that as direct and rapid genetic manipulation prolong repair and maintenance in late life, evolutionary pressures will be bypassed and we will eventually achieve at least the haphazard immortality of crockery and wineglasses.

This sketches the back-story as to why we have inherited the absurd condition of old age. Since it is very likely that we shall soon be able to do something radical to slow the process of biological aging, thinking about the evolutionary history of aging allows us to anticipate some consequences. It is worth stressing again that our current steep population increase is not mainly due to an explosive increase in new mouths to feed but to the growing number of us who linger on at the dinner table. For example, as this is written, octogenarians have become the most rapidly increasing age group in the UK. For the time being, we are not oppressed by immortality and a key concern is not how we can manage to live forever but how we can manage to live well, not abolishing death but greatly postponing decline. In the next chapter, we consider the time course of decline, and what are the factors that make some people change less rapidly than others.

Notes

1 When being made up to appear on television to celebrate her 111th birthday she sighed and remarked "One must suffer to be beautiful".
2 I do not know precisely what Bob Dylan was thinking of when he remarked, 50 years ago, that things that cannot be imitated perfectly must die, but the Hydra is a fine example.
3 Anyway, even permanently paired females often have it both ways. Prudish ornithologists were shocked to find how often females of many species of birds in apparently exclusive relationships actually sneak off to harvest genes from passing strangers.

References

[1] Hayflick, L. (1994). *How and Why we Age*. New York, Ballentine Books.
[2] Kirkwood, T. (1999). *The Time of our Lives: The Science of Human Ageing*. Oxford, Oxford University Press.
[3] Bondurianksy, R., Maklakov, A., Zajitschek, F. and Brooks, R. (2008). Sexual selection, sexual conflict and the evolution of ageing and life span. *Functional Ecology*, 22, 433–453.
[4] Loison, A., Festa-Bianchet, M., Gaillard, J-M., Jorgenson, J. T. and Jullien. J. M. (1999). Age-specific survival in five populations of ungulates: evidence of senescence. *Ecology*, 80, 2539–2554.
[5] Jacot, A., Scheuber, H. and Brinkhoff, M.W.G. (2007). The effect of age on a sexually selected acoustic display. *Ethology*, 113, 615–620.

[6] Mysterud, A., Solberg, E. and Yoccoz, N.G. (2005) Ageing and reproductive effort in male moose under variable levels of intrasexual competition. *Journal of Animal Ecology*, 74, 742–754.

[7] Sear, R. and Mace, R., (2008). Who keeps children alive? A review of the effects of kin on child survival. *Evolution and Human Behavior*, 10, 1–18.

[8] Jagger, E. (2005). Is thirty the new sixty? Dating, age and gender in a postmodern, consumer society. *Sociology*, 39, 89–106.

3

HOW FAST DO WE CHANGE?

Margaret, a distinguished industrial chemist and an admired aunt-in-law, survived into her nineties with formidable intelligence and wit intact. She used to say, with heavy authority, "The sixties are absolutely fine, the seventies are still OK but the eighties are not good – and I don't talk about the nineties". Her reports of her later decades capture important questions about how our mental abilities change as we age. When do changes first start? Once they begin, how fast do they continue? Do we lose some of our abilities earlier than others or do they all go together when they go? Do some of us change sooner and faster than others? How do behavioural changes in our mental abilities that we notice in our everyday lives or in laboratory tests relate to changes in our brains and central nervous systems? Finally, because we are anxious that we may not find what lies in wait for us particularly welcome, we want to know whether we can do anything about it.

Collecting evidence

It is simple, but laborious to gather data to answer these questions. We need only persuade a few thousand people in different age-decades – 11 to 20; 21 to 30; 31 to 40, 41 to 50 and so on – to complete as many different mental tasks as they will agree to do. Comparing average task-scores for successive decades tells us when most people reach their personal peaks, for how long they can keep this level, when their scores start to fall and, once changes begin, how fast these continue. The more different kinds of task that we can persuade them to do, the more their test scores can tell us whether aging affects some abilities earlier and more severely than others or whether things all go together when they go [1].

Many investigators have done this many times in many countries. Volunteers have usually been given tests of general intelligence, i.e. the speed with which they can make very easy decisions; the number of different words that they can learn and remember; how accurately they can recall events from their past lives; and how well they retain the information and skills that they have acquired and used over decades.

In Chapter 16, "General smarts", we shall discuss what it is that intelligence tests measure, how the concept of "intelligence" can be objectively defined and what particular parts of the brain support it. For the moment, we suggest only that intelligence test scores are a useful guide to life trajectories of mental change, because they reliably predict how well we are likely to perform in a very wide range of situations such as in school or university, in the armed services, the professions, business and industry. For cognitive gerontologists, intelligence tests have extra value because they seem to be more sensitive to mental changes in old age than any other behavioural tests we have yet developed, because they are sensitive predictors of the effects of age on everyday practical abilities and because their relationships to brain function, and to changes in the brain with aging, are beginning to be understood [2, 3, 4].

Intelligence test *scores* (as distinct from our levels of intelligence compared to others of the same age, which are the ratios conventionally termed our Intelligence Quotients, or IQs) steadily rise through childhood and adolescence and peak in the late teens or early twenties. They then remain constant for 5 to 10 years after which very small declines begin. The rate of decline gradually accelerates during the forties, fifties and sixties. Just as Aunt Margaret complained, change becomes faster during and after the late seventies and eighties. This pattern is not the same for all individuals or for all kinds of mental task. Some lucky people show little or no change until their late fifties or mid-sixties. Scores on tests of decision speed follow the same trajectories of change as scores on intelligence tests. In contrast, scores on simple tests of memory and learning seem to alter little, or not at all until the late sixties. A general finding is that changes begin surprisingly early, in the twenties and thirties, and first affect fast-paced tasks, especially if these are difficult. This is illustrated by findings that scores on a fast, complicated video game markedly fall even between 18 and 30 years [5].

It is hard to put a happy spin on this news, but despair would be premature. Declines in test scores are real, in the sense that they are extremely unlikely to happen by chance, but in absolute terms they are tiny. Readers of my age may be comforted by Figure 3.1, which shows data for AH4(1) intelligence test scores, free recall of 30 words and decision speeds on a letter/letter coding task for 6504 volunteers who were aged between 41 and 92 when they first joined the University of Manchester Longitudinal Study of Cognitive Ageing.

For the AH4(1) intelligence test, the average score between 49 and 59 was 33, between 60 and 69 it was 30.02, between 70 and 79 it was 26.0, and between 80 and 89 it was 21.

Changes in scores on most laboratory memory tests are even smaller and later. After a single reading of 30 words, the average number remembered by people aged from 50 to 59 was 9.1, for those aged 60 to 69 it was 9.4, for those aged 70 to 79 it was 8.4 and for those in their eighties it was 7.9. Declines on very simple

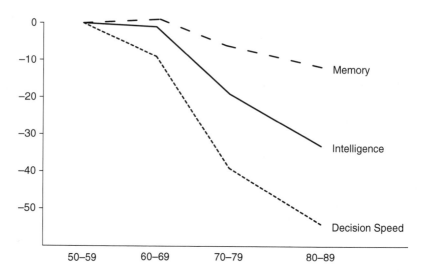

FIGURE 3.1   Percentage declines in average scores on intelligence tests, memory tests and tests of decision speed for different groups of people aged from 50 to 59, 60 to 69, 70 to 79 and 80 to 89.

tests of decision speed were much earlier and faster – nearly 60 per cent between 50 and 80+. On the simple letter/letter coding task for which we obtained these numbers, the average decision time for each item was 1.1 seconds in the fifties, 1.28 seconds in the sixties, 1.52 seconds in the seventies and 1.8 seconds in the eighties. That is, 30 years of increase in age between 55 and 85 slowed decision speed by 700 milliseconds, or 23 milliseconds per year. In general, these test data again confirm Aunt Margaret's report that until the sixties change is, at first, very slight but sharply accelerates during the seventies and eighties.

The past is another country where things were very different

We can face these numbers more comfortably if we remember that they compare individuals who were born in different historical periods and consequently, led very different lives. The youngest volunteers in Manchester and Newcastle were born in the 1940s. Compared to earlier generations, they had enjoyed much longer educations, better socio-economic circumstances, better diet and, probably most importantly, since the foundation of the UK National Health Service in 1946, free access to medical treatment and to effective guidance about how to keep healthy. In the UK, successive generations have also had increasingly less exposure to industrial toxicity. The point that they had also lived through World War II in Britain is, counter-intuitively, not a great disadvantage because the general health of the population actually seemed to improve with rationing. More people got a fair share of what food was available and diseases of surfeit such as obesity with accompanying cardiovascular problems and diabetes became less common. Older readers will be very conscious of the improvements in levels of air pollution and the decline of tobacco smoking since the mid-twentieth century. So it is an error to compare successive generations only by the calendar. Changes in our brains and bodies are the cumulative effects of internal physiological changes and of external factors. By documenting differences in individuals' lifestyles and opportunities, we can estimate what effects calendar time alone would have had if these other factors had been left out. When we do this, we find that "age" changes are much more determined by what has happened to us than by how long we have lived [6]. It is not the good years that devour us, flesh and fell and brains and all, but the sum of all the bad things that happen to us while we spin around the sun.

In the Manchester/Newcastle study, volunteers were first recruited during 1982 and 1983. The oldest of them were then aged from 60 and 90, and so had been born between 1890 and 1920 and lived through their youth and middle age in a very different and relatively impoverished world without the benefits of free life-time medical care. These older generations, who were much less advantaged in youth, also experienced faster declines in intelligence test scores as they progressed through their sixties, seventies and eighties than did those who had been born between 1930 and 1940. Over successive decades, improvements in lifestyles have increased average life expectancy in the UK by 10 to 15 years. Our rates of mental changes do not depend on how many years we have lived so much as on how long we have left. Biological age and calendar age are imperfectly related to each other. Recent convincing analyses of a well-conducted Norwegian study extend these findings. Improvements in lifetime health and survival have brought much longer preservation of mental abilities. The Manchester/Newcastle sample shows the same picture. As the 20-year survey proceeded, it became apparent that those born later were changing more slowly than their predecessors.

Geographical differences

The Newcastle/Manchester data also show that geography, as well as history, influences how long we live and so how early and how fast we begin to change. We recruited approximately equal numbers of volunteers from Greater Manchester and from Newcastle-upon-Tyne. Volunteers in these cities differed only slightly in terms of average income, socio-economic advantage, educational opportunities, general health and so also in life expectancy, but all these factors affected their scores on mental tests and the rates at which they changed as they aged. These different environments also affected men and women differently. In both cities men scored slightly higher than women on intelligence and vocabulary tests but this gap was greater in Newcastle where women of the generations we studied had less access to education than their Manchester sisters.[1] As in all other studies in the northern hemisphere, women in both cities lived longer than men. This is probably why their scores on all of our mental tests also declined more slowly as they aged. An intriguing footnote is that although men in all age groups had higher average scores on intelligence tests, women of all ages, had significantly higher scores on memory tests. This clear and persistent difference turns up in all analyses of our data. It is not due to differences in health, longevity, education or socio-economic advantage. I have not been able to think of any convincing explanation for this, but all of my female colleagues insist that it means that women have to train themselves to remember more, and more complicated things.

To fully appreciate the link between lifestyle and mortality we need only compare life expectancy in different countries shown in Table 3.1.

These huge disparities in lifespans between countries are due to differences in health related to basic resources of food, clean water, protection from violence, differences in education, incidence of disease and access to medical care. There are also marked differences even within the most prosperous nations. The USA, perhaps, overall, the most prosperous nation on Earth, is a striking example. Although for its richest inhabitants expectancies are, as are the averages in other countries, well into the mid-eighties, the overall average is dragged down by the short lives of the unfortunate to only a little above the world average at 76.8. In the UK, we find differences of 10 to 15 years between affluent and poorer London streets only 1000 yards apart. We have all noticed that people age at very different rates. It would be good for all of us if we were more aware that the main reasons for greater life expectancy and so slower cognitive aging are socio-economic advantage, quality of life and general health.

A different issue is that people who volunteer for demanding laboratory studies are, inevitably, an unusual and extremely unrepresentative minority who are atypically healthy, able and highly motivated. 60-year-old volunteers are unusually robust for their generation but 80-year-olds are extraordinary rare survivors. Because cross-sectional studies typically recruit elite octogenarians and less remarkable 60-year–olds, they greatly underestimate true rates of change [7].

Tracking individual lives

Cross-sectional comparisons between people of different ages can give only a very rough idea of when changes start and how fast they continue. They are worth

TABLE 3.1 Average life expectancies estimated in 2011.

World Average 70.5

Longest	*Average*	*Lowest*
Hong Kong, 83.4	USA, 76.8	Angola, 51.1
Japan, 82.6	China, 75.0	Botswana, 46.7
Sweden, 82.0	Bulgaria, 74.2	Congo, 48.4
Australia, 81.8	Peru, 74.2	Sierra Leone, 44.8
Belgium, 80.5	Brazil, 73.3	
Faroes, 81.9	Romania, 72.6	
Finland, 80.5	Guatemala, 70.4	
France, 81.7	India, 66.0	
Germany, 80.7		
UK, 80.8		

making because they identify factors that cause and accelerate these changes and they can even show that age affects some abilities such as intelligence, decision speed and performance on video games earlier and more severely than others such as memory for lists of words and sets of pictures [8]. To get better information we have to make longitudinal studies, during which we recruit large groups of people of different ages and repeatedly assess all of them, as often as we can, for as long as they will keep coming back.

Unfortunately, this makes the problem of volunteer self-selection far worse. Volunteers for short one-off studies are exceptional but not as extraordinary as people who sign up for many years of repeated visits, often in nasty weather, to cheerless psychological laboratories to do tasks that they do not much like. The least-able volunteers are generally also the most ill and frail and so drop out of studies earlier than others. Consequently, as any longitudinal study continues, the oldest become an increasingly elite group of exceptionally robust survivors [7]. We cannot avoid this self-selection but we can turn it into an opportunity. One way is to compute not only how people's performance changes depending both on their distance from birth and on their distance from death or from their decision that they must drop out of a study because it is becoming too taxing. When we do this, we see that people who died or withdrew from the Newcastle/Manchester study within 4 years of joining had much lower intelligence test scores when they first began than those who were destined to live for longer. When they were first assessed, people who were destined to continue with the study for 20 years were both much more able and showed far less decline over the next two decades than those who were destined to withdraw or die [9].

A different problem is that we must ask volunteers to take the same, or very similar, tests year after year. Improvements with practice may disguise declines in competence and unless we find ways to detect and measure improvement, we will underestimate true decline. Many of the first gerontologists who made longitudinal studies recognised that this was likely, but did not have the necessary statistical techniques to correct for practice and to compute true rates of change [10, 11, 12]. At first, like them, we tried to reassure ourselves that although volunteers might improve with practice, the tests that we gave them were so very simple that their gains could only be very small: we expected that even on their first attempts they would score as high as they would later in practice. They proved us wrong. A blatant example was that those who were particularly irritated by failures to correctly define some of the rarest words that they encountered in our tests looked them up in dictionaries when they got home, began to take pride in using them and scored better next time. Worse, those who were most likely to do this sneaky thing were usually proudest of their vocabularies, perhaps because they had longer educations and higher intelligence test scores. If we had not detected their dodge we might have embarrassed ourselves by a dramatic claim that people's vocabularies actually grow as they age and that those with higher scores in intelligence tests improve more than others.

Our early results made it obvious that volunteers did indeed improve with practice, even on tasks that are so simple that there is little room for improvement, and even when intervals between their successive experiences of these tasks were as long as 4 years. I was at a loss as to how to cope with this until excellent statistical collaborators, Peter Diggle in Lancaster and Mary Lunn in Oxford, wrangled ways to measure practice effects. Peter confirmed that practice gains are actually quite substantial [13]. Even more striking evidence for their reality, size and persistence was that even volunteers in their seventies and eighties who had missed an appointment for re-testing and so had a gap of 8 years before they took it again, nevertheless improved [14]. I think this is a good reason to take pride in our species because it makes the point that even very elderly people learn new tasks during a first, 10-minute trial on them, and can also retain this new expertise for nearly a decade without further practice. For cognitive gerontologists, this is an uncomfortable illustration that unless we take practice effects into account we do not properly track how the effects of biology, health, education and socio-economic factors determine the rates at which we change as we age.

Time from our beginning and from our end

We need to know how much of the mental declines that we can measure with behavioural tasks is due to the burden of pathologies and damage that accumulates over a lifetime and eventually causes death. If we track individuals over decades, we find that those who are destined to leave a study because they die or to stop

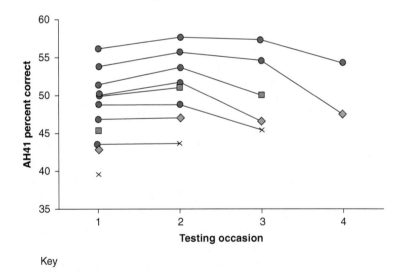

FIGURE 3.2   Death and drop-out data during the Manchester/Newcastle longitudinal study.

coming to test sessions begin to show marked declines 4 to 8 years before they become unavailable. This is not surprising because pathologies take their toll on the brain whether or not they eventually kill us. Figure 3.2 is based on analyses by Mary Lunn and her student David Wong comparing changes in intelligence test scores in individuals who survived until after the end of the 20-year University of Manchester study with those who Died (D), Withdrew and then later Died (WD) and Withdrew (W) but survived beyond the end of the study [6]. Initial scores are particularly low, and declines become steeper as death or withdrawal approach.[2]

Those excellent and robust volunteers who continued with the study until 2004 had not only scored relatively higher when they first entered the study but also showed only very slight losses over periods of between 11 and 20 years.

Mary Lunn and Ghasen Yardefagar [15] extended this analysis to test whether the rates of decline that people experience before they die vary with the particular pathologies that eventually kill them. Rates of decline before death are especially marked in people who are destined to die from cardiovascular diseases, especially if they are unlucky enough to have diabetes. Losses preceding death from infections are even larger and faster and, as we might expect, are especially big and fast for those who develop dementias before they die.

A different way to ask this question is to estimate the amounts by which different pathologies can account for the differences we find between people of different ages. If we give any mental task to all of a large group of people, we find that the differences between them are very large indeed. The total range of differences in scores between individuals (variance *between* individuals) is due to all of the multitudes of different factors that affect their performance. Unknown proportions of these differences will be due to genetics, education and lifestyle during their long lifetimes or to other factors that we may have no way to quantify. Another proportion of the differences between individuals will be associated with differences in their ages and another with differences in their health. How can we discover what proportion of age-related increase in variance between individuals is due to the effects of particular illnesses? A neat method developed by Ulman Lindenberger and Ulrich Potter [16] helps us to do this.

We first use regression equations to estimate that particular proportion of the total differences in, say, intelligence test scores *between* individuals that is associated with differences in their ages. We then do some more arithmetic to estimate what proportion of this specifically *Age-Related Variance* is associated with the presence or absence of particular pathologies.

Figure 3.3 illustrates the general idea.

For those who would like to know exactly how this works, the computational method is given at the end of the Lindenberger and Potter paper [16].

For the Manchester/Newcastle volunteers, 63 per cent of the age-related variance in intelligence test scores between people was accounted for by the presence or absence of heart disease and 61 per cent by diabetes. A more dramatic way to put this is that two-thirds of the differences in intelligence test scores that are apparently associated with differences in people's ages can be explained by whether or not

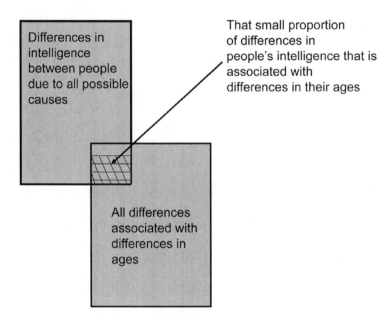

FIGURE 3.3 The diagram shows that nearly all of the considerable differences in intelligence between people (top left rectangle) are due to factors other than age. Of all the considerable differences between people that are associated with differences in their ages (bottom right rectangle) only a small proportion affect their intelligence (shaded area). Compared to all the other things that bring about differences in intelligence between people, differences in their ages has a remarkably small effect.

they suffer from one or both of two pathologies that become increasingly common in a population as it grows older.

These connections also appear in reverse. Volunteers who had relatively high intelligence test scores when they joined our study were more likely to subsequently remain healthy, live longer and so experience smaller and slower mental changes. Ian Deary and his colleagues have recently published evidence that individuals in a large Scottish sample who had higher intelligence test scores when they were first tested in the late 1940s had, 60 years later, lost less cortical brain volume than less-gifted members of their age groups [6]. A sufficient explanation is that those with higher intelligence test scores also tend to be more affluent, better educated and probably also knowledgeable enough to pay appropriate attention to their health and to seek and get medical treatment when they needed it. So, to the irritation of some elderly colleagues who greatly pride themselves on the sharpness of their wits, we cannot yet claim evidence that higher intelligence, by itself, prolongs life and delays mental decline. Being born intelligent can indeed buy us longer lives but it is likely that this is because it promotes access to education, and so greater affluence, access to medical care, wiser self-management and so better lifetime health and, consequently, slower loss of brain volume and mental capacity in old age.

Studies of thriving in infancy illustrate how complex these webs of associations are. Heavier babies thrive and grow up to become bright, relatively well-educated, and relatively well-to-do adults; and because they have led more comfortable and healthy lives, they also tend to live longer [17]. The explanation seems to be that relatively well-off parents not only tend to have fine, plump, thriving babies, but also secure for them advantages of diet, health, education and relatively good health in childhood and adolescence and so forward throughout their lives.

Clever genes and long life genes

It cannot be too strongly stressed that the clear associations between prosperity, intelligence and survival neither support nor deny other explanations such as that particular genetic factors that promote higher intelligence ("clever bloodlines") may also promote a generally more robust and efficient physiology, a better immune system and so resistance to diseases and slower decline during a longer life. It is also crucial to note that these demographic associations are not evidence that genetic differences are linked to "racial" characteristics, such as darker or lighter skin, blond, red, brown or black hair or an "oriental" epicanthal fold or proof that "master races" inevitably "rise to the top". Discussions of the scarce data that we have are made more difficult by strangely strenuous efforts by determined individuals to find evidence for racial differences in mental skills and even for personality traits. I find their evidence weak, their motivation suspicious and their insistence offensive.

It is a very different question whether, and to what extent, our genetic inheritance determines our lifespans and so also affects how long we can keep our mental abilities in old age. Unfortunate children who are born with progeria, a genetically-heritable condition, begin to show all the familiar signs of biological aging, including loss of brain tissue and consequent declines in mental ability in their teens, and live very short lives [18]. This extremely rare condition is not evidence that the rates at which the rest of us age are absolutely determined by our genes. It is quite possible that there may also be "long life" genes that increase the odds of living to a greater and also intellectually more vibrant age. It has been very hard to test this because any inherited biological advantage such as a better immune system will lead to healthy and longer life and so will help to preserve the integrity of our brains and allow us to keep our wits for longer.

It is frustrating that our analyses seldom give us complete explanations and definitive answers. This is because of the paradox that the driving force of any science is the accuracy and clarity with which we recognise what we do not know rather than the fuss we make by trumpeting illusory final solutions. Good science is smart ignorance. Correlations between the complex factors that are available for study are nearly always clues to directions for further investigation rather than definitive answers. A useful way to acknowledge this is to refer to variables such as birthweight, intelligence, health, longevity and socio-economic advantage as "markers" rather than "causes" for each other's presence or absence. This simple semantic hygiene quells the exciting bluster of wild claims to attract media attention. More importantly, it helps to keep our minds open to how complicated relationships can be, and to improve our chances of pursuing the ever-retreating target of Getting Things More Nearly Right.

Does it all go together when it goes?

A different question is whether all our mental abilities change at the same rates and by the same amounts or whether some abilities change earlier and faster than others. One problem has been that scores on tests of different mental abilities are different kinds of measurement. It is not sensible directly to compare milliseconds of slowing of reaction time with percentages of errors on particular memory tasks or with falls in points of intelligence test scores.

Because of this, psychologists have asked a rather different question: whether age has different patterns of effects across abilities in different individuals. For example, whether, in some individuals, age affects memory earlier and, possibly, proportionally more than it affects decision speed, while in others it affects decision speed proportionally more than it affects memory. To do this, investigators have tested whether the strengths of correlations between scores on different kinds of mental task are the same or different in older and in younger groups.

Computing correlations between scores on different tests taken at different ages does not tell us whether, for example, changes in intelligence are in some absolute sense, bigger or smaller than changes in memory or decision speed. It can tell us whether or not age has different patterns of effects on mental abilities in different people. If we find that correlations between scores on memory and intelligence tests within members of a group become weaker as they all age together, we suspect that this means that although age impairs everybody's memory and decision speed, for some people it affects memory more than intelligence and for others intelligence more than memory. If correlations between people's scores on different kinds of test do not change as they all grow older together, we can argue that this must be because age has the same pattern of effect on all mental abilities.

Many investigators have checked this and they have always found that correlations between scores on different kinds of task are stronger in older than in younger groups. Some of us have taken this as evidence that the effects of brain aging do not differentiate between different mental abilities. Rather, to use an ugly term that I hope is now becoming obsolete, they concluded that age "de-differentiates" abilities in the sense that the older we get, the more strongly scores on tests of any one ability predict scores on all others. One view is that this is just what we would expect if some single master factor, such as information processing speed, that we know to be very sensitive to increasing age, supports performance on all other abilities so that, as age progresses, decline in this "master" ability causes proportional changes in all the rest.

This is a bad idea because it confuses two different kinds of variability in performance across abilities. It is based on data from correlations between individuals in groups of people of different average ages. That is, the correlations tell us about *variability between individuals* and so do not answer the more interesting question as to how age may alter the relationships between scores on different mental tests for each different person (*variability within individuals*). For this we need longitudinal data and advanced statistical methods. I happened to have the data and Paolo Ghisletta, working at the University of Geneva, has the necessary brainpower and mathematical expertise. Paolo showed that variations across abilities between and within individuals can be separately estimated and that their changes could be tracked as they age [17]. Nearly two-thirds of the variance in individual differences in cognitive decline are shared across tests of memory, decision speed and intelligence. This is just what those who argue for a single common cause for declines in all mental abilities would expect. This only partly addresses a second and equally interesting question: does decline within any *particular person* tend to occur simultaneously across different cognitive abilities? Paolo concludes that, on the whole, information processing speed, memory and intelligence tend to decline in step with each other and that this is what we might expect since all abilities are affected by losses of efficiency in the entire brain brought about by cell death, losses of connections between neurones and changes in levels of neurotransmitters such as dopamine. Paolo also points out that "the present results leave considerable room for domain-specific mechanisms, accounting for the remaining 34% of non-shared variance in change" (see also [19] and [21]). That is, we do not want to promote the perspective that all variance in change is shared across a wide variety of cognitive domains. Up to one-third of the variability in these particular abilities may be independent of variability in the others. Put differently, decline in any single cognitive task does not inevitably imply decline in all other tasks. Whatever may be the mechanisms that drive average senescent changes, these are not exclusively general. This perspective is coherent with recent findings [21] that while two-fifths of change in cognitive performance appears global, one-third is domain-specific and about three-tenths are task-specific.

For elderly people who may worry about changes in their mental abilities, Paolo's analysis of the Manchester and Newcastle data offers some comfort because it means that fading of one particular talent, such as memory, is not a reason to panic that all the others must also be in equal decline. In the estuary slang of my adolescence, realising that we are losing one or two of our marbles does slightly increase the probability that we are also losing others, but this is not necessarily the case. There are slightly better odds, (i.e. two to one) that our marbles can go missing one at a time.

Some other results from the Manchester volunteers also illustrate this. Mary Lunn and Kate Hunter tracked through volunteers' test scores over the years and found that over 11 years about 55 out of 700 (13 per cent) had experienced quite severe declines in memory but only normal changes in intelligence and information speed. We took MRI scans and found that this 13 per cent had lost more tissue from their hippocampus than others of the same age. The hippocampus is an area of the brain that is well known to be essential for memory function. We have not yet published these results but, more recently, other much better studies have found some older people who have suffered more marked loss of tissue in the hippocampus than in other brain areas and who, as we might expect, showed marked declines in scores on memory tests that contrasted with relatively well-preserved performance on other mental tasks.

These findings emphasise a key point that we must always keep in mind when we are shown graphs such as Figure 3.1 that plot alarmingly remorseless declines in average levels of abilities with increasing age. Differences between individuals are very great indeed. Some change rather a lot and others hardly at all. To properly interpret these trends, we must not think of them as illustrations of the amounts and the speed of changes that apply to each and every one of us, but rather as illustrations of increases in the odds that changes will occur.

For a witty, complete and exact discussion of how the same argument must work for tables of mortality or for incidence of illnesses like cancer, heart disease or diabetes please read Michael Blastland and David Spiegelhalter's fine book, *Norm* [22]. They point out that when we discuss the effects on our longevity of bad health habits such as overeating or taking no exercise or good health habits such as drinking one (but alas no more) glass of wine a day we are not inexorably speeding up or delaying our decline but only very slightly increasing the adverse odds within a specified period. So a glass of wine a day may reduce your chances of survival by one micromort, (an increase of 1/1000 in your risk of death) while diabetes and cardiovascular problems can lose you many centi-morts (1/100) and decimorts (1/10) until you score a full mort (End Game).

It seems courteous to readers of my age to end a slightly dispiriting chapter with a micro-morsel of encouragement. As we grow old, the odds that we will suffer some losses in mental abilities do increase, but this does not completely determine our fate. We can re-adjust the odds by taking steps to keep healthy, mentally active, and so survive and preserve our abilities for longer. Similarly, it is true that an objectively detectable (rather than merely an imagined) drop in some particular mental ability, such as memory or decision speed does increase the odds that other abilities may also have become fragile but, using Paolo Ghisletta's numbers as an approximate guide, the odds of this seem to be only two out of three. Not yet cause for alarm and glum introspection, but perhaps a timely nudge to consult expert medical help in examining our lifestyles.

Notes

1 Many other studies have found that women, in general, have larger vocabularies than men of the same age. That this typical difference was reversed in the elderly Newcastle and Manchester volunteers is most probably also due to the reduced opportunities for women for access to the garrulous professions.

2 My colleagues and I used to joke that carrying on being a volunteer in the Newcastle/ Manchester Study added six healthy years to volunteers' lives. I am happy to report that, so far, this has worked for all of us as well as for the splendid volunteers.

References

[1] Rabbitt, P. (1993). Does it all go together when it goes? The nineteenth Bartlett Memorial Lecture. *Quarterly Journal of Experimental Psychology*, 46, 385–434.

[2] Duncan, J. (2010). *How Intelligence Happens*. New Haven and London, Yale University Press.

[3] Roca, M., Parr, A., Thompson, R., Woolgar, A., Torralkva, T., Antoun, A., Manes, F. and Duncan, J. (2009). Executive function and fluid intelligence after frontal lobe lesions. *Brain*, 133, 234–247.

[4] Rabbitt, P., Mogapi, O., Scott, M., Thacker, N., Lowe, C., Horan, M., Pendleton, N., Jackson, A. and Lunn, D. (2007). Effects of global atrophy, white matter lesions, and cerebral blood flow on age-related changes in speed, memory, intelligence, vocabulary, and frontal function. *Neuropsychology*, 21, 684–695.

[5] Rabbitt, P., Banerji, N. and Szymanski, A. (1989). Space fortress as an IQ test? Predictions of learning and of practised performance in a complex interactive video-game. *Acta Psychologica*, 71, 243–257.

[6] Hogan, M. J., Staff, R. T., Bunting, B. P., Murray, A. D., Ahearn, T. S., Deary, I. J. and Whalley, L. J. (2011). Cerebellar brain volume accounts for variance in cognitive performance in older adults. *Cortex*, 47(4), 441–450.

[7] Rabbitt, P., Lunn , M. and Wong, D. (2006). Understanding terminal decline in cognition and risk of death: Methodological and theoretical implications of practice and dropout effects. *European Psychologist*, 11, 164–171.

[8] Lachman, R., Lachman, J. L. and Taylor, D. W. (1982). Reallocation of mental resources over the productive lifespan: Assumptions and task analyses. In F. I. M. Craik and S. Trehub (Eds), *Aging and the Cognitive Process*. New York, Plenum Press.

[9] Rabbitt, P., Lunn, M. and Wong, D. (2005). Neglect of dropout underestimates effects of death in longitudinal studies. *Journals of Gerontology, B*, 60, 106–109.

[10] Baltes, P. B. (1968). Longitudinal and cross-sectional sequences in the study of age and generation effects. *Human Development*, 11, 145–171.

[11] Baltes, P. B. and Neselrode, J. (1970). Multivariate longitudinal and cross-sectional sequences for analysing ontogenetic and generational change: A methodological note. *Developmental Psychology*, 2, 163–168.

[12] Baltes, P. B., Cornelius, S. W. and Nesselrode, J. R. (1979). Cohort effects in developmental psychology. In J. R. Nesselrode and P. B. Baltes (Eds), *Longitudinal Research in the Study of Behaviour and Development*. New York, Academic Press.

[13] Rabbitt, P., Diggle, P., Holland, P. and McInnes, L. (2004). Practice and drop-out effects during a 17 year longitudinal study of cognitive ageing. *Journals of Gerontology, B*, 9, 84–97.

[14] Rabbitt, P., Lunn, M., Ibrahim, S. and McInnes, L. (2009). Further analyses of the effects of practice, dropout, sex, socio-economic advantage, and recruitment cohort differences during the University of Manchester longitudinal study of cognitive change in old age. *The Quarterly Journal of Experimental Psychology*, 62, 1859–1872.

[15] Rabbitt, P., Lunn, M. and Yardefagar, G. (2011). Terminal pathologies affect rates of decline to different extents and age accelerates the effects of terminal pathology on cognitive decline. *The Journals of Gerontology, B*, 66B, 325–334.

[16] Lindenberger, U. and Potter, U. (1998). The complex nature of unique and shared effects in hierarchical linear regression: Implications for developmental psychology. *Psychological Methods*, 3, 218–230.

[17] Sorensen, H. T. (1997). Birth-weight and cognition: A historical cohort study. *British Medical Journal*, 315, 401–403.

[18] Ghisletta, P., Rabbitt, P., Lunn, M. and Lindenberger, U. (2012). Two thirds of the age-based changes in fluid and crystallised intelligence, perceptual speed and memory in adulthood are shared. *Intelligence*, 40, 260–268.

[19] Anstey, K., Hofer, S. and Luszcz, M. (2003). Cross-sectional and longitudinal patterns of dedifferentiation in late-life cognitive and sensory function: The effects of age, ability, attrition, and occasion of measurement. *Journal of Experimental Psychology: General*, 132(3), 470–487.

[20] Merideth, M. A., Gordon, L. B., Clauss, S., Sachdev, V., Smith, A. C., Perry, M. B., Brewer, C. C., Zalewski, C., Kim, H. J., Solomon, B., Brooks, B. P., Gerber, L. H., Turner, M. L., Domingo, D. L., Hart, T. C., Graf, J., Reynolds, J. C., Gropman, A., Yanovski, J. A., Gerhard-Herman, M., Collins, F. S., Nabel, E. G., Cannon, R. O. 3rd, Gahl, W. A. and Introne, W. J. (2008). Phenotype and course of Hutchinson–Gilford progeria syndrome. *New England Journal of Medicine*, 358(6), 592–604.

[21] Tucker-Drob, E. M. (2011). Global and domain-specific changes in cognition throughout adulthood. *Developmental Psychology*, 47, 331–343.

[22] Blastland, M. and Spiegelhalter, D. (2013). *The Norm Chronicles: Stories and numbers about danger*. London, Profile Books.

4

HOW WELL DO WE UNDERSTAND WHAT IS HAPPENING TO US?

During the Newcastle/Manchester longitudinal study, we hoped to test several thousand elderly people many times over 5 years. We could not hope to get resources to assess them individually and so had to find pencil and paper tests of vocabulary, intelligence, memory, learning and decision speed that we could give to groups of ten or more people at once. We piloted these tests on volunteers in Oxford, a city teeming with greying academics who are all eager to confirm that they are aging exceptionally elegantly and slowly (of course, they are all quite right). Their enthusiasm was welcome and heartening but we were embarrassed that they found the tests more boring than they had hoped and were irritated by their simplicity. This was made clear while I was a timid dinner guest at All Souls College. An extremely distinguished Fellow who, unknown to me, had come to our lab to be tested out of curiosity, publicly harangued me for the childish banality of our tests, explained how I had wasted his and my time and told me that if I wanted to learn something useful about mental aging I should just ask insightful people like himself to discuss their experiences. If I had been less flustered we might both have learned something from an uncomfortable encounter. (Keeping our promise of absolute anonymity for all of our volunteers, I have never checked his intelligence test scores, but I am sure that they were, and still are, remarkable).

He had an excellent point. Humans have been thinking insightfully about their own and each other's aging for thousands of years. Conversations about personal experiences would have been a rich source of information and were just what all our volunteers wanted. They could certainly have told us more, and very different things about themselves than any of our simple tests could discover. If I had the talent to edit their anecdotes I might have produced a successor to *The View in Winter*, the remarkable book in which Ronald Blyth explored the lives of fascinating and articulate older people [1]. Since all these clever people were experts on their own aging, why could we not simply ask them to tell us about it?

Thirty years later I still think that it is a great pity that we could not organise at least some discussions and record volunteers' personal experiences of growing old. We were funded only to study how mental abilities change with age and how these changes relate to aging of the brain. A second reason was that we could not match the brilliant insights of the many novelists, biographers and philosophers who have written on old age. A third was the obstinate suspicion of an experimental psychologist that growing old may not only affect our mental abilities but also how accurately we can recognise these changes. This, at least, was a problem for which even simple questionnaires could be useful.

Asking people about their everyday competence

We used three questionnaires to probe volunteers' everyday errors and slips of memory. One was a Cognitive Failures questionnaire [2] that explored how many and what kinds of mental mistake people are aware of making during their everyday lives. A second was a Memory Failures questionnaire [3, 4] that asked people specifically about their memory failures. Vicki Abson still has enormous energy, charm, vivacity and empathy, and was very much loved by us, and by all of our volunteers. They were all eager to tell her about the difficulties of their lives and said that their most vexing and frequent lapses were forgetting where they had hidden important objects. So she designed a "Lost and Found" questionnaire to probe this distress [5].

It was delightful to see how much volunteers enjoyed responding to these questionnaires. They hinted, very politely but very often, that this was a much more sensible way of assessing their problems with old age than getting them to learn lists of random words. Their answers to the questionnaires surprised us. Those aged from 75 to 93 were just as cheerful and confident about their everyday memory competence as those aged from 41 to 74. Disconcertingly, although their scores on intelligence tests modestly predicted their scores on memory tests, neither their intelligence test scores nor their memory test scores predicted the numbers or the kinds of everyday problem that they reported [5].

This was not an accident because many convincing studies with healthy and able elderly volunteers, for example the Maastricht Longitudinal Study, have found just the same thing. A study in British Columbia [6] found that questionnaires asking elderly people to evaluate their own memory are reliable, in the sense that they give the same answers on different occasions, and do generally agree with the views of their friends and relatives. Some who complained that their memories were failing had higher than average scores on all our laboratory memory tests. Others with marginal memory test scores seemed inappropriately pleased with themselves. Their intelligence test scores also told us nothing about their everyday self-confidence. In spite of the simplicity that offended the disgruntled Fellow of All Souls, the laboratory memory tests we used are reliable and sensitive measures that sensitively identify patients whose memory problems have begun to affect their everyday lives. Why don't people's self-reports and their scores on tests of mental abilities agree?

Volunteers were not inaccurate because they had become poor at judging their abilities in any situation. For example, they could accurately judge their own performance on the laboratory memory tests that they had taken and those with higher intelligence test scores could do this more precisely [7]. The problem that all of us, of any age, have in rating our memories on an absolute scale such as "Good, Fair, Medium, Poor or Very Poor" is that we need some standard of reference. We cannot compare ourselves against an internationally accepted Metric Standard Memory.[1] We can only judge how well we meet the demands of our different lives or how our own performance compares with that of partners, friends and colleagues. If we live surrounded by extraordinarily able young colleagues or have scarily competent partners we develop modest ideas of our own abilities. Hopefully as we grow old, our acquaintances become more lenient with our failings and, perhaps because they share them, they are also less irritated by them. Our lives also begin to make fewer demands. Those, who, like me, are now classified as old/old[2] can truthfully say that we never forget any important appointments that we have. Our lives have changed earlier and faster than our brains.

Mental changes with age are slow and insidious and, until we are jolted by some painful lapse, we may not notice that we are beginning to have difficulties with that tasks we once easily performed. Our unreliability at detecting slow insidious changes contrasts with the sensitivity of young adults to the effects of sudden brain injuries that affect their memories. They usually have clear insights into the particular kinds and extents of their loss and, because their clinicians continually reassess them for hopeful improvements, their awareness of their status is continuously updated. Awareness of change also intensifies the misery of onset of dementias. Those whose dementias are advanced begin to forget how much they forget.

Feeling low and scoring low

Apart from comparing ourselves against people with whom we live and work, our ideas of our own competence are set by our general levels of confidence and optimism and by how others treat us. People's scores on any of the three questionnaires we gave them did not correlate with their scores on intelligence or memory tests but did correlate with their scores on other, quite different kinds of questionnaire that probed depression and anxiety. Happier volunteers were more confident about their ability to manage their lives. A recent study concluded that "self-report measures about cognition ought to be interpreted as expressing worries about one's cognition rather than measuring cognitive abilities themselves" [8]. This suggests that the fears of mental decline that worry many older people are more often caused by mild unhappiness than by actual mental change. Another aspect of the link between morale and self-evaluation is that people of all ages tend to give themselves higher ratings when they feel relatively pleased with their lives. Fortunately, it does not take much to make us pleased with ourselves. Many studies show that, at any age, most of us, especially men and boys, tend to overestimate our intelligence and competence.

Relationships between mild sadness and mental ability cut both ways. Self-confidence affects performance on memory tasks. There is convincing evidence that being sad and diffident not only makes us *feel* that we are less competent but also actually lowers our scores on simple tests. Older volunteers score worse if they take tests immediately after watching videos that subtly portray the old as less competent than the young [9]. People of all ages score lower on memory tasks after viewing videos that include no mention of memory or competence, but leave them feeling very slightly sad. It is not just that we are more likely to underrate our performance when we are a little unhappy. Being unhappy tends to make us perform less well. Even young people have biased judgements of their own abilities. In spite of objective evidence, young boys consistently rate their own intelligence higher than girls do. Disappointingly, parents and teachers also tend to rate boys as being more intelligent than girls of the same ages and abilities [10]. It is a good question whether this is because boys are more brash and girls are more diffident about their imagined or actual abilities or whether male-favouring bias in adults fosters illusions in the young. In either case, these biases can become self-justifying because they do affect objective performance.

Many convincing studies also show that the thoughtless biases of others can undermine us. Young black American adults perform less well on mental tasks after being exposed to material that hints at negative stereotypes of their race. Black Americans and Latino North Americans also tend to rate their own mental abilities less highly than Caucasian Americans do. Because our opinions of ourselves affect how capably we act, being needlessly humble is a self-imposed handicap rather than a winsome personality trait [11]. It matters very much that we should treat ourselves and others of all ages as generously as we possibly can.

Since we are not accurate judges of our own mental abilities, what else do we miss about ourselves? Whether we like it or not, as we grow old our health becomes an increasing preoccupation.

Judging how well we are and how long we will survive

We older people might suppose that the best possible source of information about our general health would be a complete physical examination by expert geriatricians. This is certainly the best way to check for the onset and progress of the pathologies that can beset us as we grow old but, surprisingly, for assessments of our general well-being our own subjective judgements seem to be as reliable as rigorous medical check-ups. An overall analysis (meta-analysis) of data from most epidemiological surveys made until 2006 found that after differences in sex, mobility and socio-economic advantage have all been taken into account, people who rate their health as "poor" have twice the risk of subsequently dying than those who rate their health as "excellent" [12]. This is useful to know, but such comparisons are not straightforward. Apart from the understandable effects of depression and anxiety, and of adverse socio-economic conditions in lowering our self-ratings there are subtle differences in accuracy between men and women and old and young.

A convincing study found that the accuracy with which self-ratings predict mortality varies with the age of those questioned. Old/old individuals in their late seventies and eighties are over-optimistic about their well-being, perhaps because of the greater confidence induced by their longer survival [13]. Also, as we grow older, more of us begin to suffer from illnesses that, for the moment, are still symptom-free. What we don't yet know may kill us.

Women's self-ratings of their general health predict their survival better than men's do. A large study of Australians aged over 60 when they were first seen in 1981 found that, in general, both men's and women's self-ratings predicted their chances of survival over the next 8 years [14]. Women used all the gradations of the scale to make such sensitive distinctions that the odds of survival were significantly better for those who rated their health as fair than for those who rated it as poor, better for ratings of good than for fair, and so on. Men's self-ratings did not make fine distinctions. For them only the least favourable rating, "poor", predicted greater odds of mortality than any of the others. Perhaps this is because, as other studies have shown, women worry more about their health than men do and so are more likely to become aware of even small changes and so make more subtle distinctions. Apart from pointing to a clear difference in attitudes to health by men and women this shows that even self-ratings on very simple scales are not always straightforward to interpret.

What do we compare our health against?

We can only rate our own health by knowingly or unconsciously comparing ourselves against some standard. Lynn McInnes rediscovered this in a hard way by asking Newcastle volunteers to assess their own health "Poor, Fair, Good or Excellent" either in absolute terms with no suggested standard of comparison, in relation to other people of the same age as themselves and compared to their health 5 and 10 years ago. We were surprised that global self-ratings by volunteers in their late eighties and early nineties were more optimistic than by many in their sixties and seventies. One explanation was that this actually reflected reality. Those 80-year-olds who could still agree to come to demanding testing sessions were indeed unusually healthy and so, when they compared themselves against most other people of their own age, their optimistic conclusions were justified. A telling difference was that even those who had rated their health most favourably in comparison with others of their own age were far more negative when they compared their current state of health against how they were 5 or 10 years ago. Consistent with reality, the older the volunteers were the greater declines they reported.

It seems that we oldies can not only accurately assess our general states of health but, even more accurately, can judge how much we have changed over the years. Like our judgements of our own intellectual abilities, our self-evaluations depend on the contexts and moods in which we make them. We rate our current state of well-being more poorly when we are depressed than when we are cheerful. Similarly, those who are socio-economically disadvantaged and so have a poorer quality of life rate their health as worse than do the happier and more prosperous. It is a harsh reality that the socio-economically disadvantaged do indeed live less healthy lives and do die much younger than the affluent and contented. Depression is a common consequence of disadvantage and of poor health and, when added to poor health, reduces chances of survival.[3] In many surveys, people's self-ratings of well-being remain significant predictors of how long they have to live even after differences in their levels of depression and socio-economic disadvantage have been taken into account. The large Manitoba Longitudinal Study of Aging [15] found that people's self-ratings of their general health continue to predict how long they will live even after differences in their objectively determined health status, age, sex, income, urban or rural residence, feelings of depersonalisation, levels of morale, depression and expressed level of happiness, and objectively judged levels of their own levels of health relative to those of people of their own age had all been taken into account. There are at least three explanations for this interesting finding: the proxy measures available for lifestyle variables were imperfect; elderly people's introspections give them more information or different kinds of information than they offered health professionals; or the way in which we feel about our current state of health affects both our present and our future well-being. The authors of this study prefer the last of these three different but, in my view, equally plausible contributing factors.

As we grow older, the way in which we think about ourselves probably determines our happiness and well-being even more strongly than when we are young. Even young adults are easily misled by evaluating themselves in lenient environments that make them feel more capable than they really are. At any age we cannot judge ourselves in a solipsistic vacuum. When we are asked to rate our general state of health, but are given no guidance as to what comparisons might be appropriate, it is sensible to compare ourselves against others of our own age group. We are, of course, aware that we were once healthier than we are now. We also know that our juniors are probably healthier and our seniors are probably less healthy than we are. In spite of this we seem to choose to make our judgements by, as it were, adjusting for our own ages. We can be deceived into elation or depression by making comparisons that answer different questions from those that we mean to answer.

How can we assess ourselves more accurately?

If we realise precisely what comparisons we are making, we do not seem to become less accurate as we age. As a professional observer of my own generation, I am impressed by the beady-eyed vigilance with which we watch each other for signs of change, or for dogged and pitiful failures to recognise or adapt to changes. I do not think that we have become less perceptive of changes in ourselves or that we are less prone to monitor and evaluate ourselves against each other. If we take the trouble to think carefully about the various comparisons we make to assess ourselves, we are surprisingly accurate at predicting the time we still have left. Old people evidently know a great deal about their own general state of health. More of us, particularly men, should learn to share this knowledge with physicians and others who can help us to do something about it.

Notes

1 If there were such a thing it would, of course, be carefully preserved in an elegant mahogany box with brass and ivory trimmings in the Musée des Arts et Sciences in Paris.
2 It is a convenient convention among cognitive gerontologists to refer to people aged from 55 to 65 as "young old", those aged from 65 to 75 as "old" and to those aged 75+ as "old/ old". Naturally, I insist that with the phenomenally rapid increases in life expectation and competence in later life this classification is obsolete, impertinent, politically incorrect and urgently in need of revision.
3 As Mrs Mopp, in the Tommy Handley *ITMA* show (now long forgotten by all except my generation) lugubriously declaimed every week "It's being so cheerful that keeps me going".

References

[1] Blythe, R. (1979). *The View in Winter: Reflections on Old Age.* New York, Harcourt Brace.
[2] Broadbent, D. E., Cooper, P. F., Fitzgerald, P. and Parkes, K. R. (1982). The Cognitive Failures Questionnaire and its correlates. *British Journal of Clinical Psychology*, 21, 1–16.
[3] Sunderland, J., Harris, J. E. and Baddeley, A. D. (1983). Do laboratory tests predict everyday memory. *Journal of Verbal Learning and Verbal Behaviour*, 22, 341–357.
[4] Sunderland, A. and Gleave, J. (1984). Memory failures in everyday life following severe head injury. *Journal of Clinical Neuropsychology*, 6, 127–142.
[5] Rabbitt, P. and Abson, A. (1990). Lost and found: Some logical and methodological limitations of self-report questionnaires as tools to study cognitive ageing. *British Journal of Psychology*, 81, 1–16.
[6] Hertzog, C., Dixon, R. and Hultsch, D. (1990). Relationships between meta-memory, memory predictions, and memory task performance in adults. *Psychology and Aging*, 5(2), 215–227.
[7] Rabbitt, P. and Abson, V. (1991) Do older people know how good they are? *British Journal of Psychology*, 82, 137–151.
[8] Wilhelm, O., Witthoft, M. and Schipolowski, S. (2010). Self-reported cognitive failures: Competing measurement models and self-report correlates. *Journal of Individual Differences*, 31, 1–14.
[9] Levy, B. (1996). Improving memory in old age through implicit self-stereotyping. *Journal of Personality and Social Psychology*, 71, 1092–1107.
[10] Steinmayr, R. and Spinath, R. (2009). What explains boys' stronger confidence in their own intelligence? *Sex Roles*, 61, 736–749.
[11] Kaufman, J. C. (2012) Self estimates of general, crystallized, and fluid intelligences in an ethnically diverse population. *Learning and Individual Differences*, 22, 118–122.
[12] DeSalvo, K., Bloser, N., Reynolds, K., He, Jiang and Muntner, P. (2006). Mortality prediction with a single general self-rated health question: A meta-analysis. *Journal of General Internal Medicine*, 21, 267–275.
[13] Larue, A., Bank, L., Jarvik, L. and Hetland, M. (1979). Health in old age: How do physicians' ratings and self-ratings compare? *Journal of Gerontology*, 34, 687–691.

[14] McCallum, J., Shadbolt, B. and Wang, D. (1994). Self-rated health and survival: A 7 year follow up study of Australian elderly. *American Journal of Epidemiology*, 3, 292–304.

[15] Mossey, J. M., Havens. B., Roos, N. and Shapiro, E. (1981). The Manitoba Longitudinal Study on Aging: Description and methods. *The Gerontologist*, 21(5), 551–559.

5

BODILY SIGNS OF MENTAL CHANGES

We wonder how far the signs of aging that are so easily visible to others, like greying, balding, peering, stumbling and fumbling may signal inner clouding of intelligence and memory. Do spreading wrinkles in our skins reflect even deeper creasing in our aging brains or do trivial outer changes tell us little or nothing about changes in our mental abilities?

Without change, time would be a meaningless concept. Ponderous billion-year wheeling of galaxies, heartbeats of wrens and nanosecond frenzies of fundamental particles are all clocks running at different rates. So too are the scores of different physiological processes that keep our bodies and brains alive. To measure our lives in terms of trips around the sun tells us little about how well we are or how long we have left to appreciate the Grand Contraption that we can so briefly observe.

The many clocks of our physiology run at different rates but, since they all measure the same periods of our lives, each will certainly correlate with all the others even if they have nothing whatever to do with each other. I am reminded of this every year when I visit my favourite trees in Stanton Harcourt Arboretum. Each summer they are higher and bushier and my brain has lost more neurones so that I have become slightly slower and more stupid. Tree growth and my brain decay are different clocks marking the same Sun circuits. The trees and I have nothing in common except the years that we have shared, but, nevertheless, tree burgeoning paces my decline. A neutral term for this accident is that although the trees do nothing to cause my mental changes they serve as accurate "markers" for the progress of my brain changes and savagely lopping them would do me no good at all.

Gerontologists have checked many combinations of different biological markers to discover which, if any, may be useful indicators of "biological age" (body and brain age) as distinct from "chronological age" (i.e. calendar age) [1, 2, 3]. A good guess has been that biological markers that predict our distance from death must also be indices of the progress of our general biological aging. Many markers, such as the efficiency of our cardiovascular and respiratory systems, predict our chances of survival, but no single master-marker, nor any factor computed from several different markers has yet turned out to be a uniquely good index of biological age. A comment made by the US pioneer of aging studies, Nathan Shock in 1982 [4] still stands:

> There is little evidence for the existence of a[ny] single factor that regulates the rate of aging in different functions in a specific individual. Because of the large range in the performance of most physiological variables among subjects of the same chronological age it appears that (calendar) age alone is a poor predictor of performance. Subjects who perform well on physiological tests when they are first tested, however, are more likely to be alive 10 years later than subjects who perform poorly.

Attempts to find better yardsticks of biological change still only weakly predict the sort of things that we would most like to learn, such as how long we still have to live and how well we will probably function during the time we have left. Currently the most promising is the progressive shortening in the length of telomeres – caps that preserve the integrity of chromosomes in every cell of our bodies and signal their approach to the point when they unravel and can no longer accurately replace themselves [5]. Even better indices will be found; insurance companies will be delighted, and people who have enough money and wish to find out how long they have to spend it can do so more accurately.

To be able to predict exactly how long each of us will survive would be useful but discouraging. Fortunately, no marker can yet give us death row precision of prediction of our last day and moment. Accidents will happen and the best markers can only tell us roughly how well we are now. They can only give approximate odds of the speed of future changes and of our survival if we do nothing to improve or damage our prospects. This is cheering and useful because it emphasises that we have some degree of control over our fate. The first biomarkers studied were vision, hearing and muscle strength, because these are very easy to measure and important in individuals' daily lives. In old age, differences in people's vision, hearing and balance predict differences in their intelligence, decision speed and memory [6, 7]. The interesting question is why.

The falling years

Shakespeare got it exactly right when he observed that a key symptom of old age is "most weak hamstrings". Because loss of leg muscle strength is a cause of falls that are a particular hazard in old age, this has been one of the most thoroughly researched markers of biological aging. Muscle weakness increases with calendar age [8] and differences in elderly people's leg muscle strengths predict from 2 to 9 per cent of the differences in their intelligence test scores [9, 10]. It seems strange to find such firm associations between rates of decline of ankles, calves, thighs, bums and brains, but there are many good reasons for this. People whose poor health has begun to affect their brains and central nervous systems are also likely to have become inactive and so to have lost muscle strength. Both our muscles and our central nervous systems are affected by cardiovascular or respiratory problems that reduce blood supply [11]. Atrophy of peripheral nerves that activate our leg muscles can be a symptom of more general changes in our entire nervous systems and brains and so also in our intelligence [12]. Depletion of neurotransmitters and changes in the brain affect cognition and the nerve connections between brain and muscles.

Leg muscle strength also predicts odds of survival. Loss of muscle strength is caused by prolonged inertia, and inertia is linked to faster losses of cardiovascular function that shorten our lives. Improvements in cardiovascular and respiratory efficiency brought about by aerobic exercise improve both muscle strength and mental abilities. Those of us who are sensible and disciplined enough to take regular aerobic exercise maintain higher scores on intelligence tests and faster reaction times and live longer than those whose main occupation has become "lethal sitting".[1]

Seeing and hearing our futures

In old age our acuity of vision and hearing also predicts our current intelligence and its further decline. This is not surprising because our retinas and visual pathways and the receptor cells in our inner ears are, in effect, outlying parts of our central nervous systems, so we would expect anything that affects our brains to affect them too. We lose visual acuity both because of changes in our retinas but also because of losses of computing power to interpret what our eyes tell our brains. I believe that Birren and Cunningham [13] were the first to suggest that older people's losses of visual acuity might turn out to be a useful index of how much cognitive change they have experienced and many later studies have confirmed this [14, 15, 16].

There are good reasons why changes in our brains should be directly linked to changes in our retinas and optic nerves and so our vision. However, we run into difficulties if we try to put numbers to exactly how much of the total decline in intelligence that we experience as we age is signalled by losses of visual acuity. This is because, just as for trees and brains, some proportion of the statistical relationships between changes in our eyes and brains must reflect the fact that they are clocks marking the same years. A large proportion of losses of vision are quite independent of brain or nervous system decline. Among causes of losses of vision are surface damage to the cornea, clouding of the cornea and lens, turbidity of aqueous and vitreous humours in the eyeball and increasing rigidity of the lens. It seems unlikely that these are directly related to changes in our brains. Hearing losses are not only caused by neurophysiological changes that also affect the brain but also by mechanical damage to the hair cells and other structures in our cochleas from lifetime exposure to loud noises.

We grasp that this is not a finicky and pedantic distinction when we compare relationships between calendar age, hearing thresholds and intelligence in groups of unusually healthy and less healthy old people. In both groups, hearing thresholds correlate with intelligence but, among exceptionally healthy people, these associations are weak and disappear when differences in their calendar ages are also taken into account. In less healthy groups, correlations between hearing and intelligence are much stronger and remain even after differences in age have also been considered [14]. This is because exceptionally healthy old people have not suffered illnesses that affect both their brains and their hearing. Their hearing losses are smaller and are more strongly linked to the number of years during which they have suffered mechanical damage from exposure to noise. Less healthy old people suffer much the same proportion of losses due to environmental factors and noise damage but they also have extra losses due to illnesses that have affected their auditory nerves, their brains and so also their intelligence. This is useful to know because hearing tests are much easier, quicker and cheaper tools for evaluation than complete medical examinations, and can alert us when older people's mental abilities are beginning to be affected by poor health.

Since losses of vision and hearing are markers for losses of mental abilities, we might expect that they will also predict each other. Many studies confirm that they do (e.g. [14], [15], [16], [18]). Because they are inter-related, we might also hope that by combining several of these biomarkers we might get more precise predictions of future general health, life expectancy, brain health, memory and intelligence and so, also, of our ability to manage our daily lives. Most studies do not find that this works. For example, we were able to test this with data from Manchester volunteers because a UK government agency funded us to study driving ability in older motorists. We coaxed 630 active drivers aged from 50 to 90 to let us measure their acuity of vision and hearing, leg-muscle strength, maximum expelled respiratory volume, hand-grip strength, balance and joint flexibility, and we also gave them tests of intelligence, memory and decision speed. Professional driving instructors assessed the volunteers' driving skills in their personal, familiar cars.

As we expected, the older the volunteers were the lower were their scores on all our mental and physical tests. The best predictors of their intelligence test scores were their acuity of vision and hearing, balance and strength of leg thrust. Combining these measures gave no better predictions than using any one of them on its own. Of course, we also asked the practical question that interested our sponsors: most measures, individually or together, did predict everyday driving skills, but only rather weakly. A surprising aspect of this relationship was that after we had taken into account the differences in all the biomarkers that we measured, people's calendar ages, between 50 and 90 years accounted for only 5 per cent of the differences in their intelligence test scores. If we turn this estimate around it seems even more encouraging: that is, 95 per cent of the differences in intelligence test scores between these elderly individuals were *not* associated with differences in their ages between 50 and 90. So, up to 95 per cent of differences in intelligence between people of different ages must be caused by the multitude of other factors, such as genetics, socio-economic advantage, education and health that have made them different from each other at birth and throughout their long lives. We can now go on to ask the further question of why visual and hearing acuity and balance can, nevertheless, account for that tiny 5 per cent of variance that *is* associated with differences in their ages.

Working out the exact amounts by which age affects intelligence, vision and balance

The problem is the issue of causality that we illustrated by pointing out the strong connection between the burgeoning of neighbourhood trees and the withering of our brains and wits. We can be sure that *some* of this 5 per cent of shared variance in brains, eyes, ears and balance is caused by common neurological changes, but we do not yet know *by exactly how much* because changes in balance and gait are partly caused by mechanical wear of our knee and hip joints; changes in vision are partly caused by scratched corneas and lenses; and changes in hearing are partly caused by mechanical damage from loud noise causing losses of hair cells on our basilar membranes.

The question becomes clearer when it is illustrated by a similar diagram as that used in Figure 3.3. Can we check the relative extents to which correlations between biomarkers and intelligence reflect common physiological changes and changes in functionally unrelated systems?

The argument is the same one we followed in Chapter 3. Ulman Lindenberger and Ulrich Potter, working at the Max Planck Institute in Berlin, pointed out that when we discuss changes that are associated with growing up or growing old, one of the things we most need to know is *how much* of that proportion of differences between people that is associated with differences in their ages is accounted for by other factors, such as differences in their health. They worked out a clever variant of regression analysis to calculate the proportion of this "age-related variance" that is associated with other things [19].

Ulman Lindenberger and Paul Baltes [20] used this method to estimate the percentages of age-related variance in intelligence test scores that can be predicted by simple measures of visual and auditory acuity and by walking gait. In Berlin, just as in Manchester, differences in volunteers' ages accounted for about 5.1 per cent of the differences in their intelligence test scores. Paul and Ulman then asked how much of this 5.1 per cent age-related variance in intelligence test scores that is specifically associated with differences in ages was associated with differences in vision, hearing and gait. Their dramatic finding was between 90 and 100 per cent. So, to emphasise this surprising finding, it seems that *all* of that particular part (5.1 per cent) of the variance between people that is associated with differences in their ages is also associated with differences in vision, hearing and gait. Another way to put this is that nearly all the changes that are associated with differences in people's calendar ages seem to be due to physiological changes that have also affected their vision, hearing and balance as they have grown old.

There is a strong temptation to conclude that this must mean that people whose visual acuity has sharply declined as they have grown older have also

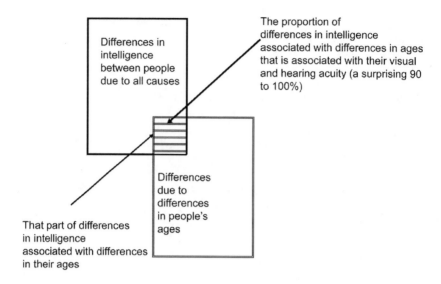

FIGURE 5.1   Differences in people's intelligence test scores are due to a great variety of things. Age also affects many abilities, but only a small proportion of differences between people's intelligence test scores (about 16 per cent) is due to differences in their ages between 50 and 90 years. A surprisingly large amount (up to 90 or even 100 per cent) of this modest 16 per cent of variance between people that is associated with differences in their ages is associated with differences in their acuity of vision and hearing. Sensory acuity is therefore, a very effective sign or "biological marker" for the amount of mental change that age has brought about.

experienced a correspondingly steep decline in their intelligence. At this point we recognise why psychologists prevaricate by using apparently weasel language like "association" and "correlation" rather than coming out loud and clear with robust conclusions about "causes" that we hope they will give us. We want to hear something like: "increasing age *causes* brain changes which *cause* losses of vision (and hearing and balance) and, because of this *also causes* losses in intelligence". Actually all that we have are correlations and, as always, we must remind ourselves that correlations cannot *prove* causes. Growing trees do not cause withering brains. Correlations are only circumstantial evidence that causes may be there to be found.

   To get out of this dilemma we need to include in our sums some direct indices of the neurophysiological efficiency of the entire brain. If changes in any global measure of brain health account for nearly all of the relationship between our scores on tests of balance and of intelligence, we can more safely conclude that, as age advances, losses in both vision and intelligence are brought about by the same losses of brain health. We found that this is, indeed, what happens [25].

Measuring and using gross changes in the brain

As we age, some of the nerve cells and their supporting tissue in our brains die and so they shrink. People's brains shrink at different rates. We can measure how much tissue any particular old person's brain has lost by using brain scans to calculate the difference between the unchanged volume of her skull and the current volume of her brain. Among older people, individual differences in amounts of brain shrinkage predict differences in their levels of performance on a variety of different mental tasks [21]. Also, as a group of people ages, more of them experience reduced blood flow in their carotid and basilar arteries and so to all parts of the their brains, but perhaps especially to the frontal cortex [22, 23]. Both age-related loss of brain volume (ARLBV) and carotid and basilar flow (CBF) are (very) rough indices of the amount of gross neurophysiological changes that have impaired our mental abilities as we have grown older. Mary Lunn and Said Ibrahim confirmed that this connection is real by showing that the rate at which levels of intelligence and speed had declined over the last 8 to 20 years in a group of Manchester volunteers were predicted by measures of their current losses of brain volume and their current carotid and basilar artery blood flow [24].

We measured the ARLBV and CBF in volunteers aged between 62 and 84 and also tested their decision speeds on very simple tasks. Volunteers' ARLBVs and CBFs accounted for between 16 and 21 per cent of the differences in their decision speeds, but differences in their calendar ages accounted for only between 11 and 12 per cent. We estimated the proportions of age-related variance in each of the two tasks that ARLBV and CBF could explain. Losses of brain volume and cerebral blood flow accounted for nearly all (i.e. 91 to 99 per cent) of that proportion of the differences in their decision speeds that were associated with differences in their ages between 62 and 84 years [25].

All these volunteers had also taken a test of balance and mobility. As usual, their balance scores correlated significantly with their decision speeds. We could therefore compute how much of that very small part of the variance in speed and

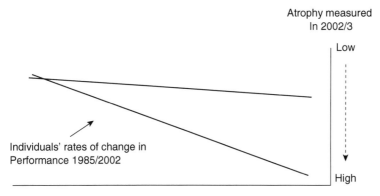

FIGURE 5.2   Mary Lunn and Said Ibrahim used data gathered during longitudinal testing of all scanned participants to predict rates of change over the previous 17 years from current levels of atrophy.

intelligence that is predicted by differences in balance is also predicted by brain volume and blood flow. The dramatic answer was – ALL. So, the strong relationships between people's balance, intelligence and decision speed are not just accidents of time-coincidence of different and independent processes. They occur because, as people grow older, they suffer brain changes that affect both their balance and their mental abilities.

It seems that changes in balance predict changes in decision speed and intelligence because, and *only* because, they also predict losses of brain volume and reduction of blood flow. Consequently, scores on tests of balance can give us a useful clue to how much brain volume and brain blood circulation we have lost as we have grown older, and by how much this has already affected our mental abilities and will continue to do so in the future unless we take appropriate steps (possibly in the most literal way by going for long pleasant walks).

We can be sure that these associations are real and so should be unsurprised that changes in biometric measures reflect our current and also our future ability

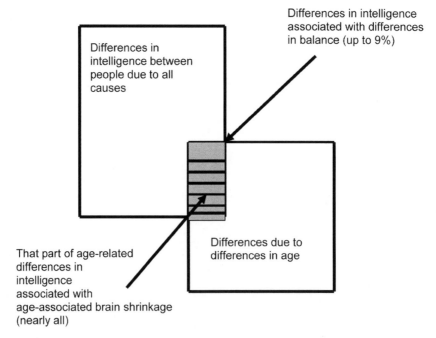

FIGURE 5.3 Differences in people's intelligence test scores are due to a great variety of things. Age also affects many abilities, but only a small proportion of differences between people's intelligence test scores (about 16 per cent) is due to differences in their ages between 50 and 90 years. Of this small proportion of age-related variance in intelligence, a surprisingly large amount (up to 90 or even 100 per cent) is associated with differences in their acuity of balance. Sensory acuity is therefore, a very effective sign or "biological marker" for the amount of mental change that age has brought about.

to manage our everyday lives. These predictions become valid quite early in life. Middle-aged and young adults aged from 45 to 68 who had weaker than average hand grip-strength suffered, 25 years later, from slower walking speed, poorer ability to get up out of chairs without support and more problems with daily self-care [26]. A large Italian study also found that hand grip-strength in middle age and early old age was a good predictor of the odds that people aged from 71 to 95 would survive for another 4 years [27]. What these associations probably mean is that those individuals who were physically slackening off in middle age because of illness or inertia tended to lose grip-strength earlier and faster than the fit and well. Grip-strength is a useful marker of maintained overall muscle efficiency and so also of the overall amount of physical activity that we take in our everyday lives. Unfortunately, those of us who feel that our slackening grip-strength does not bode well for our future cannot reverse the decline and get a firmer grasp of our futures just by suddenly beginning to exercise our hands. To improve the physiological health of our brains, as well as our hand and forearm muscles, we need to take aerobic exercise that increases our heart rate and breathing rate and also improves brain blood circulation. Strengthening our hands alone will not do the trick.

Even mild regular exercise is an effective way of preserving our health and so our wits and survival. Of course, there is much more to be done to improve our chances of enjoying a long and alert old age. Many authors have tried to define what constitutes "successful aging" and to discover what aspects of our lifestyle best promote this desirable condition. Among a group of 67-year-old North American volunteers, those who were well-educated, affluent, white, and without cardiovascular and respiratory pathologies, depression, diabetes, arthritis or hearing problems were judged to have to aged more successfully over the next 6 years. (I must emphasise that the non-Caucasians surveyed were, as a group, less fortunate only because they were socio-economically disadvantaged and very much poorer and so far more likely to be unhealthy). Apart from these easily understandable relationships, those who regularly walked more for exercise, had more close personal contacts, and were not depressed did particularly well [28].

An important factor in living a contented old age is to be free of annoying disabilities, even if these are as minor as having problems with getting up easily from chairs and beds.[2] In a recent survey of 1019 US residents aged 65, the chances of a non-disabled man surviving to 80 and remaining non-disabled until he died was 26 per cent, and for a non-disabled woman surviving to 85 and then dying without disability was 18 per cent. For both men and women, the odds of reaching the end of a long life without disability were twice as good for those who took mild regular exercise than for the more torpid [29]. Many convincing investigations of factors that make for successful aging all confirm folk wisdom. Keeping as healthy as we possibly can is the most important component of success in old age, both in its own right and also because it allows us to decline slower and live longer. It also preserves our morale. A lifestyle with a sensible diet, low stress and as much exercise as possible is key to preserving good health. Becoming socially isolated is unfortunate, both for health and morale, and is a risk for earlier cognitive decline and death. A report from a large Manitoba population stresses how important it is to remain as active as possible, in any way that is pleasant or convenient and includes a useful summary of what keeps elderly Canadians well and cheerful: "Different activities were related to different outcome measures; but generally, social and productive activities were positively related to happiness, function, and mortality. In contrast more solitary activities (e.g., handwork hobbies) were related only to happiness." The results also suggest that different kinds of activity may have different benefits. Social and productive activities afford physical benefits, as reflected in better function and greater longevity but more solitary activities, such as reading, may have more psychological benefits by providing an increased sense of engagement with life [30].

Dutch scientists are, perhaps notoriously, exact and pragmatic. A study of 599 citizens in Leiden [31] replicated nearly all of the findings we have just described, but made the extra point that after all other factors have been considered, people's attitudes to their own aging are crucial. Only 10 to 13 per cent of these Netherlanders met the stringent health and mobility criteria for "successful" or "optimal" aging. When they were interviewed about their feelings about growing old they agreed that health, mobility and keeping one's wits are very important but went on to add that maintaining health and social contacts was even more crucial for life satisfaction than absence of awareness of mild cognitive decline. The authors of this study also made the important point that aging is not a changeless state of being, but a process of adaptation. They remark that if these volunteers' adjustments to their situations are taken into account, many more of them, even those who were adversely affected by poor health, loss of mobility and social contacts, could be judged to have "aged successfully". From our personal experience, my older colleagues and I would warmly agree that it does help if you can get used to it.[3]

Notes

1 For the very best, and most convincing description of "lethal sitting" do, please, listen to the wonderful Louis Armstrong number "Ol' Rockin' Chair", particularly the version in session with Dr John.

2 Not just annoying for us, but apparently vexatious for those who have to share our lives. My personal poll of Manchester undergraduates found that a very frequent embarrassment with elderly parents and grandparents is a tendency to say "Three, Two, One. . . .Lift-off" while getting out of a deep chair, or to make explosive "OOOOFFFF" noises at random moments of mild exertion. I try very hard to avoid giving way to these and similar strangely compulsive habits.

3 When experiencing particularly difficult times some of our unusually positive volunteers were known to complain that "Old Age is like a prison". To which I once overheard the robust Lancastrian reply "Aye, but you can do your time hard or do it easy". I have no better wisdom to offer.

References

[1] Borkan, G. and Norris, A. H. (1980). Biological age in adulthood: Comparison of active and inactive US males. *Human Biology*, 52, 787–802.

[2] Clark, J. W. (1960). The aging dimension: A factorial analysis of individual differences with age on psychological and physiological measurement. *Journal of Gerontology*, 15, 183–187.

[3] Hofecker, G., Skalicky, M., Khment, A. and Niedermuller, H. (1980). Models of biological age of the rat. I. A factor model of age parameters *Mechanisms of Aging and Development*, 14, 345–360.

[4] Shock, N. W. (1984). *Normal Human Aging: The Baltimore Longitudinal Study of Aging*. N.I.H Publication No 84 -2450. National Inst. on Aging (DHHS/NIH), Bethesda, MD.

[5] Kirkwood, T. (1999). *The Time of Our Lives. The Science of Human Ageing*. Oxford, Oxford University Press.

[6] Birren, J. E., Botwinnick, J., Weiss, A. D. and Morrison, D. F. (1963). Interrelations of mental and perceptual tests given to healthy elderly men. In J. E. Birren, R. N. Butler, S. W. Greenhouse, L. Sokoloff and M. R. Yarrow (Eds), *Human Aging*. DHEW, PGS Publ, No (HSM) 71-9051. Washington, USGPO.

[7] Heron, A. and Chown, S. (1967). *Age and Function*. London, Churchill.

[8] Dean, W. (1988). *Biological Ageing Measurement: Clinical applications*. Los Angeles, Centre for Bio-Gerontology.

[9] Lord, S. R., Clark, R. D. and Webster, I. W. (1991). Physiological factors associated with falls in an elderly population. *Journal of the American Geriatrics Association*, 39, 1194–1200.

[10] Lord, S. R., McLean, D. and Stathers, G. (1992). Physiological factors associated with injurious falls in older people living in the community. *Gerontology*, 38, 338–346.

[11] Rikli, R. and Busch, S. (1986). Motor performance of women as a function of age and physical activity level. *Journal of Gerontology*, 41, 645–649.

[12] Lexell, J., Downham, D. and Sjostrom, M. (1986). What is the cause of ageing atrophy? Total number, size and proportion of different fibre types studied in whole vastus lateralis muscle from 15 to 83 year old men. *Journal of the Neurological Sciences*, 84, 275–294.

[13] Birren J. E. and Cunningham, W. (1985). Research on the psychology of aging: Principles, concepts and theory. In J. E. Birren and K. W. Schaie (Eds), pp. 3–34 *Handbook of the Psychology of Aging* (2nd edition). New York, Van Nostrand Reinhold.

[14] Anstey, K. J., Lord, S. R. and Williams, P. (1997). Strength in the lower limbs, visual contrast sensitivity and simple reaction time predict cognition in older women. *Psychology and Aging*, 12(1), 137–144.

[15] Anstey, K., Stankov, L. and Lord, S. R. (1996). Primary aging, secondary aging and intelligence. *Psychology and Aging*, 8, 562–570.

[16] Anstey, K., Luszcz, M. A., and Sanchez, L. (2001). A re-evaluation of the common factor theory of shared variance among age, sensory function and cognitive function in older adults. *Journals of Gerontology*, 56B(1), P3–P11.

[17] Granick, S., Kleban, M. H., Weiss, A. D. (1976). Relationships between hearing loss and cognition in normally hearing persons. *Journal of Gerontology*, 31, 434–440.

[18] Boxtel, M. P. J., van Beijsterveldt, C. E. M., Houx, P. J., Anteunis, L. J. C., Metsemakers, J. F. M. and Jolles, J. (2000). Mild hearing loss can reduce mental performance in a healthy adult population. *Journal of Clinical and Experimental Neurophysiology*, 22, 147–154.

[19] Lindenberger, U. and Potter, U. (1998).The complex nature of unique and shared effects in hierarchical linear regression: Implications for developmental psychology. *Psychological Methods*, 3, 218–230.

[20] Baltes, P. B. and Lindenberger, U. (1997). Emergence of a powerful connection between sensory and cognitive functions across the adult lifespan: A new window to the study of Cognitive Aging? *Psychology and Aging*, 12, 12–21.

[21] Raz, N. (2000). Aging of the brain and its impact on cognitive performance: Integration of structural and functional findings. In F. I. M. Craik and T. A. Salthouse (Eds), *The Handbook of Aging and Cognition* (2nd edition). Mahwah, NJ, Lawrence Erlbaum Associates.

[22] Gur, R. C., Gur, R. E., Orbist, W. D., Skolnick, B. E. and Reivich, M. (1987). Age and regional cerebral blood flow at rest and during cognitive activity. *Archives of General Psychiatry*, 44, 617–621.

[23] Shaw, T. G., Mortel, K. F., Meyer, J. S., Rogers, R. L., Hardenberg, J. and Cutaia, M. M. (1984). Cerebral blood flow changes in benign aging and cerebrovascular disease. *Neurology*, 34, 855–862.

[24] Rabbitt, P., Ibrahim, S., Lunn, M., Scott, M., Thacker, N., Hutchinson, C., Horan, M., Pendleton, N. and Jackson. A. (2008). Age-associated losses in brain volume predict longitudinal decline in cognitive ability over 8 to 20 years. *Neuropsychology*, 22, 3–9.

[25] Rabbitt, P. M., Scott, M., Thacker, N., Lowe, C., Horan, M., Pendleton, N., Hutchinson, C. and Jackson. A. (2006). Balance marks cognitive change in old age because it reflects global brain atrophy and cerebral blood flow. *Neuropsychologia*, 44, 1978–1983.

[26] Rantanen, T., Guralnik, J. M., Foley, D., Masaki, K., Leveille, S., Curb, J. D. and White, L. (1999). Midlife hand grip strength as a predictor of old age disability. *Journal of the American Medical Association*, 281, 558–560.

[27] Giampaoli, S., Ferrucci, L. Cecchi, F., Lo Noce, C., Poce, A., Dima, F., Santaquilani, A., Vescio, M. F. and Menotti, A.. (1999). Hand-grip strength predicts incident disability in non-disabled older men. *Age and Ageing*, 28, 283–288.

[28] Strawbridge, W. J., Cohen, R. D., Shema, S. J. and Kaplan, G. A. (1996). Successful aging: Predictors and associated activities. *American Journal of Epidemiology*, 144, 135–141.

[29] Levielle, S. G., Guralnik, J. M., Ferrucci, L. K. and Langloise, J. A. (1999). Aging successfully until death in old age: Opportunities for aging successfully. *American Journal of Epidemiology*, 149, 654–664.

[30] Menec, V. H. (2003). The relation between everyday activities and successful aging: A 6-year longitudinal study. *Journal of Gerontology, B, Psychological Sciences*, 58, 74–82.

[31] von Faber, M. A., Bootsma-van der Weil, A., van Exel, E., Gussekloo, J., Lagaay, A. M., van Dongen, E., Knook, D. L., van der Geest, S. and Westendorp, R. G. (2001). Successful aging in the oldest old: Who can be characterized as successfully aged? *Archives of Internal Medicine*, 161, 2694–2700.

PART II
Memory

6

WHAT IS MEMORY FOR?

A competent marmoset would not be seduced by a madeleine biscuit to remember past times. It would instantly recognise, seize and gobble one of the vast class of marmoset foods. Responding immediately and appropriately to each of the millions of different things in the world is a wonderful achievement for monkeys and mankind. Because we recognise each of these millions of things, their details must all be recorded in our memories, tagged with additional information about what they mean to us – whether they are attractive, unpleasant, dangerous or indifferent.[1] But memory is not just Brain Google. When our simplest and most remote ancestors began to develop nervous systems that could store representations of all the important things in their worlds and access them in milliseconds they achieved potential for prophecy – to recognise threats and benefits in advance and so anticipate what will happen next. Larger brains to store memories and the computing power to make use of them did not develop to replay the past but to anticipate the future.

To be able to use our past to predict and plan our next moves in the world is still the key advantage that marmosets and humans receive from their swift and capacious memory systems. It is unlikely that marmosets spend time ruminating their relationships or past experiences to make sense of their small lives, let alone of the entire Grand Scheme of Things. Humans do this compulsively and continually and, when we talk about our memories, we mean the theatre of the mind in which scenarios from our past lives are continually replayed and which, we fear, will one day become the only show in town. We do not appreciate that memories are not just past times but anticipations of the future based on interpretations of what has happened to us. Memories are almost the entire content of our conscious mental lives.

In the great survival game, mulling over the past is a luxury but predicting what is going to happen is essential for survival. To do this we need the vast store of details about the world that we acquire throughout our lives. Acknowledgement of failures such as "I forgot" imply that we now remember that we once decided to do something and planned how to set about doing it, but that between the intention and the act there fell a shadow.

The way in which we continuously record the information that our senses provide illustrates that memory is not a passive, dumb unselective device like a video recorder, but a busy, smart sorting compiler and interpreter of old and new information. When we feel challenged by efforts to keep up with events, we are oppressed by what seems an impossible demand to cram arriving information into a limited storage space from which it continuously and rapidly evaporates. Simple experiments confirm this impression. When we try to remember long lists of things, we find ourselves trying to retain items for longer by repeating them to ourselves as quickly and as often as we can before still more arrive. All the volunteers who discussed their memory problems with us felt that aging had particularly affected their immediate or short-term memories. As always, we listened to what they said and explored whether age had altered the longest sequences of random digits that they could immediately recall in the same order as they were given – their short-term memory spans. They misjudged themselves. Their individual memory spans varied from about seven to nine digits, but the average number recalled did not change between the ages of 40 and 80+. This was partly because all these volunteers had a lifetime's practice of remembering strings of digits and letters, such as telephone numbers and car licence plates. A more interesting point is that the task of remembering short lists of things in the exact order in which they occurred bears little resemblance to how people use their memories to interpret what is going on. Events do not unfold linearly in time like simple strings of spoken digits in which each is related to others only by the order in which they occur. We must connect all elements of a sequence of events with others that arrived earlier or later, assemble these into new meaningful patterns and relate new information, as fast as we can, to what we have just acquired and what we have known for many years. This needs the continual active engagement of a bustling system that can update, sort and re-order information and extract meaning from it by referring it to data about the world already held in long-term memory. Recognition of these dynamic characteristics of memory convinced Alan Baddeley and Graham Hitch [1] to call this activity Working Memory.

Memory is busy brain bustle

Old age seems to have little effect on simple recall for unaltered sequences of items but it does sharply degrade working memory. We see this when we ask people to re-order sequences of items that they have heard, even in simple ways such as reporting lists of digits backwards rather than forwards. Older people now do much worse than the young, as they also do when we ask them to add the last two of seven digits read to them, to then say this sum aloud and to then recall the whole previous sequence in the order that they heard it. Or distract them by giving them an additional short easy extra task, such as comparing the sizes and colours of two squares or reporting back a second short sequence of items before they recalled the first string of items that they heard.

Alan and Graham showed that we have different dedicated storage spaces to temporarily hold and organise information from different sensory systems: one that they called the "articulatory loop" continuously accepts and cycles sequences of sounds for later identification as words to be recalled. Another that they called the "scratch pad" holds rapidly fading visual images. Evidence that these are separate storage spaces is that memory for lists of letters or digits is disrupted by speaking nonsense words aloud or even by repeating "la, la, la" but is little affected by doing another task that does not involve words, such as using a pencil to track a wavy line on a rotating disc. Tracking, however, interferes with memory for spatial relationships. Age greatly increases the effects of distracting tasks on any kind of material held in working memory.

A good example of the limitations of working memory is the so-called "Cocktail Party Problem" of making sense of what two different people say simultaneously [2]. In experiments to illustrate this problem, two different sequences of words are simultaneously played, one to each ear. When sequences are short, young adults correctly report what they heard in both ears. They do this much more accurately when they are allowed to first report what was said to one ear and then what was said to the other [3]. As people grow old they can usually correctly report the message heard in one ear but, while they do this, the message to the other ear has to briefly queue to be reported and is more likely to be lost. This becomes more likely as we grow old and causes us problems when trying to follow fast-moving conversations among a group of people. These difficulties are not mainly caused by deafness or failures to selectively attend to one ear and then to the other, although these also play their part. They occur mainly because memory traces decay faster so that words spoken to one ear are lost while those spoken to the other are being recognised and reported [4, 5].

Over the last 40 years, many colleagues have expanded Alan Baddeley's first experiments into a vast body of research. It is now accepted that the busy systems

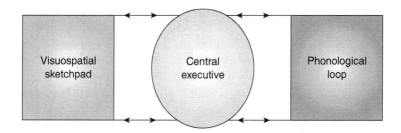

FIGURE 6.1   Alan Baddeley's first conception of "Working Memory" Reprinted by permission from Macmillan Publishers Ltd: [Nature Reviews Neuroscience] (4, 10), Copyright (2003).

that the brain uses to do these tasks must involve not only different, dedicated storage areas for different kinds of information such as the sounds of words and visual images, but must also involve what Alan and Graham called a "Central Executive". This is an overtaxed functionary that controls which parts of the clamour of information competing for our attention we select and recognise and also organises how it is re-ordered and related to other relevant information that has earlier been permanently entered into long-term memory. The central executive must also devise, or at least access, plans to achieve what needs to be done with this information to meet goals that alter from moment to moment with the changing demands that our worlds make of us. This is a complicated process: selecting relevant from among irrelevant information; referring to information available in long-term memory and updating this as needed; deciding what needs to be done; forming an intention to do this one thing and not another; devising an appropriate plan to fulfil this intention; monitoring progress of the plan as it unfolds; and abandoning or altering it as necessary. All this must take place while continually holding goals in mind so that we recognise if and when we reach them. It seems that these complex computations are the activities of the working memory system that are most severely degraded by aging of the brain.

Patients who have suffered local damage to the frontal and temporal lobes of their brains have severe problems with working memory. This suggests that these areas support the complicated processes that constitute our active interface with the world and so steer us through our lives [6]. There is also evidence that age affects our frontal and temporal lobes earlier and more severely than any other parts of our brains [7]. This seems to happen because, as age progresses, brain blood circulation becomes less efficient and frontal lobes are vulnerable to these changes earlier than other areas. Some neat experiments by Lynn Hasher and Rose Zacks [8] took up the idea of "frontal ageing" and tested whether increasing age impairs working memory tasks that involve selection and re-ordering of information sooner and more severely than other mental abilities. In my view, their evidence is not strong because other well-conducted studies have given different results. I think that this is mainly because it is very difficult to recruit groups of more than 20 to 50 elderly people to do laboratory experiments. Those who volunteer are atypically well and healthy and so less likely than most to have suffered age-related neurological changes. Also the rate, amount and location of changes in older brains vary so greatly between individuals that even groups of 50 elderly people are probably not big enough to always include enough individuals with marked local frontal and temporal losses to affect group-average scores on "frontal" tests.

Now that brain scans are easily available, we can directly identify and compare older individuals who have suffered greater and less loss of frontal and temporal lobe volume. This allows us to directly test how far losses in working memory efficiency are due to changes in these specific areas and how far they are due to global changes in the entire brain. This model also suggests some things that we can do to maintain our working memory. To boost our brain circulation and keep our frontal and temporal lobes healthy and efficient we can increase the amount of exercise we take. We must, in all senses, jog our memories.

Note

1 A point made far better 400 years ago by Andrew Marvell: "The mind, that ocean where each kind, Does straight its own resemblance find."

References

[1] Baddeley, A. D. and Hitch, G. J. (1975). Working memory. *The Psychology of Learning and Motivation*, 8, 47–89.

[2] Cherry, C. (1953). The Cocktail Party Problem. *Journal of the Acoustical Society of America*, 25, 975–979.

[3] Broadbent, D. R. (1958). *Perception and Communication*. Oxford, Pergamon Press.

[4] Inglis, J. and Caird, W. K. (1963). Age differences in successive responses to simultaneous stimulation. *Canadian Journal of Psychology*, 17, 98–105.

[5] Clark, L. E. and Knowles, J. B. (1973). Age differences in dichotic listening performance. *Journal of Gerontology*, 28, 173–178.

[6] Owen, A. M., Downes, J. J., Sahakian, B. J., Polkey, C. E. and Robbins, T. W. (1990). Planning and spatial working memory following frontal lobe lesions in man. *Neuropsychologia*, 28, 1021–1034.

[7] Brody, H. (1994). Structural changes in the ageing brain. In J. R. M. Copeland, M. T. Abou-Saleh and D. Blazer (Eds), pp. 30–33, *Principles and Practice of Geriatric Psychiatry*. Chichester, Wiley.

[8] Hasher, L., Stoltzfus, E. R., Zacks, R. T. and Rypma, B. (1991). Age and inhibition. *Journal of Experimental Psychology, Learning, Memory and Cognition*, 17, 163–169.

7

REMEMBERING TO DO THINGS

Working memory holds the information and runs the programs that we need to tell us what to do next. In this sense it is time travel – our best guess at how we shall cope with the future. Failures can occur at one or more successive stages: my forecast may be wrong so that my plan is inappropriate; I correctly work out what is going to happen and also what to do and when to begin to do it but fail to recognise a cue to activate my plan; or I may get even further and recognise a need for a drink, plan a good route to get to it, stand up and start walking but at some point forget the goal and then pause, banjaxed, making the best of befuddlement by doing something else that seems vaguely appropriate to the new place in which I find myself. I rely on information held in my long-term memory as to where drinks are to be found, how to get there and even, to reassure myself that my modest standards have not slipped, that I shall also need to find a cup to drink from. My working memory has to hold the intention, the route and the entire detailed plan of action, to continually check and update my progress through this plan while constantly keeping the goal clearly enough in mind to know when it has been achieved so that, rehydrated, I can get on with my day.

We learn a great deal from studying failures of our plans. While I worked in Manchester, I had the benefit of frequent conversations with Jim Reason, a British expert on human errors in managing complex and fraught processes such as landing aircraft, avoiding railway accidents, carrying out surgery and managing nuclear power stations [1]. To identify individuals who are particularly prone to failures of intention and execution in such tasks Jim, over many years, developed questionnaires probing what he termed the "slips of action" that occur in everyday life. Donald Broadbent, who was the pre-eminent British psychologist between 1958 and 1992, used to describe examples from his own life. One was going out last thing at night to carefully put empty milk bottles in the rabbit hutch and a lettuce on his doorstep. Another was going into his bedroom to change to go out to dinner only to find that he had put on his pyjamas and tucked himself into bed (he was a rather shy man and did not enjoy social encounters much).

Jim's questionnaires [2] did, indeed, identify people who reported errors in translating their intentions into plans or in completing plans they had successfully begun. They are reliable in the sense that people give consistent answers on different occasions. They are also valid in the sense that people's self-descriptions agree with their families', friends' and colleagues' accounts of their behaviour. We took advantage of Jim's work and asked older people to complete one of his questionnaires and tell us about their slips of action. The oldest made more errors on simple laboratory memory tasks and were also less reliable at remembering when they had agreed to visit our lab to take tests. Their answers to Jim's questionnaire certainly gave us more information about them than we could gain from their performance on laboratory memory tasks such as recalling sets of pictures or lists of words. Nevertheless, to our surprise, on Jim's questionnaire, just as on all others that we had used to probe their everyday competence, (see Chapter 3) older volunteers reported no more, and often significantly fewer lapses than much younger and, objectively, much more able persons.

This again shows that successfully making, remembering, initiating, playing out and monitoring and eventually completing and terminating plans in everyday life is a different and much more complex skill than learning and remembering lists of unrelated words. A key issue is that age not only changes people's brains and so affects their minds. It also transforms their lives. Young/old volunteers in their sixties are still challenged by many unpredictable and rapidly changing demands. The old/old in their late seventies and eighties are no longer under the same pressures and nearly all their needs are met by unchanging, thoroughly tested and well-remembered routines. Also, because the demands that their lives still make on them are often pressing and important, the failures experienced by 60-year-olds are more painful and memorable. Errors made by the old/old, aged 75 or over, are often less consequential and so barely noticed and harmlessly forgotten.

Looking for things

Consciousness of my own lapses gives me some insights into what has already happened to me and what lies ahead. Common crises include locating things such as spectacles, keys and pens. Even allowing that my living space is cluttered beyond the endurance of my patient partner, the amount of time I spend scrabbling around is becoming ominous. A common derailment is that searching for one thing reveals others that I have previously lost and these suddenly seem important and grab my interest. New activities triggered by these discoveries take over and a previous plan evaporates. A different kind of failure is incompetent management of searches.

I once asked elderly people to look for a particular pamphlet buried in the clutter of my laboratory office in Manchester (compared to my own endless groping their searches caused trivial disturbance). They rarely used even the simplest systematic strategy of scanning through all documents on one end of a desk or shelf and moving gradually to the other. Like me, they randomly rummaged and often re-inspected the same locations. The intervals between these repeated scans were startlingly brief. It was as if they felt, for no obvious reason that the pamphlet was more likely to be on some parts of the desk-tops or shelves than others, and they repeatedly poked through these hot locations. Although they always remembered exactly what they were looking for, they often forgot where they had just looked. It was harder to see whether, like me, they were likely to be distracted by finding irrelevant but tempting objects. There were always many things on my work surfaces to catch my interest but little to intrigue them. The closest approximation to these problems of search derailment that I could find was to ask them to look for two or more things at once. Like me, when searching for a single thing they would almost always recognise it as soon as they saw it but when searching for two or more things they might repeatedly ignore one of them, though they had glanced at it and handled it. The older the volunteers were, the more difficult it was for them to hold two or more search targets in mind. An undeservedly neglected paper long ago made the point that as we age we become worse at visual search because we tend to forget what we are looking for [3].

I have never tried to publish the results of this amateurish search experiment, but I hope that this tale illustrates how making and carrying through plans depends on prospective memory and planning. I have found mathematical descriptions of more and less good search strategies, (e.g. [4]) and so am aware that there are clever ways to compare the efficiency of search strategies that people devise for themselves, but I have not yet come across any experimental studies of elderly rummaging. I think that this is because a vast body of research on what psychologists have called prospective memory has followed different lines.

The earliest prospective memory experiments were simple, laboratory studies of how well people can do things they have been asked to do precisely when they have been asked to do them. These have found differences in efficiency at "time-based" and "event-based" tasks. In time-based tasks, people break off an on-going activity to do something else at a particular moment in clock-time, specified in advance. In event-based tasks, they are asked to break off when some other particular event or signal occurs. Many studies have found that older people perform less well than young adults on both kinds of task, but especially on time-based tasks [5, 6].

While working in our Manchester laboratory, Elizabeth Maylor made witty studies of the difficulties that older people experience in these situations. In a pleasantly naturalistic experiment, she asked volunteers to telephone her from their homes either at an exactly specified time or within a specified interval such as "between three and four pm" [7]. On this task, changes in efficiency with greater age were offset by the use of strategies. Volunteers aged between 45 and 65 tended to rely on "interval cueing" relying solely on their memories to ring at the arranged times. The confidence of younger volunteers in their ability to wing it was often misplaced. Some who tried to remember without self-devised external prompts did less well than those older people who arranged cues to remind themselves. Their reminders were sometimes odd and laboriously complex, such as piling up items of furniture around the telephone, but they seemed to work. Many older people coped because they had learned to distrust their memories and to invent aids to help them.

Louise Phillips, another valued Manchester colleague now a distinguished Professor in Aberdeen, draws attention to what she calls the "Age Paradox" [8]. Older people always perform less well than young adults on boring and seemingly pointless laboratory tasks such as learning lists of words. This is not just because these tasks are tedious and exasperating but rather because we do become less efficient at learning anything new as we grow older. Louise and her associates point out that in contrast to their problems in unfamiliar laboratory tasks in situations that more closely mimic the demands made by their daily lives and, particularly when they can organise their environments to help them, older people often creatively invent strategies that allow them to function as well as, or even better than the young. Perhaps their long life experience and their recognition of increasingly frequent memory lapses makes them realise when they should not be over-confident and they develop techniques to cope. In contrast, young people do not yet bother to invent useful techniques because their abilities have seldom let them down and, whether realistically or not, they remain confident of their ability to manage without these aids.

Elizabeth's telephone experiment pointed out a key fact that our success at remembering to do the right thing at the right moment depends on how well we can recognise and use what Fergus Craik [9] has called "environmental support": attending to external events that can trigger needed actions at appropriate times. Elizabeth guessed that people with higher intelligence test scores might be better at her tasks, reasoning that they might be better able to recognise when they need environmental support and invent clever dodges to cope. This was not what she found. Perhaps to recognise the need to find support we not only need intelligence but also the humility born of previous failures. The clever have failed less often. Elizabeth also gave her volunteers questionnaires on which they reported the number and kinds of lapse that they made during their everyday lives Their self-reports did not predict their performance on simple learning and memory tasks but those who reported frequent everyday lapses were also less effective on prospective memory tasks. It seems that it is not enough to experience failures, or even to recognise that one is prone to failures. Having recognised that we are at risk we must take the next step and find something to do about it.

In another experiment, Elizabeth asked volunteers aged from 50 to 80+ to name, in turn, each of many pictures of faces of famous people and to draw circles on their answer sheets to tag those wearing spectacles [10]. She found that young/old volunteers recognised more faces and also more often remembered to mark pictures of spectacled faces. Again, she found no evidence that those with higher intelligence test scores did better than others. This is surprising because in general volunteers' intelligence test scores predicted their performance on all the other memory tasks that they were given as part of the longitudinal study in which they were enrolled. The strong relationships between people's performance on intelligence tests and on simple memory tasks, on tests of decision speed and on vocabulary tests contrasted with their lack of prediction for just those tasks of face recognition, planning and planned control of performance that, intuitively, heavily depend on intelligence.

Once again this raises the question of how far even the most able of us monitor our own performance sensitively enough to become aware of our failures of intention. Clinical patients assessed for the effects of sudden brain injuries are immediately aware of losses of memory efficiency that affect their daily lives [11]. Undamaged normal elderly can also assess their own everyday memory competence, since their self-descriptions in their answers to questionnaires agree with those of their friends, family or carers. A problem with interpreting people's answers to questionnaires is the difference between their awareness that they make lapses and their ability to judge whether these are more or less frequent and serious than the average for people of their generation and lifestyle. The best we can do is to compare ourselves in relation to what we can observe of others. Those who live in lenient environments cocooned in the support of helpful families, friends and colleagues may make very few lapses and so remain unaware that their abilities are declining below levels adequate for more exacting lives. The capacity for these insights also varies. Healthy elderly people's accounts of their own abilities agree very well with the objective descriptions of their behaviour made by those who know them best. (Of course, this may partly be because family, friends and carers can be quite forceful in drawing their attention to their lapses.) In contrast, people fading into dementias become increasingly unaware of their problems and claim that they make few, if any, slips [11]. Like these patients, some of us may begin to forget that we forget.

We are beginning to recognise some of the changes in aging brains that underlie these problems. Our ability to remember and to plan ahead is impaired by losses of brain tissue, specifically in the hippocampus and temporal lobes of our brains.

Biochemical and hormonal changes also alter memory efficiency, as menopausal women well know. Many Manchester volunteers complained that they made more lapses than usual on days on which they felt physically below par. It seems that our memory abilities are also affected by very mild changes in emotional state. Matthias Kliegel and his colleagues showed that making volunteers even very slightly depressed by showing them a sad video lowered their subsequent scores on a prospective memory task [12]. It seems that even prospective memory tasks that seem trivially easy, are nevertheless taxing enough to stretch older people to the limits of their capabilities, leaving them with little reserve of capacity to buffer themselves against the distraction of even very mild indisposition or emotional discomfort.

Most of us feel that distractions make it harder to form and carry through plans and all the experimental evidence confirms this. If we try to do two tasks at once, we find that we must choose between making errors on both or coping with one at the expense of the other. Very many studies have found that switching between tasks or attempting to do two things at the same time becomes much harder as we grow older [13].

Formal theories of prospective memory suggest that it can be thought of as a label for the functions of the much wider system that Alan Baddeley first termed "working memory". Working memory is a descriptive term for those aspects of memory function that are concerned with processing new information, briefly holding it while it is sorted and rearranged, and relating it to plans that are already formulated and held in mind.

In his earliest experiments to explore working memory, Alan asked volunteers to do two tasks at once. They found this much harder if both made very similar demands. The same logic has been used to test what, precisely, are the demands made by prospective memory tasks. As we might expect, the more demanding a prospective memory task, the more it is disrupted by other tasks. This may seem to be an uninteresting re-statement of the obvious truism that it is harder to do two difficult than two easy things at once. Nevertheless, we must always remember that humans have been strenuously thinking about themselves and their minds for thousands of years, so that much of what psychologists have had to do during the last two centuries is to codify, experimentally validate, document and quantify ancient intuitions. Those who are comfortable with simple analogies between mental activities and computer hardware may like to think of mutual interference between simultaneous tasks as similar to the problem of a machine that has only one central processor to deal with information needed for one kind of decision at a time, so that other information, needed for different decisions must queue to be dealt with. The difference is that, in contrast to computer hardware memories, short-term wetware memories can hold queuing information for only very brief intervals before it decays and is lost. It also seems that our brains have separate dedicated processers for different kinds of sensory information, such as sounds (words) and patterns (vision) or for hand and leg movements. These can work in parallel, so that different kinds of information can be processed simultaneously but similar information has to queue to be dealt with.

At this level of description, a convenient way to summarise the effects of brain aging on working memory, including prospective memory, is that it reduces the speed at which information can be processed and also increases the rate at which any item of information that is waiting to be processed will decay. There is also good evidence that, at all ages, people take longer to shift between different signals to which they have to attend and that old age disproportionately increases this switching time between different tasks [13]. Slowing of this switching time and difficulties in managing two or more tasks simultaneously also result from damage to the frontal lobes [14] and this is consistent with evidence that aging affects the frontal lobes earlier and more severely than other systems in the brain. Consequently, as we age we become increasingly handicapped at dealing with competing sources of information and so we become increasingly vulnerable to distractions causing failures to do what we had planned.

Unconscious awareness of plans

We need not constantly remain consciously aware of our intentions or of the plans that we have made to carry them out, of the critical event that should trigger the next stage in an unfolding plan or of what we must do when these cues appear. We also need not remain consciously aware of the goals that this internal preparation and activity are supposed to attain. It seems to be possible to hold all these stages in completing planned actions in the dark of the mind until they are activated by appropriate cues and moments. This ability to maintain an unconsciously lurking attention for critical changes in our surroundings was certainly a powerful advance in the evolutionary brain race in which our ancestors did so well. Our multi-great-grandparent tree shrews found a better way to anticipate the next moves that the world might make on them than to hold continually, in the forefront of whatever dim consciousness they had, all the possible threats and rewards and contingent strategies of their lives. Some prospective memory experiments reveal this unconscious awareness. One study measured the times that older and younger people need to identify some brief signals and to make different "reject" responses to other irrelevant signals [15]. The nice result was that older volunteers not only took longer to recognise valid target signals but were also unusually slow whenever they made errors by classifying a valid signal as a "reject". It is as if, when momentary glitches of attention occurred, the intention to make the correct, valid response was present but partly blocked. The valid signals had been recognised at some level, but this rapid and unconscious detection failed to gain control of action. A follow up to this study also showed that the same brief patterns of brain waves (cortical evoked potentials) that occur when valid targets are correctly recognised and answered are also present when they are missed and no response is made to them [16].

We are mostly unaware of the extraordinarily fast and complicated processes of working memory that steer us through every decision every moment of our lives. This unawareness contrasts with our vivid familiarity with the familiar pictures and stories in our minds that we tend to refer to, collectively, as our "memories". These have been termed by psychologists "episodic memory" and we will discuss them in the next chapter.

References

[1] Reason, J. (2000). Human error: Models and management. *BMJ: British Medical Journal*, 320, 768.

[2] Reason, J. and Lucas, D. (1984). Absent-mindedness in shops: Its incidence, correlates and consequences. *British Journal of Clinical Psychology*, 23, 121–131.

[3] Broadbent, D. E. and Heron, A. (1962). Effects of a subsidiary task on performance involving immediate memory by younger and older men. *British Journal of Psychology*, 53, 189–198.

[4] Zollner, P. A. and Lima, S. L. (1999). Search strategies for landscape-level interpatch movements. *Ecology*, 80, 1019–1030.

[5] Einstein, G. O., Holland, L. J., McDaniel, M. A. and Guynn, M. J. (1992). Age-related deficits in prospective memory: The influence of task complexity. *Psychology and Aging*, 7, 471–478.

[6] Einstein, G. O. and McDaniel, M. A. (1990). Normal aging and prospective memory. *Journal of Experimental Psychology: Learning, Memory, and Cognition*, 16, 717–726.

[7] Maylor, E. A. (1990). Age and prospective memory. *Quarterly Journal of Experimental Psychology*, 42, 471–493.

[8] Phillips, L. H., Henry, J. D. and Martin, M. (2008). Adult aging and prospective memory: The importance of ecological validity. In M. Kliegel, M. A. McDaniel and G. Einstein (Eds), pp. 161–185, *Prospective Memory. Cognitive neuroscience, developmental and applied perspectives*. New York, Taylor and Francis.

[9] Craik, F. I. (1994). Memory changes in normal aging. *Current Directions in Psychological Science*, 3, 155–158.

[10] Maylor, E. A. (1996). Age-related impairment in an event-based prospective memory task. *Psychology and Aging*, 11, 74–78.

[11] Roche, N. L., Fleming, J. M. and Shum, D. H. (2002). Self-awareness of prospective memory failure in adults with traumatic brain injury. *Brain Injury*, 16, 931–945.

[12] Kliegel, M., Jager, T., Phillips, L. H., Federspiel, E., Imfeld, A., Keller, M. and Zimprich, D. (2005). Effects of sad mood on time-based prospective memory. *Cognition and Emotion*, 19, 1199–1293.

[13] Kray, J. and Lindenberger, U. (2000). Adult age differences in task switching. *Psychology and Aging*, 15, 126–133.

[14] Rushworth, M. F. S., Hadland, K. A., Paus, T. and Sipila, P. K. (2002). Role of the human medial frontal cortex in task switching: A combined fMRI and TMS study. *Journal of Neurophysiology*, 87, 2577–2592.

[15] West, R. and Craik, F. I. (2001). Influences on the efficiency of prospective memory in younger and older adults. *Psychology and Aging*, 16, 682–691.

[16] West, R. and Covell, E. (2001). Effects of aging on event-related neural activity related to prospective memory. *Neuroreport*, 12, 2855–2858.

8

WHO SAID THAT?

A common problem in old age is remembering what was said but not who said it. A possibly more embarrassing problem is that we remember anecdotes perfectly but bore our friends because we forget how often we have already told them. Psychologists call memory for where we got information "source memory" and agree that it becomes less reliable as we age. This is inconvenient because, particularly in busy group conversations, it adds to other difficulties of age, such as deafness. If we are deaf, as well as not hearing what has been said, and so answering questions that no one has asked, we lose the plot by forgetting who said what.

During the 1970s, Subhash Vyas and I were still too young to be much troubled by such lapses, but our older volunteers insisted that they are a serious nuisance and that we should study them. We videotaped four speakers who each, in turn, made a different remark on the same topic such as lettuce, ducks or clouds. We played these to people aged between 50 and 80 who had high intelligence test scores (these were easy to find in this intimidating Oxford sample). We asked them to recall all the comments and tell us which speaker had made each one. People of all ages could remember exactly what had been said, but the oldest found it harder to recall who had said what and often misattributed even statements that they perfectly recalled. This agreed with earlier findings that people of all ages can remember most words in lists read to them in alternation by a male and a female speaker, but the older less accurately remember whether any given word was spoken by the man or the woman [1]. Other studies have explored situations in which failures of source memory make it more difficult for older people to cope with everyday life. An example is having to act as a witness in a court of law. People aged from 16 to 33 and from 60 to 82 could immediately recall videotaped simulations of crimes and subsequently identify the "perpetrator" in simulated line-ups of physically similar people. Thirty-five minutes later, the older volunteers were still as good as the younger, both at remembering exactly what happened and at identifying the perpetrator. A week later, they remembered fewer details and failed to identify the perpetrator more often than the young [2].

Lapses of source memory are not just a problem for older people. Young children have relatively poor source memory and are less able than adults to distinguish between events that they actually experienced and others that they had only imagined [3]. Elderly adults have the same problem [4]. An analysis of the descriptions of true and false memories for information given during a laboratory experiment found that young adults provide accurate accounts of concrete details of complex events that they have witnessed but that older people tend to dwell on the thoughts and feelings that the events provoked. Perhaps it is not too fanciful to suggest that younger adults are more firmly anchored to reality by their reliable memory for actual, concrete details of events while, for the old, the boundaries between what was perceived and emotional and imagined responses to it begin to dissolve. Another way to put this is that we become less able to monitor our memories and so lose distinctions between our memories of what was actually said and our memories of our reactions to it. So detachment from sources is a scary step towards losing connection with the reality of our past [5, 6]. Weakness of source memory and the consequent risk of confusion is also found in young patients who have damage to the medial temporal and frontal lobes of their brains.

Apart from changes in the temporal and frontal lobes, there is a simple logical reason why we find it harder to remember sources than content. We have to concentrate on the content of what is said because, without this information, remembering who spoke provides us with no more than a tally of those present. After content has been given its necessary priority, remembering sources places an extra demand on attention and memory.

Dan Schacter [7] suggested that it is difficult to remember where information came from because, while the content of a statement is usually unique, there may be many possible sources. To remember sources we must solve a "many to one mapping" problem, deciding from which of several plausible sources each particular piece of information came. This does not seem to be the only explanation. Dan also tested situations in which there was only one possible source for each item of information to be remembered but found that, even with equal numbers of items and sources, items were remembered better.

Tim Perfect [8] pointed out that in experiments to study source memory volunteers are usually asked first to recall items of information and then to remember their sources. He reversed this routine and asked volunteers to first recall each source and then the information that it provided. In this case, older people did not find it harder to remember sources than content. It seems that older people can do this quite well if they know in advance that they must prioritise sources. They only seem to have problems with sources when it is most efficient to prioritise memory for content over memory for sources. So when age makes attention and memory weaker, content is sensibly prioritised and sources become less likely to be registered. The practical lesson is that we should flexibly prioritise sources or content according to what we most need to do. We may also more easily manage to remember who said what if we try to think of speakers in turn to cue our memory for what each said.

Linking sources to content

As we grow older, even though we can still correctly remember many different items of information, we seem to have more trouble remembering connections between them. Psychologists term this process "binding" of disparate pieces of information to constitute a coherent memory. One test of this was to ask a male and a female assistant to show pictures of former US Presidents to older and younger people [9]. Older people recognised more presidents but, in spite of this, less accurately remembered which of the assistants had shown each. Here very familiar faces were cues to recall the sex of their presenters. The connections between presenters and faces were arbitrary as a face provided no information as to who was more likely to have shown it. Since the two presenters were physically present throughout the experiment they could hardly be forgotten. What the experiment showed was that older people find it harder to remember unfamiliar connections, even between very familiar things, even if one of these things is still present while they are asked to recall.

If the instructions had been reversed and people had been asked to remember which faces each presenter had shown, then the old might have benefitted more than the young because they knew more presidents and so had better chances of also retrieving the links. Once again this suggests that a practical strategy to ease our problems with source memory is not to begin by asking ourselves "who said this?" but by asking "what did each person say?"

Forgetting to whom you told your story

Failures to remember links between people and events can become an embarrassing issue in another way. Anything interesting that happens to us becomes a potential entry in our mental archive of topics to bring up during conversations. Unfortunately, although these events and thoughts may be unique and, if we are lucky, may even be quite interesting, we become increasingly likely to tell them repeatedly to the same people. Here the linking problem becomes "one to many" rather than "many to one". We remember our stories far too well but forget on which of our companions we have inflicted them. If they are prickly, our companions may take offence because they feel that we have regarded our previous encounters with them as being less significant and memorable than they would like to believe.

It does seem that as we grow old, source memory becomes harder to manage. This may be because we interrogate our memories in a less efficient way, or for other reasons. A simple explanation is that making the effort to remember connections between different items is an additional task, and this is harder than remembering just the items themselves independently of each other. The more difficult a memory task becomes, the greater is the difference between old and young. A different possibility is that to remember links we may have to use particular brain structures and that aging affects these particular dedicated systems earlier and more severely than other parts of the brain. Work on this possibility is in progress.

References

[1] Craik, F. I. and Kirsner, K. (1974). The effect of speaker's voice on word recognition. *The Quarterly Journal of Experimental Psychology*, 2, 274–284.

[2] Memon, A., Bartlett, J., Rose, R. and Gray, C. (2003) The aging eye-witness: Effects of age on face, delay and source memory ability. *Journal of Gerontology, B*, 58, 338–345.

[3] Lindsay, D. S., Johnson, M. K. and Kwon, P. (1991). Developmental changes in source memory monitoring. *Journal of Experimental Child Psychology*, 52, 297–318.

[4] Cohen, G. and Faulkner, D. (1989). Age differences in source forgetting: Effects on reality monitoring and on eyewitness testimony. *Psychology and Aging*, 4, 10.

[5] Henkel, L. A., Franklin, N. and Johnson, M. K. (2000). Cross-modal source monitoring confusions between perceived and imagined events. *Journal of Experimental Psychology: Learning, Memory, and Cognition*, 26, 321–325.

[6] Hastroudi, S., Johnson, M. and Chrisniak, L. D. (1990). Aging and qualitative characteristics of memories for perceived and imagined complex events. *Psychology and Aging*, 5, 119–126.

[7] Schacter, D. L., Osowiecki, D., Kaszniak, A. W., Kihlstrom, J. F. and Valdiserri, M. (1994). Source memory: Extending the boundaries of age-related deficits. *Psychology and Aging*, 9(1), 81–89.

[8] Tree, J. J. and Perfect, T. J. (2004). A re-examination of source monitoring deficits in the elderly: Evidence for independent age deficits of item and source memory. *Brain Impairment*, 5, 138–144.

[9] Bayer, Z. C., Hernandez, R. J., Morris, A. M., Salomonczyk, D., Pirogovsky, E. and Gilbert, P. E. (2011). Age-related source memory deficits persist despite superior item memory. *Experimental Aging Research*, 37, 473–480.

9

LOSING AND FINDING WORDS AND NAMES

Most of us can expect to keep most of our words up to the end of long lives but among the frequent vexations and anxieties of old age are brief failures to find particular words that we can easily produce at other times – usually when we no longer need them. These brief memory blocks are remembered because they often happen in conversations during which we have fallen into embarrassed stammering while the particular word we seek stays stuck in some crevice of the mind. Groping for a word in public becomes even more embarrassing and memorable when it is the name of someone known and admired for forty years, as I found when toasting my partner and her family at her birthday party and, for ten alarming seconds, lost "Owen", the first name of an excellent brother-in-law.

These blocks occur at any age and have been named "Tip of the Tongue States" (or for psychologists, who love inventing terse, business-like acronyms, TOTs). Questions about these small griefs are: do TOTs really become more frequent in old age or do we simply notice them more because they seem threats of impending decrepitude? Are TOTs premonitions of more drastic memory losses to come? Are some kinds of word more likely to go missing than others? Are proper names especially troublesome? What other factors, apart from advancing age, block words from recall? If word finding does become more difficult as we grow old, what particular brain changes cause this?

We try to provoke TOTs in laboratory experiments in many different ways: by giving people exact dictionary definitions and asking for the single words that best fit them; by asking general knowledge questions that can be answered by single words; or by recording the accuracy and speed with which people can name pictures of rarely encountered objects such as casements, astrolabes or gyroscopes. Their general finding has been that word-finding problems occur often in childhood, are less frequent in young adults and become increasingly frequent in old age.

A review of the literature on picture naming concluded that the older people become the more often they have word-finding problems [1]. The author also made the important point that the number of years that people have lived makes little or no difference to their problems with word finding if their levels of education and lifetime occupations and their general health are also taken into account. This is theoretically important because it once again shows that older people's competence at remembering words is determined by the amount that they have learned during their lifetimes and by their general health rather than by tallies of the years of their lives. It is also comforting because we cannot slow or check the passage of time but there are effective ways to maintain brain health and so access to our words.

The natural history of TOTs

Laboratory experiments are so tightly controlled that they often do not tell us what we would most like to know and they tend to answer questions that we did not wish to ask. Evidence that is more satisfying comes from a naturalistic approach, such as asking people to keep diaries of times when they blocked while finding a word that they were, rightly, convinced that they knew. Debbie Burke, the North American doyenne of TOTs, asked her volunteers to keep diaries of their lapses. These confirmed that TOTs do indeed increase with age. She also found that words most often TOTted are relatively rare and, more often than we would expect by chance, are proper names [2]. We all recognise her additional finding that a particular vexation of finding oneself in a TOT state is the number of incorrect alternatives that jostle for attention. This is reassuring, in a way. Since we confidently reject intrusive alternatives we must, at some level, still retain enough information about the word we seek to instantly reject incorrect alternatives and immediately recognise it when it comes to mind or is spoken by somebody else. Debbie found that most of the competing alternatives that our minds throw up are words with similar sounds but different meanings to the ones we seek. Incorrect alternatives are also usually words of the same grammatical class of nouns, adjectives, adverbs or verbs as the elusive target.

A useful question is whether we can use this babble of wrong guesses to get ourselves out of TOT states. A test was whether people could escape from TOTs that occurred when they searched for single-word answers to general knowledge questions [3]. Before being asked each question they read aloud words that sounded similar to the one that they would later be asked to find. This rehearsal of similar-sounding words reduced the number of TOTs that they later made. Unfortunately, the further result of this experiment will be familiar to all who have been vexed by the false answers that throng for attention whenever we block on a word. If, after a person had blocked on a word, other words that sound similar to it were read aloud the number of TOTs increased. This seems consistent with our experience because the incorrect alternative answers that we generate while blocking on a TOT are also usually words that sound similar to the one for which we are searching. However, before we decide that this must be a complete explanation we must ask, as did another study [4], whether some kinds of similarity between blocked words and distracters are more helpful than others. People responded to general knowledge questions by saying "Know", "Don't Know" or "TOT" and then read lists of ten words that included three that had the same first, middle or last syllable as any unresolved TOT word. Words with the same middle or last syllable did not help. Words with the same initial syllable did help the young and middle aged and also the young/old (60 to 70s) but not the old/old (75+).

Those of us who have long passed the significant day on which we officially became old/old, (and have been rather too enthusiastically congratulated by colleagues on this transition) take what comfort we can from a study that compared TOTs between people aged 17 to 29, 30 to 49 and 50 to 82 years. As usual, the young and middle aged did not differ from each other, but they experienced fewer TOTs than the old. Better news is that when differences in their general knowledge were taken into account, those aged from 50 to 80 did as well as younger adults [5]. Those who had little general knowledge also made fewer TOTs. (In empty minds there seem to be fewer words to intrude.) Also, instead of signalling a TOT, these volunteers could claim confident ignorance.

This raises the fascinating question as to how any of us, at any age, knows whether or not we know something that we cannot, at the moment, precisely recall; also whether our accuracy at knowing what we know (but can't at the moment recall) changes as we grow old. Although research on this almost metaphysical question is still rather sparse (it is, rather pompously, termed "metamemory"), some studies find that the accuracy with which we can decide whether we know or do not know a word or fact that we cannot currently recall does not decline with age, though the confidence with which we make these judgements may be affected [6]. However, other studies do find some loss of accuracy of feelings of knowing in old age that are correlated with scores on behavioural tests of frontal lobe function, on which older people perform less well [7]. A particularly well-conducted study found that even demented patients who have lost much of their vocabulary do not seem to have lost the ability to decide whether or not a word is familiar enough to be retrieved on a later occasion [8]. However, at least one other research group has found that metamemory is impaired in patients with "mild cognitive impairment" who may, of course, be in the early stages of dementias [9]. Studies of brain-damaged patients agree with the behavioural evidence that the frontal lobes of the brain are involved in metamemory, since patients with lesions to the right prefrontal cortex have less accurate feelings of knowing [10]. Brain images obtained from intact and conscious volunteers agree with this [7] and also point out that, although the right and left inferior frontal gyri are involved in "feeling of knowing" judgements, they are not involved in direct recall of immediately remembered information [11].

I'll never forget what's-his-name

Most experimenters find that efforts to recall proper names of people and places are especially likely to produce TOTs. Many would also comment that problems specifically with remembering proper names become greater as we age. In one study, volunteers were asked to name photographs of current and former celebrities [12]. All, especially the oldest, made errors and experienced TOTs, especially for names of those celebrities then past their peak fame. It is understandable that TOTs should occur for the names of lesser-known and infrequently encountered celebrities because even when their faces are familiar their names are harder to retrieve than those of the more recently famous. But why do proper names seem to be particularly troublesome even when we often use them?

Possibly because when we lose them, this is always embarrassing and may even seem neglectful and rude. One suggestion has been that proper names actually are harder to recall than other kinds of word because they are arbitrary labels that convey no information about their owners. Many surnames such as Bishop, Carpenter, Farmer, Mason, Priest and so on do have meanings but, except for rare coincidences, are no longer valid job-descriptions. Other proper names such as Bull, Fox and Lamb are also meaningful words that can be deliberately associated with vivid concrete images and, for this reason, they may be easy to remember. Since entering primary school I have strongly argued that surnames are arbitrary labels that tell us nothing whatsoever about their owners. Many, perhaps most, surnames are just sound-tokens with no meaning at all.

Gill Cohen illustrated these problems by showing volunteers pictures of 12 people they did not know and asking them to remember, for each, a proper name and also some other items of information such as an occupation or a possession [13]. Their names were recalled less well than anything else about them, particularly when the proper name was the name of an occupation such as Weaver or Carpenter that might be mistaken for one of the job descriptions that they also had to remember. The relative difficulty in remembering different kinds of information about people also seemed to be affected by the order in which they were recalled. Occupations were the easiest to remember and were usually recalled first; surnames and possessions only later. Gill suggests that information about who a person "is" prominently includes a role in life and that it is the most useful index in our mental directory of people. Apart from being a banal opener for a conversation with a stranger the trite question "What do you do?" may also serve to index them in our mental contact list.[1]

Gill's finding that there are strong contingencies in the order in which we recall different kinds of information about people suggests that we become skilful at building up systematic networks of associations to remember what we most need to know about individuals. If we do this, we can use each detail to find another still lost in the shadows of the mind. George Temple a loveable, distinguished, elderly mathematician, complained to me that his problems in remembering colleagues' names were being made worse by the recent tendency for their wives to keep their original surnames. In the past, he could often remember a husband's lost surname by imaging a partner who shared the same label. Alas, no more.

George's spouse-finding strategy makes a point about how our brains link words to their meanings. The same noise that makes up the name "Jones" may be linked to other very different entities. Briefly losing a link between a name-noise and a particular person does not imply loss of the name-noise, but only loss of one of many possible connections between this noise and other people, things and events. It is unlikely that the brain stores a separate representation of the name-noise Jones for each of many different kinds of association. Prompting with the word Jones encourages retrieval of all entities with that label. When we fail to retrieve the right entity, what seems to have gone missing is one of many *links* of association. Once the image of Jones-female is found in memory, retrieval of the quite different link between her and her surname allows us to locate Jones-male.

Another point is that even a complete, accurate and vivid description of an entity whose name we have mislaid may not help. Jones, in three-dimensional solidity, with his profession, personal habits and emotional aura all blatant, does not necessarily prompt his name. Circumlocution or circum-mnesis can take complicated paths. I once tried to tell my patient partner that I would cook Saffron Chicken for lunch but could only manage "chicken in a crocus-stamen sauce". She expressed revulsion until I remembered the fine author Luis Zafron who gave me what I needed – the *noise* of a word for which I already had the correct meaning.

I buy this story, but distinguished colleagues would disagree. Elizabeth Maylor (the British as distinct from the North American doyenne of TOTs) suggests that difficulties with names occur because they are usually quite rarely used compared to other words [14]. Another study [15] found that if we allow for their lower frequency of use, proper names are not harder to bring to mind than other words. I find this plausible, but still feel that to show that the relative frequencies of proper names (and of all other words) affects the ease with which we can recall them does not mean that other factors such as the multiple associations of particular names with many different people do not also play a part. It is useful to ask what makes *any* words hard to recall, whether they are proper names or not. Rare words by definition are those that are seldom encountered or used and these produce more TOTs than common words. Similarly, proper names that have not been recalled for some time are less easily found and so are more often TOTted. To show that recall of proper names does not disproportionately decline with age compared to recall of other words, after all those factors that make proper names harder to recall have been, statistically or experimentally, factored out, does not mean that older people do not, daily, have greater trouble with proper names nor contradict earlier findings. This only means that anything that makes recall harder for the young makes it even harder for the old. The difficulties encountered by the old are not qualitatively different from, but only exaggerations of, those encountered by the young.

There are more positive aspects to name rarity. A very rare name is distinctive because it is not shared by other people that we know. Also, the people we know usually have at least two labels, a first and a second name. We must distinguish the many Smiths we know by their first names or by other facts about them. Their first names may also be more or less rare and so distinctive. Balthazar Smith may be easier to remember than plain John Smith. This may make a difference when we try to cue our recall of a person by his first or second name. The unique Balthazar may cue the correct one of many Smiths better than the common Smith cues the rare Balthazar. Perhaps because our own names are illustrations of rarity and frequency Steve Jones and I picked up on this idea and tested how well elderly volunteers could retrieve common second names when cued by rare and common first names and vice versa [16]. We found moderate support for the value of distinctiveness as a cue, and as a help for problems of name retrieval that become more frequent in old age.

Naming faces

A more definitive experiment compared how well young adults could name photographs of celebrities who had rare or common names and more or less distinctive faces. Distinctive faces were correctly named faster than were less distinctive faces and celebrities with rare names were named faster than those with common names – but only if their faces were also distinctive. When volunteers were taught names for unfamiliar faces, they learned familiar faster than unfamiliar names. Both the general frequency of words and the familiarity of names affect how well they are recalled, but these factors also interact with the distinctiveness of a face. If one wishes to be swiftly recognised and correctly named, having a unique face is an asset. As, in some ways, is having a unique name [17].

A different factor that determines how easily we can recall words is the age at which we first learned them. Since children usually learn very common words first, the effects of rarity and age of learning are confounded but can be separated by clever experiments. In a study neatly titled "Last in First Out", old and young volunteers were equated in terms of other measures of their total vocabularies and compared on the speed and accuracy with which they could name pictures of objects [18]. All the volunteers found it harder to remember long object names than short object names. The visual complexity of the pictures and the relative ease with which they could be imaged had no effect on recall. Allowing for this, and also for the relative frequency with which the object names are used in everyday life, older volunteers recalled fewer names than the young, and people of all ages were better at recalling object names that they had learned early in their lives.

A similar point was made by another comparison of the speed and accuracy with which people can name photographs of celebrities [19]. Celebrity names learned earlier in life were recalled faster and more accurately. The authors caution us that names that have been learned when we were young have, no doubt, also been recalled more often over the years. Names that were first encountered early in life may also benefit from having been learned in youth when learning is more efficient. Youthful learning may be more durable. Possibly, also, a name or a word that we have recalled at intervals over a long period of our life is better remembered than one we have used just as often, but over a shorter period. This last comparison would be difficult to make and, as far as I know, has not been tried.

Words in the brain

Is memory for faces and names supported by particular areas of the brain, different from those that support memory for other kinds of pictures or words? If so, does advancing age affect these areas more than others? Since the 1960s, many studies have shown that damage or change of the hippocampus and the nearby medial temporal lobes markedly reduces memory efficiency.

During the 1860s, a French neurologist Pierre Paul Broca studied two patients with brain damage that affected their ability to find even common words. Their damage was in what is now known as "Broca's area" in the left frontal lobe of the brain, more precisely labelled the pars opercularis and pars triangularis of the inferior frontal gyrus. Patients with damage to this area, usually resulting from strokes, have severe difficulties in finding words. Their frequent word-finding failures superficially resemble TOTs and, just like undamaged people, they try to resolve them by paraphrases such as "holding water" for a drinking tumbler. They can, nevertheless, still understand words that they cannot immediately bring to mind. Different language problems are experienced by patients who have damage to Wernicke's area in the medial temporal lobe, including underlying white matter damage, which isolates the occipital, temporal and parietal regions. Because they can produce language but have difficulty understanding it, their condition is termed "receptive aphasia" to distinguish it from "expressive aphasia", which is caused by damage to Broca's area and results in an inability to produce the correct words for things or events. Receptive aphasics have difficulty understanding either spoken or written language although, curiously, they can talk using normal grammatical constructions and intonations but meaning is poorly conveyed. It seems likely that age-related minor losses of tissue specifically in Broca's area would increase TOTting without necessarily causing the severe problems that would be diagnosed as expressive aphasia. The phenomenon of using paraphrases of forgotten words that occurs in Broca's aphasia also occurs in older (and even in younger!) people who are momentarily blocked.

Problems with finding people's names are different from difficulties with recognising their faces. A severe problem with face-recognition is termed prosopagnosia and results from damage to the fusiform gyrus, which is located along the lower margins of the temporal lobes of the brain. This seems to be a highly specialised area since those with severe damage to it cannot recognise faces at all but have little or no difficulty with all other means of identifying individuals such as their voices, habitual clothes or body language. Prosopagnosia also does not seem to be an all-or-none condition. It can be genetically transmitted and occurs in up to 2.5 per cent of the normal population whose greater or lesser difficulties in recognising faces, vary from "being rather bad with faces" to having quite severe problems. It is possible that some people whose brain aging causes greater than usual losses of brain tissue, specifically in their fusiform gyrus, find it especially difficult to recognise faces. The various problems of finding words and names for faces that we have discussed could be caused by specific losses in each of these areas or, since they are rather far apart in the brain, to losses in the richness of the connections between them. This is also an illustration that all brains do not age in the same way. General, diffuse changes affect us all, but, superimposed on these, we may experience different patterns of decline as changes in circulation with age affect different local systems in our brains.

Note

1 In contrast, the allegedly classic Royal Conversation Opener "Have You Come Far?" seems to acknowledge lack of interest in remembering anything at all about the person greeted.

References

[1] Goulette, P., Ska, B. and Kahn, H. J. (1994). Is there a decline in picture-naming in advanced age? *Journal of Speech and Hearing Research*, 37, 629–644.

[2] Burke, D. M., MacKay, D. G., Worthley, J. S. and Wade, E. (1991). On the tip of the tongue: What causes word finding failures in young and older adults? *Journal of Memory and Language*, 30, 542–579.

[3] James, L. E. and Burke, D. M. (2000). Phonological priming effects on word retrieval and tip-of-the-tongue experiences in young and older adults. *Journal of Experimental Psychology: Learning, Memory, and Cognition*, 26, 1378–1391.

[4] White, K. K. and Abrams, L. (2002). Does priming specific syllables during tip-of-the-tongue states facilitate word retrieval in older adults? *Psychology and Aging*, 17(2), 226–235.

[5] Dahlgren, D. J. (1998). Impact of knowledge and age on tip-of-the-tongue rates. *Experimental Aging Research*, 24, 139–153.

[6] Allen-Burge, R. and Storandt, M. (2000). Age equivalence in feeling-of-knowing experiences. *The Journals of Gerontology Series B: Psychological Sciences and Social Sciences*, 55(4), 214–223.

[7] Souchay, C., Isingrini, M. and Espagnet, L. (2000). Aging, episodic memory feeling-of-knowing, and frontal functioning. *Neuropsychology*, 14(2), 299–309.

[8] Moulin, C. J., James, N., Perfect, T. J. and Jones, R. W. (2003). Knowing what you cannot recognise: Further evidence for intact metacognition in Alzheimer's disease. *Aging, Neuropsychology, and Cognition*, 10(1), 74–82.

[9] Perrotin, A., Belleville, S. and Isingrini, M. (2007). Metamemory monitoring in mild cognitive impairment: Evidence of a less accurate episodic feeling-of-knowing. *Neuropsychologia*, 45(12), 2811–2826.

[10] Schnyer, D. M., Verfaellie, M., Alexander, M. P., LaFleche, G., Nicholls, L. and Kaszniak, A. W. (2004). A role for right medial prefrontal cortex in accurate feeling-of-knowing judgments: Evidence from patients with lesions to frontal cortex. *Neuropsychologia*, 42(7), 957–966.

[11] Kikyo, H., Ohki, K. and Miyashita, Y. (2002). Neural correlates for feeling-of-knowing: An fMRI parametric analysis. *Neuron*, 36(1), 177–186.

[12] Evrade, M. (2002). Ageing and lexical access to common and proper names in picture naming. *Brain and Language*, 81, 174–179.

[13] Cohen, G. (1990). Recognition and retrieval of proper names: Age differences in the fan effect. *European Journal of Cognitive Psychology*, 2, 193–204.

[14] Maylor, E. A. (1997). Proper name retrieval in old age: Converging evidence against disproportionate impairment. *Aging, Neuropsychology, and Cognition*, 4, 211–226.

[15] Rendell, P. G., Castel, A. D. and Craik, F. I. (2005). Memory for proper names in old age: A disproportionate impairment? *The Quarterly Journal of Experimental Psychology Section A*, 58, 54–71.

[16] Jones, S. J. and Rabbitt, P. M. A. (1994). Effects of age on the ability to remember common and rare proper names. *The Quarterly Journal of Experimental Psychology*, 47, 1001–1014.

[17] Valentine, T. and Moore, V. (1995). Naming faces: The effects of facial distinctiveness and surname frequency. *The Quarterly Journal of Experimental Psychology*, 48, 849–878.

[18] Hodgeson, C. and Ellis, A. W. (1998). Last in first to go: Age of acquisition and naming in the elderly. *Brain and Language*, 64, 146–163.

[19] Valentine, V. M. T. (1998). The effect of age of acquisition on speed and accuracy of naming famous faces. *The Quarterly Journal of Experimental Psychology: Section A*, 51, 485–513.

10

REMEMBERING THE BEGINNINGS OF OUR LIVES

It may seem out of place to discuss our earliest memories in a book about old age. On the other hand, most of my older friends say how very much they enjoy thinking about their remote past and even the first events that they can recall from their infancies. Perhaps this is because these contrast pleasantly with a perplexing present. I also think that old age is a time in which we try to interpret our lives and try to understand how the past has shaped who we now are.

It is a plot-spoiler to begin by confessing that I know of no evidence that increasing age affects the dates or the accuracy of our earliest memories, or even how often we recall them. Nevertheless, studies of our earliest memories do make important points about the nature of memories: their reliability, their relation to the original experiences that they purport to record and, most of all, their extreme selectivity – the reasons why we remember some things and not others. Some useful guiding questions are: what is the earliest age from which we can remember anything at all? Do some of us have much earlier childhood memories than others and, if so, why? Is there anything about our very earliest memories that makes them different from later ones? For example, are our earliest memories unusually vivid or emotionally charged? How accurate are they? Are they, unlike later memories, only apparently unchanging snapshots of past realities or do they also become less accessible and accurate as we age?

Large surveys have found that few adults remember things, people or events that they encountered before they were 18 to 25 months old. Parents know that this is not because infants cannot remember anything from day to day. They are charmed to see how their toddlers can recognise objects, animals and people many weeks after a single previous encounter. Formal experiments endorse their pleasure but also show that, although infants retain enough information from day to day to interpret their simple lives, by the time they are adolescents they have forgotten almost everything they once remembered about their early childhoods. Why?

Freud was a master-minter of aphorisms, and the Goethe Prize for Literature was possibly his best-deserved distinction. Noticing how sparse our memories from early childhood are he coined the phrase "infantile amnesia" that is still used as a label for this curiosity. He believed that memories of earliest childhood are few and bland because all the threatening stuff is edited out. He saw infancy as an exceptionally stressful time during which we struggle to reconcile our helplessness and dependence with our fierce inappropriate desires. Memories associated with these infantile conflicts are so distressing that, although (as Freud believed) they stay with us throughout our lives, we expend considerable mental energy suppressing them so that they remain inaccessible unless triggered by accidental reminders or skilfully managed therapeutic conversations. Some of Freud's writings suggest that he doubted that any detail of any event in our entire lives is ever lost rather than being actively suppressed. In his elegant book *The Psychopathology of Everyday Life* [1] he implied that every detail of our lives is recorded in memory and, although censorship and distortions of memory occur, these can be resolved by therapy to reveal underlying true memories. Unacknowledged hurtful memories and the energy-sapping effort required to keep these out of consciousness, distort our interpretations of ourselves and of others throughout our lives.

Wordsworth, a much better poet and only slightly less ambitious psychologist, had earlier offered the pleasant romantic idea that our memories of earliest childhood are not only rich and plentiful but especially significant and vivid and nourishing because they come "apparelled in celestial light, the glory and the freshness of a dream". His optimism survived through the early nineteenth century until Freud's bleaker view took over and the blue remembered hills of the land of lost content began to be strip-mined for anguish to explain current distress. Are the few early memories that we can access just too bland to need exorcism or camouflage? As we age, do we increasingly forget our early childhoods or do we remember and dwell on them until, perhaps, they at last become the main content of our mental lives?

My personal earliest memories are congenially insignificant, not especially vivid and I recall them seldom. The clearest, from about 2.5 years is not a snapshot of a single event but a collage of many episodes of being watched until I fell asleep in the hot dark by a pungent, chain-bidi-smoking soft-voiced Ayah, underpaid to minimise my impact on my parents' lives. She eased our boredom with plot-less descriptions of glittering Rajahs and Ranis, with warriors riding elephants and horses decorated in silver, gold, scarlet and green. During tepid Oxford insomnias, I can still imagine no better progress to oblivion.

Blight out of mind?

The idea that most of us have far fiercer mental Ayahs who actively censor our memories of childhood pain is topical because of legal confrontations between agonised adults who claim to have "recovered" repressed memories of parental abuse that is desperately repudiated by their distraught families. A distinguished forensic psychologist, Elizabeth Loftus, found that all of the many legal claims of "recovered memory" that she was asked to analyse collapsed under detailed investigation [2]. Her studies, and many other revelations of the implantation of false memories of childhood abuse during careless psychotherapy, erode confidence that these "recovered memories" are evidence for Freud's ideas about repression. It is obviously very difficult to design laboratory experiments to test claims of this kind, but controlled studies can give us some information.

One study recorded childhood memories from 429 adults, of whom 19.8 per cent had been sexually abused, 11.5 per cent emotionally abused and 14.9 per cent physically abused [3]. All who had been abused in any way said that they could remember even painful incidents but also that they now deliberately and consciously avoided doing this. The vividness and number of the neutral and pleasant childhood memories that they could recall were not related to the kind of abuse that they had suffered. The authors found no evidence that memories of abuse were unavailable until released by appropriate therapy, that memories associated with sexual abuse are especially hard to recall or that being abused as a child, in any way, makes it harder to recall other neutral or pleasant childhood memories.

Other studies also raise doubts as to whether memories of childhood traumas are repressed but can later be recovered. It is much harder to prove that childhood memories, particularly memories of sexual abuse, are *never*, in Freud's terms, "repressed". For example, a study of 129 women who had been sexual victims in childhood found that, when questioned, 38 per cent claimed not to remember abuse that they had experienced 17 years earlier and that had been documented at that time [4].

A different question is whether trauma and stress in childhood affect all mental abilities, including memory, in later life. A small study found that 21 survivors of childhood sexual abuse had lower scores on tests of logical reasoning and of short-term memory than 20 non-abused controls [5]. There is also evidence that stress in early life can cause brain changes that affect later competence. Many studies show that rats that are stressed when they are young, experience changes in the hippocampus and frontal cortex and learn less rapidly when they mature. The stressed rats also experience changes in corticosteroid and neurotransmitter function and become less engaged in social play with other animals [6, 7].

When we think about this conflicting and incomplete evidence, it is useful to distinguish three different possibilities. One is that we actively suppress memories of abuse, and so may be unconscious that they are still held somewhere in our minds; another is that experiencing abuse and other stresses causes brain changes that make us permanently less competent at learning anything new and also at remembering even innocuous life experiences. A third, very different, idea is that we know very well what is in our memory but just do not go there, even avoiding recalling things that, by association, may bring up things that we would rather shun. I think that while there is persuasive evidence for all these possibilities the evidence for specific, unconscious repression of particular memories is the weakest. I am biased by some convincing objections to the methodology of experiments that have claimed to demonstrate repression [8].

Deliberate repression or avoidance of painful memories is only one of many explanations why childhood memories are few and innocuous. A neurophysiological explanation is that while we are infants, and even in our early adolescence, our brains undergo greater changes than they will ever experience again. Before the age of four, infants lose more nerve cells (neurones) more rapidly than at any later age. We continue to lose and alter connections between neurones until adolescence [9]. One idea is that this is necessary because the infant brain has to physically organise itself to learn to interpret the world. Those nerve cells and the connections between them that become included in new pathways and networks survive, but others are lost, presumably with any memories they store. A different idea is that infant brains do not, at first, work as well as they eventually will because the gradual development of fatty surrounding sheaths for connections between neurones (myelinisation) gradually improves their efficiency. This process is not complete until late adolescence. Infant memories may be sparse because the young brain re-wires itself, because they are recorded in a sub-optimal and rapidly changing system, or for both these reasons.

Language and early memories

A different explanation, at the level of actions and behaviour rather than of neurones and neurophysiology, is that the ability to recognise something and to be able to recall it is different from the ability to tell others about it. Parents know that their infants can recognise particular pets, places, toys and people long before they can talk about them. One study [10] tested infants' memories for things, events and people that they had first seen at about 13, 16 or 20 months. Nine months to three years later, there was little evidence that they could remember any experiences from age 13 or 16 months. Their vocabularies were also tested at 13, 16 and 20 months. Those who knew more words earlier could remember more events, earlier events and more details of each event.

This might mean either that infants need to learn language before they can properly interpret, record and describe things that happen to them or that, although they do record impressions and images of things and events, they cannot communicate these until they have the words to do so. A subtly different possibility is that language gives us an additional way of recording our experiences and is also the most convenient index system for the filing cabinets of our minds. Our memories are partly made up of verbal descriptions. Our words are our best way of getting at our memories and may even be an integral part of the representations of the past in our minds.

A problem in discussing earliest memories is whether they are unaltered original impressions of events or memories of memories that we have often rehearsed and edited in private and even discussed with others. Children's early memories are likely to be discussed with their parents or other adults so that, over time, they become collaborative constructions. We can check details of children's memories with those of adults who were also present. There is usually good agreement between accounts given by children and accompanying adults but this may just mean that they have often talked together about their shared experiences. For better evidence, we can check children's memories for particular striking events against reliable independent records that have not been seen either by the children or by adults who shared them. Records of hospital treatment provide this opportunity and allowed psychologists to compare how well toddlers who were aged from 13 to 36 months when they were treated for accidents, remembered what had happened to them 6, 12, 18 and 24 months later. The youngest had scanty recall but a few 2-year-olds, who had little language at the time of the accident, could recall some visual images of what had happened. Those children who had most language when the accidents happened remembered them best. As we might expect, the older the children were when their accidents happened the more plentiful and accurate were the details they remembered. The amount of stress that children had suffered, judged both from their own accounts and from those of others and from their hospital records, did not seem to affect how well they recalled their accidents. Older children, and those with more words, who could more easily talk with their parents about their experiences would also have benefitted from longer and more frequent discussions. This suggests, though it cannot conclusively prove, that at least some childhood memories may be stable records of original impressions rather than post hoc collaborative constructs [11].

Do our earliest memories alter in old age?

Whether or not some of our earliest memories are collaborative constructs, what happens to them as we grow old? Do we lose some of them? Do we mull them over more or less often? Lynn McInnes [12] asked a few hundred elderly volunteers to describe and date their earliest memories, to tell us whether they were associated with any particular emotions and to rate how vivid they now seem. Volunteers' ages between 54 and 83 years made no difference to the number of childhood events that they now remembered, how vivid they said that these memories now were, how early in life the remembered events had occurred or how often they now thought about them. Their earliest memories often involved little or no action and seemed to resemble snapshots or, more rarely, recorded sound bites rather than sound and vision replays. The average age of first memories was 3.6 years with a range from 2 to 8 years and was not affected by the age at which they were recalled. Most memories were ordinary and unexciting impressions of places, people, animals or objects. Some were memories of striking public events, such as the beginning of the Jarrow hunger march. Most were not particularly vivid or emotionally charged. In contrast to other studies, both men and women seemed to remember the same kinds of thing in much the same ways and women did not remember events from younger ages than men. The only difference was that those who produced the earliest first memories also had significantly higher scores on two tests of fluid intelligence that they took in their old age. This provokes some ideas.

As children grow up, they become faster at solving difficult novel problems and so achieve increasingly higher scores on intelligence tests. However, intelligence tests are designed to be stable so that as they grow up, and even into their old age, the rank order of people's first test scores with respect to each other changes little or not at all. This means that if we had been able to invent a time machine to travel back and give our volunteers an intelligence test when they were very young the rank order of their scores with respect to each other would have been much the same as we found in their old age. Those who could recall events from earlier in their lives would also have had relatively high test scores as young children. One explanation is that clever infants are alert to life earlier and record more of what is going on around them. This seems plausible, but a more specific, and perhaps more testable, idea is that more intelligent children master words earlier in childhood and so can recall events better because they have learnt more words to describe these events to themselves and to discuss them with others and also to help to later retrieve them.

The variety of possible explanations for this finding makes us realise how hard it is to argue for any single explanation for individual differences in reports of memories from any age. We have noticed that the completeness and persistence of infant memories depends on how fast their brains develop. Those infants whose brains develop earlier also earlier attain conscious awareness and language, and better understand and remember what is going on about them. This seems likely but it is certainly not the whole story. Children who have relatively high intelligence test scores also tend to have relatively able parents who are, consequently, usually also relatively well-off. These luckier children have better childhoods and lifelong general health, nutrition and longer education. In advantaged families we might also expect more frequent and detailed discussions between parents and children and, perhaps, also a greater mutual interest in discussing their shared past.

Clever and intellectually curious young children may begin to explore and date events in their lives at an earlier age and will be more likely to continue to do this as they grow up and earlier begin an active archaeology of their infant memories. It is disquieting to realise that our memories are so greatly edited and altered during frequent recall that they become, in effect, memories of memories rather than fading records of original impressions.

It is hard for us to be confident about the precise dates of the memories that we report. Time, by itself, leaves no trace, so we cannot work out when an event happened except by its relationships with other events. In response to the question "How do you know that this is your earliest memory?", most Newcastle citizens offered comments such as "it must have been after 1936 because my younger sister was there". Others, who could find no evidence in their memories to bracket possible dates, puzzled which of several different recollections was actually earliest and often had to weakly conclude that some just seemed earlier than others. Evidently much selection and editing had gone on, and what they offered us would often be the earliest memory that was plausibly dateable by circumstantial evidence rather than what may have been an actual, but not verifiable, first memory.

Unfortunately, as is usual in psychology, several explanations are equally plausible and they all may work together. Those we have just listed are upstaged by yet another: intelligent children, especially if they have acquired language early, are more likely to discuss their memories with their parents and other adults. Most studies (though not ours) find that girls mature faster than boys and, age for age, tend to have bigger vocabularies. Girls also tend to talk more with their parents and siblings and to become interested in sharing their experiences with others earlier in their lives. Findings that children in socially advantaged families consistently have earlier first memories may mean that these lucky ones are somewhat more intelligent and learn more words somewhat earlier but also that more affluent parents also tend to be better educated, more successful throughout their lives and more inclined to talk at length with their children about daily events.

How our early memories construct our life stories

Consistent differences between men and women throw some light on the idea that many, perhaps most, of our earliest memories are collaborations. Mary Mullen [13] asked 768 people to tell her the number, date and kind of their earliest memories. Like other investigators, she found that women reported more and earlier memories than men. Eldest children of both sexes also reported more and slightly earlier memories than their younger brothers and sisters. Mullen suggests that this could be because parents tend to talk more with their first children than with those who arrive later into a busier household; also that parents, particularly mothers, tend to talk more to their daughters than to their sons. She suggests that women may report earlier memories both because they gain enough words to describe and retrieve them earlier and also because they benefit from earlier and more frequent involvements in the development of a family saga of incidents that are often collaboratively recalled, discussed, edited and dated.

Most Newcastle volunteers reported bland and trivial incidents as their first memories. They said that these were, on the whole, mildly pleasant to recall and unconnected to any other important or interesting events in their lives. Very few reported painful or disturbing memories. Other studies have also found that people tend to avoid recalling painful events and choose to replay harmless and pleasant memories. Since pleasant memories are brought to mind more often, it may be harder to retrieve painful memories not because they have been unconsciously repressed but because they have faded from neglect. To decide whether painful memories are especially likely to be forgotten or repressed, we need better evidence than simple counts of their number and emotional tones.

All these points emphasise the key issue that, unlike photographs or DVDs, memories are not passive records that become randomly corrupted or lost as we age. They are constantly and actively altered as new information from before and after the remembered event comes to light, by our changing ideas about what most probably happened to us and by collaborative editing and additions by others who shared our experiences or merely discussed them with us. Our memories include all of this diverse information but not always records of how we came by it or what the originals of our memories were. Our recall of the details of particular occurrences is also modified by the way we interpret them in relation to other happenings at different times and places and both before and after them. The importance of our memories to us is often not their literal accuracy but their meaning as defined in the fabric of our personal myths. Our personal interpretations of our lives are made up of our memories and, it seems, by the subtle impressions and clues passed on to us by our immediate families, to determine what is and is not important to remember and how we should interpret it. These influences determine what experiences we remember, how we later recall them and how we evaluate them and weave them into the tales that we spin to explain our lives to ourselves.

Wang Qui illustrated this by comparing childhood memories reported by Caucasian Americans and Chinese Americans. Chinese earliest memories were, on average, about 6 months later than Caucasian [14]. In a later study, she watched Chinese and Caucasian mothers interact with their young children [15]. Caucasian mothers intensively involved themselves with their children to construct elaborate joint memories. Mother and child continually added additional details and built on each other's recollections. Both strongly focussed on the child's personal reactions to events and feelings about them. Chinese mothers initiated much less embellishment and interpretation, added less detail and opinion and focussed on moral principles and guides to appropriate behaviour that might be gained from the event. Wang Qui showed that these different styles of children's interactions with their mothers affect both the content and the style of the earliest memories that they can later recall. Caucasian children's early memories focussed on their personal reactions to events and on their inner feelings about them. Chinese early memories were sparser in detail, played down personal feelings, were more modest, less judgemental and less self-centred. Chinese adults tended to remember and describe their own actions neutrally in terms of their personal roles in the social contexts in which the incidents had occurred. Parents and families form, shape and edit our memories and so also our interpretations of ourselves and our actions, our attitudes and especially our memories of our own past lives.

References

[1]   Freud, S. (1901). *The Psychopathology of Everyday Life* (trans. A. Brill). London, Unwin.

[2]   Loftus, E. and Ketcham, K. (1996). *The Myth of Repressed Memory: False memories and allegations of sexual abuse.* London, St. Martin's Griffin.

[3]   Melchert, T. P. and Parker, R. L. (1997). Different forms of childhood abuse and memory. *Child Abuse & Neglect*, 21, 125–135.

[4]   Williams, L. M. (1997). Recall of childhood trauma: A prospective study of women's memories of sexual abuse. *Journal of Consulting and Clinical Psychology*, 62, 1167–1176.

[5]   Bremner, J. D., Randall, P., Scott, T.M., Capelli, S., Delaney, R., McCarthy, G. and Charney, D. S. (1995). Deficits in short-term memory in adult survivors of childhood abuse. *Psychiatry Research*, 59, 97–107.

[6] Meaney, M. J., Aitken, D. H., Van Berkel, C., Bhatnagar, S. and Sapolsky, R. M. (1988). Effect of neonatal handling on age-related impairments associated with the hippocampus. *Science*, 239(4841), 766–768.

[7] Meaney, M. J. and Stewart, J. (1981). Neonatal androgens influence the social play of prepubescent rats. *Hormones and Behavior*, 15 197–213.

[8] Hudson, J. I. (1995). Can memories of childhood sexual abuse be repressed? *Psychological Medicine*, 25, 121–126.

[9] Huttenlocher, P. R. (1990). Morphometric study of human cerebral cortex development. *Neuropsychologia*, 28(6), 517–527.

[10] Bauer, P. J., Kroupina, M. G., Schwade, J. A., Dropik, P. L. and Wewerka, S. S. (1998). If memory serves, will language? Later verbal accessibility of early memories. *Development and Psychopathology*, 10, 655–679.

[11] Peterson, C. and Bell, M. (1996). Children's memory for traumatic injury. *Child Development*, 67, 3045–3070.

[12] Rabbitt, P. and McInnes, L. (1988). Do clever old people have earlier and richer first memories? *Psychology and Aging*, 3, 338–341.

[13] Mullen, M. K. (1994). Earliest recollections of childhood: A demographic analysis. *Cognition*, 52, 55–79.

[14] Wang, Q. (2004). The emergence of cultural self-constructs: Autobiographical memory and self-description in European American and Chinese children. *Developmental Psychology*, 40, 3.

[15] Wang, Q. (2001). Culture effects on adults' earliest childhood recollection and self-description: Implications for the relation between memory and the self. *Journal of Personality and Social Psychology*, 81, 220.

11

REMEMBERING THE REST OF OUR LIVES

It seems a stretch to say that our memory that records and interprets the entire story of our past life is mainly used to predict the future, but there is direct and touching evidence. Henry Molaison, a Canadian, had both the right and left medial temporal lobes of his brain surgically removed in 1953. This left him unable to remember anything that happened to him, from day to day during the remaining 45 years of his life. During this time he was studied intensively by a number of brilliant neuropsychologists but it is possible that, "HM", as one of the most widely discussed and interesting cases in the literature, is now better remembered than any of them. Suzanne Corkin explains his existential situation and value to science in a humane and clever book, *Permanent Present Tense* [1], in which the first page records his response to the commonplace conversational gambit "What will you do tomorrow?" Henry's placid answer "Whatever is beneficial" points to both the sweetness of his nature and to the sad fact that with no guidance from his yesterdays he could not make even vague predictions about his tomorrows.

Henry's permanent present illustrates that our memories are our archives and the sources of our expectations. Our sparse earliest memories show us that even apparent snapshots of trivial incidents are not passive records but active constructions and re-organisations of information from many different times and sources. Since our memories are selected, organised and edited with or without our conscious control, it seems a good plan to choose what structures we impose on them so as to best remember what is most useful to us. Some ways of doing this are described in Chapter 24, where I describe some formal systems for remembering things, many of which were invented and used in classical Greece and Rome.

Discovering formal systems of ordering information that improve how efficiently we attend to, order, store and retrieve information gave Greeks and Romans useful practical mind tools. They did not yet realise that even if we do not consciously learn and use formal mnemonic systems, we nevertheless automatically develop and unconsciously use systems of mental organisation that determine what we notice and recall. This was shown by Frederick Bartlett while working in Cambridge UK during the early 1930s [2] and using experiments that seem sometimes to have been very informal indeed. During Cambridge garden parties he would ask acquaintances to recall an anthropological story, "The War of the Ghosts" that he had read to them months or years earlier in a more formal laboratory setting. This describes a quarrel between members of two rival tribes, Egulak and Calama, whose environments and strange beliefs and consequently odd behaviour Bartlett had chosen to be as different as possible from suburban Cambridge. He noticed that if his acquaintances were prompted within a few hours or days of first hearing this tale, they could accurately recall many of the original, bizarre, details. A few months later, they would have forgotten most of the extreme oddities but still remembered much of the more conventional information. Bartlett's insight was that memory failures are not random. People distorted the plot by introducing new incorrect details because they increasingly tended to, in his term, "conventionalise" the story to better fit in with their own experience. Alternatively, some details that are too striking and unusual to be modified in this way may be preserved intact, though they then emerge as discrepant fragments in an otherwise coherent story since much of the information that once linked them has been lost or altered. Even many years after first telling them his tale, Bartlett seems to have been so persistent in following up his victims during random social occasions that I imagine them experiencing severe heart-sink and briskly beetling off as the bulky, eminent figure lurked towards them. Yet again.

Bartlett's observations are stronger and more convincing than the common theme of many detective stories: witnesses remember what they expect and forget or misremember what they misinterpret or incompletely understand. Bartlett's key insight was that our memories are not passively recorded and unchanged except by random losses. They are always active re-constructions and interpretations guided by the techniques of interpreting relations between things, people and events that we have built up during our everyday lives. He called these interpretive systems "schemata" that we develop and use to understand and organise new information in memory, both while we first encounter it and also when we later try to retrieve and assemble the fragments left by inevitable memory losses into consistent recollections. Bartlett completed this work before the computer age. If he had shared the concepts of modern information technology, it would have been natural to talk of memory programs that selectively pick up some kinds of information but not others and that fill gaps in recollection by extrapolation from data acquired before or after the events that we remember.

Bartlett's ideas have helped us to understand some of the difficulties that older people experience with their memories. Gill Cohen illustrated how Bartlett's theory of schemata implies that older people may have difficulties remembering because they take in information more slowly, retain less information and forget faster what they once learned [3]. They may also have problems because they do not have appropriate organising systems or because the ones that they use are not fit for purpose. One study showed the consequences of these systems of expectation and reconstruction for people trying to remember the spatial layout of imaginary houses. Older volunteers did much less well when house plans were bizarre than when they agreed with their expectations [4]. We are all prone to remember the familiar and expected better than the odd and the novel, and this difference increases as we age. This has important consequences in everyday life, for example in medical consultations during which older patients are likely to forget or misremember details that are unfamiliar or do not fit their expectations or their understanding of their own medical problems [5]. An experiment to illustrate this found that older people remember sequences of words nearly as well as the young when they are related by previous associations but not when they are randomly selected [6]. Another showed that older adults can remember pictures nearly as well as young adults if the relationships between their component parts are familiar but not if they are chaotically disarranged [7]. So, in general, people of any age are handicapped if they cannot recognise and use structures in the information they must remember, and this disadvantage becomes much greater as they grow older. Convincing experiments also show that older eye-witnesses are more dependent on their preconceptions, and so more apt to falsely "recall" the most likely sequence of events, to miss details that do not fit their expectations of what might have happened so that, like Bartlett's acquaintances, they begin to insert false details that seem to them to make the best sense of an incomplete recollection. As we grow old, our recall of events becomes increasingly dependent on and controlled by context and expectation.

Which parts of our lives do we remember best?

The problems that experimentalists feel competent to explore are different from and, at first sight, disappointingly more simple-minded than those that Freud discussed. These are whether we can remember more events more clearly from particular periods of our lives; whether, as in a computer system, our total memory capacity is limited so that information about past events is progressively over-written and obliterated by more recent material; and whether, as we age, memories from our early lives are better recalled because they were registered when our brains were younger and more efficient or whether young memories are selectively lost because they have had longer to fade over time.

If all our memory traces inevitably fade over time, the number and vividness of the memories that we can recover should steadily rise from early childhood through adult life to peak in the recent past. If memories are most completely and durably recorded by young brains and more weakly and fuzzily by old brains their number, richness and reliability should steadily decline as we age. This benefit for younger memories may be enhanced by the increased odds that they have been recalled more often. These processes may, of course, work together. We might, for example, expect that all distant memories except those that have been frequently recalled and rehearsed should become increasingly sparse and replaced by more recent memories.

Depending on what we assume about the relative time courses and strengths of these opposing processes, we might expect our retrievals of events to peak at different ages.

To find out what actually happens, psychologists ask people to recall as many events as they can from all parts of their lives, either spontaneously or when prompted by associations with random words. Both methods give the same results. Even in old age, the proportion of the total number of memories recalled increases steadily after the low point of infantile amnesia to peak in the recent past. This is unsurprising because the older we are the more memories we acquire and we have an increasingly large stock of memories on which to draw.

Does this mean that all memories steadily decay over time so that earlier memories are progressively lost and, perhaps, over-written and replaced by later ones? We can test this by comparing the number of memories retrieved from different periods in the lifespan. The number of events an individual recalls does not smoothly increase from infancy to old age. Some periods of people's lives produce a larger number of more vivid memories than others. These periods of unusually plentiful and vivid memories are sometimes termed "reminiscence bumps", and usually date from young adult life or early middle age. Because reminiscence bumps tend to occur at slightly different ages for different people, when results for many different people are pooled and averaged, their different reminiscence bumps and troughs tend to cancel each other out and show a fairly smooth average increase over time. Even so, in some large studies, averages of pooled scores do show a rapid rise from a very low number from infancy and childhood to a much

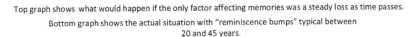

Top graph shows what would happen if the only factor affecting memories was a steady loss as time passes. Bottom graph shows the actual situation with "reminiscence bumps" typical between 20 and 45 years.

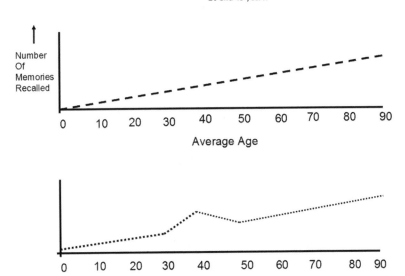

FIGURE 11.1 Reminiscence bumps.

larger number from young adult life followed by a slight drop during middle age and another rise for the very recent past.

An excellent review of the literature on autobiographical memory by David Rubin [8] emphasises that for people of all ages, reminiscence bumps or peaks tend to coincide with their periods of greatest and most engrossing activity and most involvement in personal and community crises. For example, people who lived through a particularly eventful historical period, such as World War II, the Korean War or the Vietnam War during their forties or fifties might remember many events from their middle age, while those who experienced these wars in their twenties and thirties might show correspondingly earlier reminiscence peaks. Apart from the effects of exceptionally dramatic periods of life, there is also evidence that most people's reminiscence peaks occur in the period between adolescence and early middle age. A wry speculation is that this is because more interesting and important things happen to us during these periods of our lives. We think of them and discuss them more often than we recall and talk about more prosaic happenings. A cosier version is that, just as in fairy stories after initial struggles princes and princesses go on living secure, serene and happy lives that are too boringly repetitive to merit record. It is also during early life that experiences occur for the very first time. Details of first loves and, less romantically, of first jobs seem to be particularly well recorded. Also, whether because of their intrinsic importance or because of the excitement of their then novelty, youthful memories make more interesting topics for private entertainment or for conversation and are more often mulled over and so better preserved (though possibly also more thoroughly edited and re-shaped by frequent rumination and discussion).

A study of 1241 people aged between 20 and 93 asked for happy and sad memories, and also for an interesting category of "involuntary memories" – the kind of images or scenarios that come to mind spontaneously, without apparent cause or prompting, and bear no relation to what we may be doing at the time. Older people showed a clear peak for happy memories from their twenties. In contrast, sad and traumatic memories were rare in youth and increased with age. Involuntary memories were strongly biased towards happiness rather than sadness. The authors suggest that the life periods for which reminiscence bumps occur must also be affected by a tendency to rehearse and replay happy youthful memories and to avoid recalling unpleasant events [9]. A different study also showed that this bias towards happy memories affects the plots that we work out for the life stories that we construct for ourselves out of our memories that give us a sense of personal identity, of who we have been and what we have become [10]. Post hoc crafted patchworks of recollection are our only source for speculations on the plots and the meanings of our lives.

A problem for objective research is that any recollection with which a courteous older person tries to oblige a tediously persistent psychologist will never be a first recall of an event. This is particularly true of earliest memories, because people cannot identify which of their memories are earlier than others without going through some long process of recollection, mulling and comparing candidate recollections.

The fact that a request to produce a first memory is, almost invariably, very rapidly answered should convince us that this is not a first-ever act of retrieval. The process of sifting, comparing, discussing and dating the memory against others has obviously been so thorough that details are very likely to have been lost, added, distorted or blurred. Our first memories are also very likely to be those incidents from our most remote past that, for whatever reason, we have most frequently recalled.

Flashbulb memories

Folklore insists that age does not wither nor custom stale memories of unique, dramatic or emotionally highly charged events. Typical phrases used to describe their distinct quality are "It is as if I were still there" and "I shall remember every little detail for as long as I live". Such exceptional memories have been nick-named "flashbulb memories". They are useful to study because they can often be accurately dated and checked against public records and the recollections of others. Unfortunately, for just these reasons, they are also likely to have been altered by frequent discussion. Striking events are thoroughly documented and media retrospectives are frequent so it is hard to separate details of our original first-hand impressions from those obtained from the media just after they happened or even much later in retrospective articles.

To try to separate memories of public and personal details, researchers ask people to remember what they, personally, were doing when they first heard of unexpected and significant events such as the Kennedy assassination, the Lockerby bombing, the September 11 atrocity or Princess Diana's death. People often say that their memories of their personal situations when they first heard of striking events are still highly charged with emotion, exceptionally vivid, accurate, rich in detail and have resisted normal fading over time. Are flashbulb memories so different from all others that age does not alter them?

A problem with many of the earliest studies was that investigators tested recall of events weeks or months after they happened. This allowed plenty of time for the original memories to become distorted by new information from media coverage and by the greater than usual discussion with others of where we were, what we were doing and how we felt and reacted to the news. Better-planned studies now use very early initial de-briefing after a flashbulb event with several later probes of recollection. These improved experiments have not yet found convincing evidence that people's memories of their situations when first hearing of unexpected, highly emotionally charged events are more accurate than for events of mild or no significance. In spite of their reported vividness, the point that people supply more details for flashbulb than for more ordinary memories can be explained by evidence that dramatic events are more often discussed with others. Evidence for this is that individuals' second and later reports of flashbulb memories are often richer and more detailed than their first and earlier ones, and they may even introduce new details that are discrepant with those they originally recalled. Flashbulb memories are interesting but, so far, their main message has been that subjective vividness of memories is a weak guarantee of their reliability. Analyses of flashbulb memories show, once again, that memory is not a passive unalterable record of what we see, hear and feel but the result of a continuous active construction of plausible scenarios from information obtained before, during and even after the events we recall.

Old age does not spare flashbulb memories and the emotional poignancy and the vividness of the images they recall do not guarantee their accuracy. It is interesting that while age makes recollection of details more unreliable and sparse, the emotional charge and subjective vividness of memories do not seem to fade. These aspects of stirring memories are caught by phrases like "I'll remember every tiny detail forever", which are not used less often as aging continues. It seems likely that, in old age, people's impressions of the vividness and detail of their flashbulb memories become deceptively greater because they are continuously updated and enhanced by frequent recall and increasingly contrast with the relative fuzziness of less exciting and less visited recollections.

Remembering what we have learned

A difficulty in exploring people's memories is that they can usually tell us a great deal about what has happened to them but neither we, nor they, can be sure how reliable their recollections are. To get around this, we must find independent sources of information. A convenient source is their present memory for subjects that they studied at school or university. Archived syllabuses and examination papers are permanent records of what they were once taught and their examination results give us some idea of how well they once learned it. We can give people multiple-choice questionnaires of the material that they once studied or even, if we are pitiless, give them the same examinations again.

Bahrick tested middle-aged and elderly people's memory for the Spanish that they had learned in US High Schools [11]. He was able to follow forgetting of Spanish over periods of 50 years. The amount of forgetting was less for those whose initial learning had been richer and more effective. Rapid loss during the first 3 years after high-school graduation was followed by an apparent plateau with a further decline in old age. In another study, Bahrick found similar results for memory for High School algebra and arithmetic with the additional depressing detail that those who had not gone on to study mathematics at university or use maths in their professions were accurate at only chance levels in their old age [12]. This will surprise few of us. Bahrick's demonstration is neat because the students had all studied Spanish and maths at the same ages but this also meant that he could not test whether the age at which people first learn something affects the rate with which they forget it. Martin Conway and Gill Cohen could do this because of the UK's Open University, a splendid institution that offers courses to students of all ages from adolescence to 80 or even 90. Gill and Martin compared students' former psychology course records with their present memories for information that they had once known very well indeed. Their results confirmed and extended Bahrick's findings of an initially rapid decline over the first 36 months followed by an above chance plateau [13]. The new detail was that those who had studied psychology at ages ranging from 25 to 77 showed greater loss of detailed information but no greater loss of arguments and concepts [14]. On the whole, these experiments are an inspiring demonstration that highly motivated and able old people can learn a new subject as effectively as young adults, and can sometimes be as good as young adults at retaining their new knowledge.

We should interpret these results cautiously because, like those from all natural history experiments, they are affected by variables that cannot be completely controlled or documented. We cannot, for example, conclude that we retain fewer memories from middle age *only* because our slightly older brains had then begun to learn more slowly and to forget faster. There are also differences in motivation between young adults who learn new information to get academic degrees as credentials to further their careers and older students who do not need professional advancement, study only out of interest and do not have later careers that make use of their acquired knowledge. Differences in their reasons for studying a subject may also affect the desire and the opportunity to talk about what they have learned, or to expand their knowledge by general reading. Laboratory experiments can be tightly controlled to eliminate variables that may affect results or by rigorously selecting and intensively documenting participants. Unfortunately, these useful constraints also mean that the models that we can derive from them are only valid for a correspondingly limited reality, do not resonate with our personal subjective experiences of the world and certainly do not address all the questions that we would most like to ask. Data gained in real-life situations, such as the Open University studies, do give us some interesting information but also need so much qualification that they tend to provoke rather than resolve debates. Nevertheless, the general conclusions from these studies are clear, dependable and not too discouraging. Even information that we have spent years of hard effort acquiring will be gradually lost unless we continually revise and refurbish it. On the other hand, the greatest losses occur during the first 3 years after learning. As we grow older, it becomes harder and takes longer to acquire new information, but even when we are very old indeed we can learn new skills to gratifyingly high levels of competence and can retain what we have learned nearly as well as we would have done when we were young if we diligently keep revising. Use it or lose it seems a fair description of our predicament.

References

[1] Corkin, S. (2013). *Permanent Present Tense: The unforgettable life of the amnesic patient.* New York, H. M. Basic Books.
[2] Bartlett, F. F. C. and Bartlett, F. C. (1995). *Remembering: A study in experimental and social psychology Vol 14.* Cambridge, Cambridge University Press.
[3] Cohen, G. (1993). 10 age differences in memory for texts: Production deficiency or processing limitations? In L. L. Light and D. M. Burke (Eds), 171–190, *Language, Memory, and Aging.* Cambridge, Cambridge University Press.
[4] Arbuckle, T. Y., Cooney, R., Milne, J. and Melchior, A. (1994). Memory for spatial layouts in relation to age and schema typicality. *Psychology and Aging,* 9, 467–480.

[5] Ley, P. (1979). Memory for medical information. *British Journal of Social and Clinical Psychology*, 18(2), 245–255.

[6] Thompson, L. A. and Kliegl, R. (1991). Adult age effects of plausibility on memory: The role of time constraints during encoding. *Journal of Experimental Psychology: Learning, Memory, and Cognition*, 17, 542–555.

[7] Hess, T. M., Flannagan, D. A. and Tate, C. S. (1993). Aging and memory for schematically vs taxonomically organized verbal materials. *Journal of Gerontology*, 48, 37–44.

[8] Rubin, D. C. (2002). Autobiographical memory across the lifespan. In P. Grat and N. Ohta (Eds), pp. 159–184, *Lifespan Development of Human Memory*. Boston, MIT Press.

[9] Rubin, D. C. and Berntsen, D. (2003). Life scripts help to maintain autobiographical memories of highly positive, but not highly negative, events. *Memory & Cognition*, 31, 1–14.

[10] Berntsen, D. and Rubin, D. C. (2002). Emotionally charged autobiographical memories across the life span: The recall of happy, sad, traumatic and involuntary memories. *Psychology and Aging*, 17, 636–652.

[11] Bahrick, H. P. (1984). Semantic memory content in permastore: Fifty years of memory for Spanish learned in school. *Journal of Experimental Psychology: General*, 113, 1–29.

[12] Bahrick, H. P. and Hall, L. K. (1991). Lifetime maintenance of high school mathematics content. *Journal of Experimental Psychology: General*, 120, 20–33.

[13] Conway, M. A., Cohen, G. and Stanhope, N. (1991). On the very long-term retention of knowledge acquired through formal education: Twelve years of cognitive psychology. *Journal of Experimental Psychology: General*, 120, 395–409.

[14] Cohen, G., Stanhope, N. and Conway, M. A. (1992). Age differences in the retention of knowledge by young and elderly students. *British Journal of Developmental Psychology*, 10, 153–164.

PART III
Senses

12

SEEING

Our brains are marvellous 1.3 kilo lumps of fats and proteins living in dark bone boxes. They control nearly all of our bodily processes: breaths, heartbeats, some gut functions and many other chores of which we are, gratefully, unconscious. Almost as a sideline, they receive and keep all the information we get about our worlds, ourselves and the shifting and muddled representations and projections of present, past and future that we call our "consciousness". What is really out there we conjecture only through heavy mathematics. Particles caper about in a space that it is inappropriate to call either dark or light, because photons, the smallest bits of light, are part of the same dance. The glitter and buzz of our conscious experiences are not out there in reality but only exist in the models of the world that our brains fabricate. The only information on which our brains can base these models to guide our trundling around is within the tiny range that our sense organs can register — tastes, smells, touch, texture, temperature, pain and pressure and, most importantly for us as for most other primates, light and sound. If we were pigeons, we would build information about the Earth's magnetic field into our mental constructs and so would perceive and imagine wide spaces and our positions in them quite differently. If we were electric eels, lateral line organs on our flanks would send out electric pulses and pick up returning echoes to help us make a radar map of the nearest inches of surrounding mud-banks, sludge, reeds and their edible or noxious inhabitants. Our worlds are interpretations and records and, in effect, maps and models derived from the very limited kinds of information that our receptors can give us.

When we were young, our eyes and ears were marvellously efficient. Our eyes could register the smallest possible packages of light energy, single photons, and so, on a dark night, make out a lit candle more than a mile away. As we age, these wonderful sensors become less efficient and our brains must base their guesses about the nature of surrounding reality on increasingly degraded information. Age also reduces the efficiency of our computing brains, so that the interpretation of such information as we can still receive becomes less reliable.

Because our brains control our entire bodies, it is an appealing whimsy that they must also have planned and controlled the evolution of our sense organs to improve the information that they receive from the world. The British physiologist, Sir Charles Sherrington, was the first to suggest that, contrariwise, developing sense organs led to the need to grow brains to make the best use of them. A crucial evolutionary step for the simplest early organisms was developing receptors on their surfaces that could register changes in the chemicals in the fluids in which they lived. This allowed them to detect molecules water-borne from sources that were many of their body-diameters away from them. These were the first "distance receptors" and gave access to information that, if they could develop the computing power to use it, could be used to foretell important impending events such as whether they were about to have or to become lunch. They could only use this information if they grew brains to interpret it.

Interpreting sensory information to predict the immediate future gave even these very simple creatures the foundations of physics and philosophy: the ability to perceive time (soon, less soon); the relation of time to distance and movement (fast or not so fast); and probability (opportune, risky or futile to dodge or pounce). I think that to draw a parallel between evolutionary receptor-races and the history of science is not a trivial conceit. Our theories about the world have been repeatedly challenged and transformed by inventions of new extra receptor systems such as microscopes, optical and radio telescopes, X-ray cameras and brain scanners that extend the limits of our biological sense organs. Each new receptor technology has provided new information that contradicted our earlier assumptions about the nature of reality. To interpret this, we had to change our theories of how things are and got to be this way and no other. Richard Gregory, an admired teacher and friend, took this idea a stage further, insisting throughout his long and entertaining

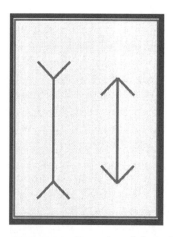 

FIGURE 12.1 Examples of classic illusions.

career that perceptual systems, like scientists, continuously make and improve their best guesses about what is going on by developing, trying out and adopting hypotheses to fit the information available. If this information is inadequate or misleading, we tend to make incorrect judgements. If these hypotheses are persistently discrepant from reality, we call them "illusions" [1].

Our best guesses about reality

Visual illusions show that there are many different levels at which the changes that age brings to our nervous systems affect our interpretations of the world. Even slight mechanical or optical changes limit our sensory acuity – the dimmest flashes of light, the softest sounds, the weakest traces of smell and taste and the lightest touches that we can sense. Aging of sense organs also restricts the number of distinctions we can make, such as the number of different colours that we can distinguish and the subtle cues of perspective that allow us to judge the relative sizes of distant objects. Tiny sensory changes can lose us the particular information of shading or slight colour changes with distance that we need to derive a representation of a third dimension in the world from the two-dimensional images on the flat retinas of our eyes. For example, how far away things are; whether two distant things are bigger or smaller than each other; how fast we and other things are moving; and if and when collisions will occur. Designing computer systems to guide moving objects has taught us that these computations can be mathematically very complicated but the tiny brains of ants, bees and hover-flies manage them brilliantly. A third level at which loss occurs is in the computing power of the brain itself. Like blurred digital photographs, degraded sensory information can be cleaned up by the brain to resolve details but loss of computing power makes this less efficient.

A look at the eye

The grid of light-sensitive cells at the back of the eye is called the retina (Latin for a "net") that acts like the grid of pixels in a digital camera, each of which registers whether, and how much light falls on it. Figure 12.2 shows that before light can reach these receptors it has to pass through several transparent structures. First the cornea, the window between the eye and air; then through a fluid called the aqueous humour; then through a hole of adjustable size (the pupil) in a semi-opaque membrane (the iris); then through an adjustable lens that focuses the light to give an upside-down image of the world which finally passes through a jelly of vitreous humour and is cast on the screen of the retina at the back of the eye.

At each of these stages, physical changes affect the amount and kinds of light that travel through the eye and thus the quality of the image on the retina. The cornea, like a carelessly handled spectacle lens, gradually becomes scratched and damaged. It also takes on a yellow clouding. Corneal damage scatters light and blurs the eventual image on the retina. Clouding reduces the amount of light that

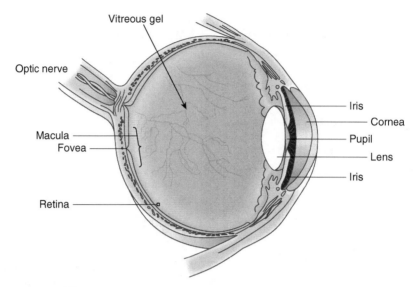

FIGURE 12.2 The eye.

can get into the eye and selectively dims light at the blue end of the spectrum. In normal young eyes, pupils flexibly expand and contract to let through more light in dim situations and less light in bright illuminations. Age reduces pupil flexibility. In bright light, unalterably wider pupils allow glare and in dim light, smaller pupils keep out much of the light available. While we are young, our lenses are flexible enough for muscles attached to their edges to tug them to focus the clearest possible image on the retina. Lenses grow rigid with age and can no longer be tugged into focus and become set to give the long-sightedness that forces us to comically hold newspapers and watches at arms' length. The lens also yellows and becomes slightly more opaque, further filtering out blue light in favour of yellow.

Hardening of the lens first becomes noticeable around age 40 and some particular striking visual failure prompts a visit to an optician and an ever-remembered pang of the first prosthesis. (My personal middle-aged-eyes crisis happened on the Victoria Line of the London Underground when I failed to orient a group of patiently courteous Japanese schoolchildren because, for different reasons, neither they nor I could make sense of the tiny Tube Map in my pocket diary.)

Another problem with the lens is gradual deposition of fats eventually resulting in occluding cataracts. Viewed through a thickening film of suet, the world becomes dimmed and jaundiced: street-lights at night do gain attractive halos but this fringe benefit makes night driving uncomfortable and unsafe. Painless cataract removal almost instantly returns us to a brighter, crisper and bluer world.

When the image focused by the lens reaches the retina it is upside-down with reference to our bodily orientation. Our brains have to adjust to this inversion to "perceive" and to "feel" the inverted world as the "right way up". Since the late nineteenth century, doughty observers have worn lenses that re-reversed their retinal images for a week or longer [2]. They eventually begin to perceive upside-down as normal and can again walk, write, read and even intrepidly ride bicycles.[1] The brain is plastic, in the sense that it can re-program itself, even in old age.

On their way from the lens to the retina, photons of light face an additional challenge: a jelly-like packing in the eye, the vitreous humour, which in old age is increasingly contaminated by bits of organic detritus that opticians call "float-ers". When we turn our closed eyelids to a bright light these drift across our visual fields like shoals of crinkling corpses of amoebae. As we grow old, floater swarms become increasingly dense, block out more light and, literally, give us a dim view of the world. Apart from blocking out light, the sudden shifts of floater-shoals are often mistaken for moving objects in peripheral vision. They should be taken seriously because high densities of floaters, especially if they occur suddenly, may be a warning of a detaching retina that urgently demands medical help to forestall blindness.

On the surface of the retina, an opaque yellow pigment stealthily accumulates. This further dims light of all wavelengths but, once again, most particularly blue. Because older people see the world through this increasingly dense yellow filter they also become less accurate at judging subtle differences between colours. The losses caused by each of these different obstructions are quite small, but for many people in their eighties their cumulating effects reduce the amount of light that our retinas once received when we and our eyes were young by more than 80 per cent and our worlds correspondingly fade.

When photons of light at last reach the retina they hit receptor cells that we call cones and rods because of their different shapes. These, contain photosensitive pigments, rhodopsin and iodopsin, that, when bleached by light, trigger electrical impulses to the next layers of retinal cells, bipolar and then ganglion cells. Groups of many cones, and even larger clusters of rods, connect to the same bipolar cell and many bipolars connect to the same ganglion cell. This progressive many-to-one coding-down allows for computation before the ganglion cells communicate with cells in the optic nerves. Here, after further computation and re-direction at a point where the nerves from both eyes join at the optic chiasma and partly cross-over to the opposite side of the brain, further neuronal channels fan out to the visual cortex at the very back of the brain and to the parietal lobes on both its rear side-surfaces. It is these structures that make the computations that give us the rich, bright, shimmering and mobile world that we take for granted as the arena of our lives.

We may not yet know all that happens at the retina. A biologist, Michael Russell, made the surprising discovery, for some years rejected by vision scientists, that the retina also contains ganglion cells that are sensitive to differences between light and dark but apparently bypass our consciousness (for an excellent discussion of the remarkable phenomenon of this and other cases of this kind of "blindsight" see [3]). Patients who are completely blind protest that they cannot consciously tell whether lights are on or off. Nevertheless, if they are forced to make irritated guesses they do this correctly. This, and other demonstrations of blindsight [3] convince us that there is much less to consciousness than meets the eye or is recognised by the brain.

The cones, in the middle (fovea) of the retina, on which the image of what we are looking at is centred, register only relatively bright light. They come in three varieties sensitive to red, green and blue light and, acting in combination, give us colour vision. Towards the periphery of the eye, rods increasingly replace cones. Rods are completely bleached by bright light and so cannot again register changes until they recover in low illuminations when they allow vision, but with less acuity and no colour sensitivity. (This is why, notoriously, in the night all cats are "grey"). Age culls both cones and rods, impairing acuity in bright light and reducing sensitivity of night vision. Earlier and greater losses of rods than cones cause peripheral vision to be lost earlier than central vision, so that older people may increasingly experience tunnel vision. Age also lengthens the time that retinal receptors, particularly rods, need to regenerate after they have been bleached out. This increases the dark-adaptation time needed to recover from dazzle. Because of this, we older people take longer to gain our maximum sensitivity of vision in dim light and, unfortunately, even at its best our dark vision is never again as good as it was when we were young.

All these changes degrade the information that the eye can give the brain. This affects our view of the world in obvious ways, such as blurring of vision even with appropriate spectacle lenses; and an insidious leaching of light from the world, the poignancy of which Thomas Nashe captured in his wonderful line "Brightness falls from the Air".[2] Slower adaptation to night vision can turn night strolls into blundering misadventures. Most of us learn this too well and too soon but, because the changes are so slow and insidious there is a risk that we may not recognise them in time. There is evidence from a study of elderly motorists made in Marin County California that elderly people become aware of their visual problems and take timely steps to safeguard themselves. Even though in this extremely car-dependent culture, older people are obliged to continue to drive almost as a basic necessity of life, substantial numbers of elderly people recognised that night driving was becoming increasingly hazardous and voluntarily gave it up.

This debate continues. When I published research on the behaviour of elderly drivers, I was aware of strong opposing pressures on how to interpret my findings. The police felt that unacknowledged visual deficits by elderly drivers contribute to many of the accidents in which they are involved. This view was based on data from surveys and roadside checks which sometimes found some elderly people who were continuing to drive with dangerously poor levels of vision. I do not know of data that convince me that such cases are common enough to justify new legislation. The occasional discovery of individual visually handicapped elderly motorists should be considered in the context of repeated findings from many countries that accident rates among drivers over 70 are only slightly greater than for the safest age group in the population, the middle aged, and very much lower than for drivers younger than 30. This remains true even when the numbers are adjusted to take into account that the elderly make fewer and shorter trips than the young. An opposite pressure came from elderly drivers who were alarmed that my research might become a platform to launch legal restrictions. The dilemma is real and important. Because visual changes are insidious they may go unnoticed for a dangerously long time, but many, and probably most, older drivers pick up that they are gradually becoming at risk, are well aware of this, consult their doctors and opticians and give up driving if and when they must. The issue is becoming more urgent because, as I write this in 2013, the number of people in Britain who are aged 70 and over and still have driving licenses has, for the first time, exceeded 1 million. The oldest is 103.

Elderly people become well aware of serious losses of vision but much less of how small changes in visual sensitivity affect how well they remember and interpret what they see. Christine Dickenson and I illustrated this by persuading young undergraduate ophthalmologists to briefly wear cylindrical lenses that caused very mild distortion of vision. This did not affect how fast or accurately they could read printed text but did reduce how much they could remember of what they had read. The small extra effort needed to make out the text is borrowed from a general pool of information processing capacity, or bandwidth, that we also use to remember it. These and more recent experiments confirm that reduced clarity of vision makes reading more difficult and this extra difficulty prevents older people from rapidly making correct inferences about what they have correctly read [4, 5]. Christine and I continue to try to persuade middle-aging colleagues that a timely trip to an optician or, nowadays, turning up the print-size on their e-readers, can sharpen their comprehension as well as aid their vision.

We also lose some sensitivity of colour vision. German research identifies yellowing of the cornea and lens and, in particular, accumulation of yellow pigment in the retina as a main reason for losses of colour sensitivity but there is evidence that high-order computation systems for colour perception are also involved. Recent research suggests that, probably because of their loss of sensitivity to small differences in colours, elderly people tend to group large numbers of colours under the same label: for example, they apply the terms "orange" or "blue" to broader ranges of shades than the young do. Colour mixers and decorators whose living depends on the ability to make very subtle colour distinctions, and convey them by terms such as "blush pink" or "eau de nil", are particularly inconvenienced.

As old age proceeds, changes in the eye accelerate and bring unexpected hazards. Losses of the edges of the visual field can be dangerous in driving and other situations in which we need to be aware of things in the corners of our eyes. We depend much more than we realise on peripheral vision to maintain stability when walking over even mildly rough and irregular surfaces. Narrowing of peripheral vision contributes to the risk of falls that can be catastrophic for frail elderly people.

Aging also affects the interpreting brain. Loss of brain computing power adds to changes in the eye to affect how well we can judge the relative sizes of distant objects (size constancy), the rate at which objects are moving, and the relative brightness of near and distant parts of our visual fields. This can have hazardous consequences. Carol Holland and I [6] found that even alert and capable elderly Manchester volunteers were less good at predicting the speed of oncoming road traffic as they stood on the pavements of Oxford Road outside the main University buildings. Better-controlled laboratory studies have found that as people age they become increasingly prone to overestimate the speed of moving objects and are less effective at judging if and when two moving objects will collide. Lessons for metro-geriatrics are obvious.

There are also hints that age reduces the efficiency with which we can integrate visual information to recognise complex scenes and things. We shall discuss the effects of age on face recognition in a different chapter, because faces are a special case and are especially important to us and other primates. There is evidence that old age affects the higher-order brain functions that resolve complex ambiguous information into meaningful scenarios. Vision scientists, and indeed philosophers, have been intrigued by ambiguous figures that can be equally easily or convincingly interpreted in either of two, or more different ways, such as the "Necker cube", the "Schroeder staircase", Wittgenstein's line drawing that might be either a duck or a rabbit or Boring's uncharitably titled "wife/mother-in-Law illusion" (see Figure 12.3, and also <www.grand-illusions.com> for a wide range of optical illusions).

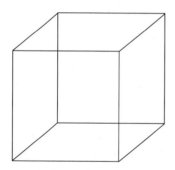

FIGURE 12.3A Necker cube.

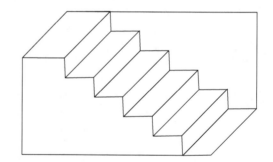

FIGURE 12.3B Schroeder staircase.

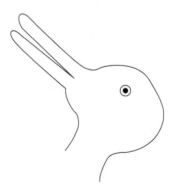

FIGURE 12.3C Wittgenstein's
duck-rabbit.

FIGURE 12.3 Reversible figures.

An interesting thing about these reversible figures is that we only perceive them in one aspect at a time – one or the other orientation of a cube or a staircase, either a duck or a rabbit, a beauty or a crone, but never both at once. If we stare long enough, we spontaneously or deliberately shift from one perception to the other. This shows that perception is not merely a "bottom-up" process in which any information that arrives at the retina, as it were, finds its match in an archive held in the brain. What we see is determined by what we think is most likely to be there. We do not completely lose the ability to switch between alternative interpretations in old age but there is evidence that we experience fewer switches between the alternative possible aspects of reversible figures [7]. Consequently, as we grow older, interpretations of complex scenes take longer and we find it much harder to find letters or numbers that are embedded in distracting visual clutter [8]. Anything that the young find hard to make out is even more difficult for the old. No doubt the few of our ancestral hunter/gatherers who survived into old age found it a grave disadvantage to miss the fruit among the foliage or the snake in the grass or the leopard in the tree. Being occasionally baffled by complex scenarios on TV is not nearly so inconvenient. It is pleasant to record that these fading skills of identifying objects among visual clutter and resolving ambiguous information greatly improve with practice, even in old age [9].

Notes

1 In Cambridge UK, which seems to have been a centre for such weird activities, dangerously illegal upside-down driving of cars was rumoured, as was riding a bicycle around the top of a narrow brick wall formerly surrounding an Anatomy building in the (old) Downing Street Science Area (Dr Kenneth Craik). An eminent mathematician, John Conway, went even further and devised lenses that allowed him to sample information as if from an extra dimension in the hope that this would train him to better imagine multidimensional topology. It is reported that he successfully learned his four-dimensional way round and round a College mulberry tree and got quite used to the experience (see Alexander Masters' "The genius in my basement"). It is not surprising that few elderly scientists have subjected themselves to such emetic experiences. Those who have say that adapting to inverted images takes much longer is less complete and is subject to alarming, sudden reversions.

2 I reject the terrible idea that he actually wrote "Brightness falls from the hair" which was wrongly transcribed. Of course, in our age, he could have become a brilliant copywriter for shampoo advertisements but, luckily for us, he had to make a far harder, less opulent but more brilliant living.

References

[1] Gregory, R. L. (1997). *Eye and Brain: The psychology of seeing*, (5th edition). Princeton NJ, Princeton University Press.

[2] Stratton, G. M. (1896). Some preliminary experiments on vision without inversion of the retinal image. *Psychological Review*, 3, 611–617.

[3] Cowey, A. and Stoerig, P. (1991). The neurobiology of blindsight. *Trends in Neurosciences*, 14(4), 140–145.

[4] Dickenson, C. M. and Rabbitt, P. M. A. (1991). Simulated visual impairment: Effects on text comprehension and reading speed. *Clinical Vision Science*, 6, 301–308.

[5] Sass, S. M., Legge, G. E. and Lee, H-W. (2006). Low vision reading speed: Influences of linguistic inferences and aging. *Optometry and Vision Science*, 83, 166–177.

[6] Holland, C. and Rabbitt, P. M. A. (1992). People's awareness of their age-related sensory and cognitive deficits and the implications for road safety. *Applied Cognitive Psychology*, 6, 217–231.

[7] Beer, J., Beer, J., Markeley, R. P. and Camp, C. J. (1989). Age and living conditions as related to perceptions of ambiguous figures. *Psychological Reports*, 64, 1027–1033.

[8] Heath, H. L. and Orbach, J. (1963). Reversibility of the necker cube, IV responses of older people. *Perceptual and Motor Skills*, 17, 625–626.

[9] Klein, D. W., Culler, M. P. and Suce, J. (1977). Differences in inconspicuous word identification as a function of age and reversible-figure training. *Experimental Aging Research*, 3, 203–213.

13

HEARING

We hear by detecting tiny fast changes in air pressure. These vibrations are funnelled by the elaborate whorled outer ear, the pinna, which focusses their energy along the auditory canal to reach the eardrum. Humans underestimate the value of having an outer ear because, within the range of ear sizes that our species currently grows, large external pinnae do not bring sufficient gains in sound detection to compensate for their possible inconveniences. People with damaged outer ears do lose some sensitivity and, in particular, find it harder to recognise where, in the space about them, sounds come from. The large, elaborate and delightful outer ears of foxes who live by locating rabbit-rustling, and of rabbits who survive by detecting fox-creeping, show how useful pinnae can be for collecting and channelling sound. The charming ear-twitches of foxes and dogs also show that partially rotatable pinnae can be an advantage in checking a sound direction and in maximising the sound available. Few humans can furl and twist their ears but we manage, though less well than dogs and foxes, to get fixes on faint noises by turning our heads about.

The ear

Sound vibrations travel down the auditory pathway until they agitate the eardrum: a neat descriptive term for a membrane stretched across the ear canal. Vibrations of the eardrum are picked up by three tiny, articulated bones, the hammer, the anvil and the stirrup. This is a mechanical lever system that magnifies the vibrations at the oval window of the cochlea, a fluid-filled tunnel shaped like a snail shell. Stretched along the inner length of the winding cochlea is a flaccid sheet of tissue, the basilar membrane, on which sensory cells are mounted. They are called hair cells because each of them sprouts a slender thread-like filament that is agitated as the basilar membrane is vibrated within the fluid that fills the cochlea. It is convenient, and not too grossly misleading, to think of these as acting like the strings or wires in harps or pianos, each tuned to a particular frequency of vibration. Agitations of the hair cells cause them to send electrical impulses, first to a way-station, the cochlear nucleus, where much elaborate computation and further coding is carried on, and then on through the auditory nerves to the auditory centres on both sides of the brain. Here complicated jumbles of impulses from different cells are sorted and analysed to give us all that we know of the richness and emotional power of music, the subtleties of speech and all the bangs, whistles, crunches and buzz of the world. As illustrated in textbooks, the ear has always seemed to me to be a clumsy, Heath-Robinson structure in which bits of skin are wobbled by little bits of bone and these wobbles travel down a fluid-filled tube to shake some parts more than other parts of a flabby curtain of tissue so jerking stronger signals from some than from other nerve cells mounted on it. This is a dull failure of my imagination because audiologists compute that, when in perfect working order, this apparently clumsy fleshy system works at the extreme practical upper limit of sensitivity. If it were any more sensitive the faintest sounds that it could register would be masked by random vibrations of air molecules.

Hearing where things are

A seemingly odd design feature of the auditory system is that the right and left hemispheres of the brain do not each independently deal with input from the right and left ears. Information from each ear, as from each eye, goes to both hemispheres. This cross-connectivity is crucial because we not only need to know what sounds are but also where they come from, and we can only work this out by comparing the loudness and phases of sounds picked up by both ears. One cue is that because our heads separate our ears they make a sound shadow so that the noises are louder

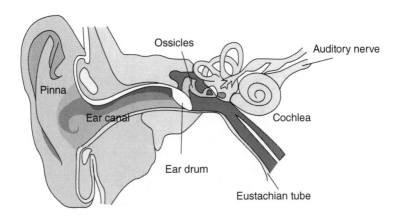

FIGURE 13.1 Schematic of the ear.

on the side from which they come. More subtle cues are the extents to which the sounds reaching the two ears are out of phase, and also differences in the micro-moments of their onsets due to differences in their directions and so the distances that they must travel to each ear. It is impressive to realise that, when in their best youthful condition, our ears, nervous systems and brains can register differences as minute as the time it takes a sound, travelling at more than 600 miles an hour, to traverse the width of a human head. When we are young, we learn to use this information to make remarkably accurate judgements of where sounds come from. As we age, we make these decisions less efficiently and so become less accurate at judging where sound-sources are. No doubt this increasing uncertainty might be a crucial loss for mythic virtuosos such as Zen Master Archers who, allegedly, could launch a second arrow to split a first located only by the noise of impact (the past is where miracles always happen). This loss of sound localization does not seem to me to be a serious problem for an average free-range urban oldie but it does make some differences. Unless we are blind, we do not twig that we use even very faint sound and echoes of the noises of our own movements to map the space around us in the dark. When I was young, I used to notice that whenever I entered a room empty of furniture I immediately got a feeling of greater space – that curiously seemed to be mapped on my skin rather than in sound-space about me. As my ears fail, my sense of the space immediately around me becomes much less precise. Nowadays "heard space" seems to have contracted close about my head. If I were blind, loss of echolocation would be a big problem rather than just an interesting change in experience. I could now no longer train myself, as young blind people do, to use echoes of my own movements or speech to accurately locate objects about me or to hear whether a wall is wood, brick or concrete well before I bump into it. Wandering gently about Oxford this only causes mild regret that the world has lost the differences of texture provided by accurate hearing and a sense of the amplitudes and differences between the spaces about me.

Particular hearing losses

Hearing loss in old age has such a characteristic pattern that it has been given the clinical label "elderly presbycusis". We become increasingly deaf to sounds of higher frequencies. This process starts early and is progressive. The very young can hear the high-pitched squeaks that bats make to detect obstacles as insubstantial as slender hanging threads and even to pinpoint midges.[1] As we move into middle age, we gradually lose upper frequencies. Higher voices in the dawn chorus are gradually muffled. For most of us, a much greater problem with selective loss of high frequencies and losses of nerve fibres conveying information from the ear to the brain is the effect on ease of understanding what is said to us. Vowels get through, but differences between consonants such as "K" and "P" or "S" and "F" are muffled, particularly when listening to squeaky children and women rather than gruff men. Presbycusis is almost universal, and starts quite early in life. Very large American surveys [2] find that hearing losses in both ears, especially for the upper frequencies, affect 23 per cent of people aged between 65 and 75 and 40 per cent of those aged 76 and older. It used to be thought that a sufficient explanation is selective mechanical damage from sound exposure to the hair cells on the parts of the basilar membrane that are tuned to detect high frequencies. Recent research shows that we also lose cells in the cochlear nucleus and the auditory pathways, and consequently become less sensitive at discriminating the temporal order of different speech sounds that rapidly follow each other [2, 3]. This ability of separating the order in which sounds occur is crucial for recognising spoken words and needs additional and more elaborate computation than simply registering differences in their pitch. Studies of senior gerbils [3] show that animals who have spent their young lives in quiet surroundings experience smaller losses of auditory nerve fibres and have better hearing than litter-mates who have led less quiet infancies. Gerbils' losses are especially marked in those nerve fibres with low spontaneous rates of firing. If the same is true for humans, losses of these particular fibres would explain some of the characteristic problems that older people have in understanding speech in a noisy background and in using combined information from both ears to locate the sources of sounds in space. The general point is that old age not only muffles the earliest stages of sound registration but also degrades the first computations in the auditory nerve and cochlear nucleus that filter and shape information for further interpretation deeper in the auditory cortex of the brain.

Losses of nerve cells from the auditory pathway with consequent knock-on effects on higher-level computing ability may explain why many older people find that even hearing aids that can selectively amplify the high frequencies in the speech spectrum do not completely overcome their problems of understanding spoken words.

Progressive losses of cells in the auditory pathways happen for many different reasons. For example, prolonged, inadequately controlled diabetes causes patterns of hearing loss characteristically different from that usually described as the "normal presbycusis" due to aging of the auditory system. Epidemiological studies also find that deafness increases with systolic blood pressure. Reports from a large and convincing Norwegian survey [4, 5] found that from 30 to 58 per cent of hearing losses "could be explained by age alone" but that an additional 1 to 6 per cent was due to lifetime exposure to noise and by other factors such as diabetes and infections. Hearing losses were slightly smaller in women than in men, possibly because the women were less likely to have been exposed to very noisy environments. Differences in noise exposure do not entirely explain these sex differences because the advantages for women seem related to their better health. Slight hearing loss seems to be a minor one among many other vexatious inconveniences of menopause and, like these, can be arrested or reversed by hormone replacement therapy.

The Norwegian study also checked whether amounts of hearing losses are related to the increase in the use of portable sound systems during people's lifetimes but found no evidence that this was so. However, because their elderly sample had not commonly used headphones in their youth they may have underestimated the effects of this source of noise exposure. There is some evidence that increasing use of personal music systems has affected the outlook for later generations. In the USA, incidence of hearing losses among adolescents increased markedly from 14.9 per cent in 1988/1994 to 19.5 per cent in 2005/2006 [6]. During this time, increases in hearing losses largely reflected losses of higher frequencies, and the incidence of losses in a single ear rather than in both ears, also rose. Again, losses were slightly less in women than in men. As usual, the presence and extent of hearing losses were greater in socially disadvantaged groups, probably because of their greater risk of exposure to industrial noise and to less protection from the wide range of difficulties from which affluence shields us.

Discoveries of substantial and progressive hearing losses during adolescence are ominous for old age. A study charmingly titled "Evidence of a misspent youth" [7] found that rats exposed to loud noise when young not only showed immediate neural degeneration and consequent hearing losses, but also further, greater and accelerating losses as they aged.

There are other intriguing, but as yet incompletely explained, sex differences. In their mutual old age, auditory thresholds seem to be more similar between sisters than between brothers. One possible explanation for this is that women may share very similar environments, especially if they are housewives, while men earn their living in more or less noisy jobs. A study comparing hearing thresholds of husbands and wives and brothers and sisters found no relationship between thresholds for genetically unrelated husbands and wives, but that thresholds for parents and children and for brothers and sisters were more similar than we would expect to occur by chance [8]. So hearing acuity seems to be determined both by biological relationships and by shared lifestyles and environments. Another intriguing sex difference was that genetic associations in hearing thresholds were stronger between related women than between related men, though this may again happen because the women were more likely than the men to share similar noise environments. Most participants in this study were young or middle aged and, because the differences in thresholds appeared for low and medium as well as for high frequencies, these results do not yet show whether genetic and environmental associations not only determine the amounts of hearing losses in old age but also the ages at which they first appear. As a general rule, hearing losses that occur in youth and middle age seem to persist and increase as life continues.

Even for happily functioning oldies it is a downer to be told that some degree of hearing loss is inevitable, that it not only affects high-pitched sounds but also the ability to make subtle distinctions between the temporal order of sounds, and that it is partly caused and accelerated by, sometimes unavoidable, exposure to loud noises. We have noticed that loss of discrimination of the temporal order of noises makes it more difficult to locate sounds in space and harder to recognise speech. For most of us, the main issue is how and by how much these changes are likely to affect our daily lives. There are obvious minor regrets: we have noticed the loss of the full spectrum of birdsong and other natural noises. The effects of losses must extend to music but this is less of a problem than it was for our parents because technologies now allow easy amplification of music and, more crucially, sensitively selective adjustments of loudness across different sound frequencies so that when losses of high frequencies become a problem, we can selectively amplify them. Growing hearing loss is an occupational hazard among musicians, who are often exposed to noisy environments, but older musicians I have talked to say that while this is a nuisance it by no means ruins their pleasure. Losses of the peripheral sound system seem to be compensated by the music stored and heard in the head. The most common problems are with understanding speech. Hearing aids do help, and they can now selectively amplify the particular parts of the sound spectrum that we lose, most typically the higher frequencies. Unfortunately, one of the characteristics of age-related deafness is that background noises, such as clatter and chatter in a crowded restaurant, become a problem. Hearing aid designers do not yet seem to have solved this. Hearing aids are a particular boon when listening to the wireless or watching TV among people who would find our preferred volume levels uncomfortable. They are also very useful during conversations with a single speaker in a quiet environment, but work much less well at a lively party, in a busy restaurant or a wind-buffeted beach.

Obvious and less obvious problems of being deaf

Conversation is one of the great joys of life. Its degradation is a major loss. It is at the core of our relationships, and is the main medium through which we learn how others feel and express ourselves to them. During the distant 1970s, Subhash Vyas and I made a small unpublished questionnaire study of the ways in which older people who are becoming slightly deaf cope with problems in group conversations. Volunteers generally agreed that, even without a hearing aid, talking with one person at a time is usually quite comfortable and easy. This is partly because during one-to-one encounters people rapidly attune to each other's difficulties and modify not only how loud and with what pitch they speak, but also favour listeners by using common rather than rare words, choose words less likely to be misheard, shorten their sentences and adjust their speech patterns. Conversations between people with markedly different accents are also a matter of subtle accommodations and compromises. It is also surprising how much information we can get by lip-reading, even though we may be quite unconscious of picking this up. Unfortunately, in old age we find lip reading harder to learn and so gain less help from it. It is clear that the more familiar is a voice or an accent, the easier things are. We can recognise what family members and close friends say much more easily than we can understand strangers. Especially during telephone conversations, unfamiliar accents can be very difficult. Glaswegian and Bangladeshi cold-calling salespersons never make me offers that I can't refuse; only offers that I can't understand. A very common complaint is that even when we can correctly make out what is said, mild deafness increases the time that we need to do this. This problem becomes worse as we age because we become slower both at recognising signals of any kind and at making decisions about them. An uncomfortable outcome is that, because we are slow to make them, the wit and cogency of our responses get lost as the most apt and clever rejoinder will fall lame as soon as its moment has passed. Choking back undelivered aphorisms is an insufficiently acknowledged curse of deafness (at least among the intensely eloquent volunteers that Subhash and I polled). For the same reasons, it is a trial for even slightly deaf people to interact with speakers who talk very fast. Even more so if they solicitously pause to check that you are keeping up before gabbling on again. To mishear things completely and to answer questions that you have not been asked is not comfortable but, as a deaf person, I have found that a briskly flowing conversation can absorb even quite surreal changes of topic. It is an enormous benefit to have partners, children and friends who know you so well that they remain vigilant for such occasions and can be relied on to silence an entire room full of people while they patiently and clearly explain your lapses to you and to each other. Bless you every one.

For those deeper in deafness than I yet am, there are worse social hazards that stem from our attempts at compensatory strategies. Those who are seriously deaf often have to choose between passively practising extreme social smiling or taking an initiative and monologuing to grasp and keep control. You never miss changes of topic if you make all of them yourself, and you never mishear questions or comments for which you leave no space. Whether to appear silent and stupid or, worse, silent and resentful or to ruthlessly treat your company as a lecture audience can be an interesting choice.

Other coping strategies are simpler and more sophisticated. Over the last 50 years, I have noticed that academic colleagues begin to talk more slowly as they have aged. This effect was very marked in a revered teacher, Alan Welford, the distinguished founder of cognitive gerontology in Britain. His sentences were excruciatingly slow, but always perfectly constructed and cogent. His leisurely progress through exquisitely framed prose had the effect of slowing down those to whom he spoke, so that conversations took place on a different, geological, time scale. His audience could predict the end of each sentence long before it came, and we felt, at the end of the academic hour, as if we had given his lecture to ourselves. Perhaps this is why I learned so much more from him than from brisker tutors.

A hazard of the inevitable coupling of growing peripheral hearing losses with increasing slowness of mental computation is that this can make our conversation seem much duller than it actually is. Finely honed aphorisms come too late, sluggish interpretations and mis-hearings can be mistaken for slow-wittedness or incomprehension. There are also other problems. When young adults are asked to do two things at once, such as carrying out mental arithmetic on short lists of numbers that they must also later remember, they try harder, take longer and forget more. It takes effort to successfully enter information into memory, even briefly into short-term memory. Having to spend more mental bandwidth and time to hear what is said borrows from the limited information processing bandwidth that we have. We fail to enter into consciousness some of the information that we struggle to hold in mind. I was once hired to test the effects of crackle on comprehension of speech over noisy telephone lines. Most of the young people I tested did very well at recognising even single random words that they could barely make out. Unexpectedly, they poorly remembered sentences that they had correctly heard and repeated when they were first played to them [8]. This was because they had to try harder to recognise words so they had less reserve processing capacity to encode them and enter them into their memories. Many years later, intrigued by some of the practical problems of carrying out conversations under unfavourable conditions, Subhash Vyas and I tested whether mildly deaf older people suffered similar problems. They did, because even when they could correctly repeat all the words they heard, they later remembered fewer of them [9]. Much more thorough studies have since confirmed and extended these findings [10].

Subhash's and my companion finding, pleasing to our clever sample of elderly Oxford residents, was that the higher their intelligence test scores, the faster they could recognise speech and make correct inferences, and so the less their hearing losses affected their memory for what they had heard [11]. This obviously also reduces the speed and the accuracy with which we can make correct inferences from all that has occurred during a lecture or a conversation and so makes our responses less apt and precise, and our insights less acute than we would otherwise have managed. Some of our own studies with Manchester volunteers extended these findings by showing that even slight deafness makes it much harder to attend to long lectures, especially if the topics are both stodgy and intellectually demanding (unpublished study). This could have been anticipated from work carried out during and after World War II, which showed that military personnel who have to monitor radar displays for rare signals for periods of 60 minutes or more begin to lose concentration and so miss events that they should detect. If the radar displays are also noisy and signals are difficult to make out, the effect is much more marked, and signals begin to be missed after 20 minutes or less.

Because older people's problems with deafness are eased if they still retain high intelligence we have to regretfully agree that, in this restricted practical sense, deafness does indeed reduce ones conversational intelligence. I do not like this way of putting it but cling to the comforting thought that I can considerably raise my conversational and lecture-listening intelligence by simply using my hearing aids.

Note

1 Think also of the success of the "mosquito device" installed in some shopping precincts to discourage adolescent loitering. This produces an intense high-frequency sound irritating to young adults and dogs and cats but unnoticeable by middle age.

References

[1] Tremblay, K. L., Piskosz, M. and Souza, P. (2003). Effects of age and of age-related hearing loss on the neural representation of speech cues. *Clinical Neurophysiology*, 114, 1332–1343.
[2] Seidman, M. D., Ahmad, N. and Bai, U. (2002). Molecular mechanisms of age-related hearing loss. *Ageing Research Reviews*, 1, 331–343.
[3] Mendelson, J. R. and Ricketts, C. (2001). Age-related temporal processing speed deterioration in auditory cortex. *Hearing Research*, 158, 84–94.

[4] Schmiedt, R. A., Mills, J. H. and Boettcher, F. A. (1996). Age-related loss of activity of auditory nerve-fibres. *Journal of Neurophysiology*, 76, 2799–2803.

[5] Borchgrevink, H. M., Tambs, K. and Hoffman, H. J. (2005). The Nord-Trøndelag Norway Audiometric Survey 1996–98: Unscreened thresholds and prevalence of hearing impairment for adults > 20 years. *Noise and Health*, 71.

[6] Tambs, K., Hoffman, H. J., Borchgevink, H. M., Holmen, J. and Samuelson, S. O. (2003). Hearing loss induced by noise, ear infections and head injuries: Results from the Nord-Trøndelag Hearing Loss Study. *International Journal of Audiology*, 42(2), 89–105.

[7] Shargorodsky, J., Curhan, S. G., Curhan, G. C. and Eavey, R. (2010). Change in prevalence of hearing loss in US adolescents. *Journal of the American Medical Association*, 2010, 772–778.

[8] Kujawa, S. G. and Liberman, M. C. (2006). Acceleration of age-related hearing loss by early noise exposure: Evidence of a misspent Youth. *Journal of Neuroscience*, 26, 2115–2123.

[9] Gates, G. A., Curopmitree, M. P. H. and Myers, R. H. (1999). Genetic associations in age-related hearing thresholds. *Archives of Otolaryngology Head Neck Surgery*, 195, 654–659.

[10] Rabbitt, P. M. A. (1966). Recognition: Memory for words correctly heard in noise. *Psychonomic Science*, 6, 383–384.

[11] Wingfield, A., Tun, P. and McCoy, S. (2005). Hearing loss in older adulthood: What it is and how it interacts with cognitive performance. *Current Directions in Psychological Science*, 14, 144–148.

[12] Rabbitt, P. (1991). Mild hearing loss can cause apparent memory failures which increase with age and reduce with IQ. *Acta Oto-laryngologica*, 111, 167–176.

14

TASTE AND SMELL

I can still smell the sharp, smoky urban winter and the rich nasal pleasure of a fish and chip shop, and strategic ducting of warm baking smells in supermarkets work for me. I now unreliably distinguish between some spices or judge when a garbage bin is becoming over-ripe. I wince to remember how my colleagues and I used to smile at the force of perfume and aftershave when groups of elderly people came to testing days. My sense of taste, which is closely linked to my sense of smell, is also blunted. I now could not possibly become a coffee or tea-taster and I keep quiet when friends enthuse about subtle distinctions between wines. It is no comfort that I am not alone. In 1994, the US National Centre for Health [1] collected data on the problems with taste and smell experienced by people aged over 18. They estimated that 2.7 million (1.4 per cent) had olfactory problems and 1.1 million (0.6 per cent) had taste problems. The proportion with these difficulties increased markedly with age. Of people aged 65 or older almost 40 per cent (1.5 million) had problems with either smell or taste or both. Losses of smell and taste significantly predicted levels of general health, other sensory problems such as losses of vision or hearing, difficulty standing or bending and depression. Changes in sensitivity of taste and smell are small inconveniences but are also hints to be alert for other health issues. Apart from this, some authors suggest that losses of taste perception can be causes as well as symptoms of poor health because they make us more likely to inadvertently eat too much sugar. Also, food without excessive quantities of salt seems tasteless and we may use increasing quantities of salt to mask bitter tastes. Others are concerned that losses of taste and smell sensitivity that cause all foods to taste equally bland may lead to dangerous losses of appetite and to poor dietary choices [2, 3, 4].

When we are young, our acuity of smell is remarkable. We breathe air-born molecules into our noses, which are shaped to channel air flow over olfactory recep-tor cells embedded in the olfactory epithelium in the inner lining of the nostrils.

Molecules of volatile compounds bind to proteins in these receptors and cause these to fire-off signals. Different kinds of receptor may be sensitive to different classes of molecule, so that the patterns of their different degrees of excitement are codes that our brains must crack to register subtle distinctions between the thousands of different complex combinations of molecules that we can distinguish from each other. Individual receptors also produce different, characteristic temporal codes of pulses for different volatile molecules. Pulses from receptor cells trigger bipolar cells, the next neurones in a long chain that leads to the brain. These, again, act as many-to-one coding networks with groups of bipolar cells producing different patterns of firing, characteristic to particular odours, to activate the next neurones in these many-to-one coding chains. Neurones clump together in structures called glomeruli in the olfactory bulb, an area of the brain where more complicated decoding takes place. Like taste receptors, smell receptors have brief lives and are replaced about every thirty days. As aging continues, replacement becomes less efficient and some receptors that are damaged or destroyed by inhaling toxic chemicals such as tobacco smoke are permanently lost. Our total number of receptors steadily declines throughout our lives. Individuals vary greatly in the number of taste receptors that they have, and so in the range and intensity of flavours that they distinguish. Some are born with many more receptors than most of us; women seem, in general, to have more taste receptors than men, and some of them become privileged "super-tasters" who can make good livings in the food industry and have to protect their fortune by insuring their taste sensitivity for surprising sums.

Our olfactory system is fragile in many ways. Impacts to the nose, such as blows or knocks from falls can shear bipolar cells and damage the olfactory bulb. As life goes on, accumulating mechanical damage and increased likelihood of falls add to incidence of losses of smell. Other causes are viral damage from respiratory infections, some prescription medicines and high concentrations of volatile chemicals in industrial environments. Convincing surveys show that people who spend their working lives on factory floors experience greater losses of smell, and consequently also greater blunting of taste than those in less polluted environments [5]. The working poor not only cannot afford the tastes and smells that pleasure the affluent; they become less able to appreciate what they can get.

The brain regions neighbouring the olfactory bulb are part of a system, including the amygdala, that is involved in feelings of strong emotions and the hippocampus, which is a control centre for registering memories of all kinds. The interesting juxtaposition of emotional, memory and sensory computational systems in the brain suggests an explanation for why smells are so effective at evoking poignant emotional memories. For this we must blame remote shrew-like and less distant primate ancestors for whom smell was a far more important sense than it now is for us. Having important memories of distress and fear, or of food and other alarms and satisfactions instantly and powerfully triggered by smells has been a good survival plan that still survives to enrich literature.[1]

The intensity and complexity of taste also very much depends on our smell receptors. When we relish or reject food it is difficult to know which components of the experience come from either sense. Other animals, most notably dogs, can distinguish between many thousands more smells than we can, detect odours we can never sense and interpret them with amazing accuracy. Dogs can detect faint traces of sweat, body odours and deposits of other molecules in footprints and (we do not yet know how) tell in which direction a tracked person or animal walked. Their advantage is not only the vastly greater number of their receptor cells, and the greater membrane surfaces over which they are distributed; they also have an extra adaptation: they can transfer molecules from their saliva with their tongues to an additional smell receptor surface. They can taste as well as smell an immense and rich chemical world that is unimaginable to us, and a much larger proportion of their brains is dedicated to analysing this greatly enriched information. If dogs had languages, they would have to include a vast vocabulary for many thousands of smells and modifiers for their relative persistence, freshness and durations. Humans have a relatively impoverished range of receptors for smell and taste, each variety of which responds, with some degree of specificity, to different kinds of chemical. Taste receptors in the mouth are clustered in taste buds on the upper surface of the tongue, the base of the tongue and its margins with the cheeks, the soft palate, pharynx, larynx, uvula and, surprisingly, the upper oesophagus and far down our gullets. Other researchers have found similar chemical, taste-bud-like structures in the linings of the stomach and intestine. This distribution of receptor cells over the entire upper digestive tract gives some plausibility to the comic swilling, rinsing and gargling practised by connoisseurs of wine, tea and coffee. The existence of receptors as far down the gastric system as the stomach and intestine also contributes to feelings of gastric satisfaction (happy tummy) and also distressing aspects of digestive miseries. The wide spatial distribution of receptors in our mouths means that the tastes that we get from items of food or drink change over time as they progress on the way to the gullet and beyond, producing what pretentious oenophiles describe as "wine song", a sequence of taste-notes proceeding from first grateful sensations on the tongue to later and richer sensations from the palate and tongue-cheek margins. I am willing to believe that people I have seen swilling and rinsing are virtuosi, cunningly ordering sensation sequences into masterpieces that those who are as mouth-deaf as I am can never comprehend. At least I am lucky enough not to wear dentures which, by covering the palate, especially blunt the richer and more subtle tastes of chocolate that we can access by pressing lush chunks against the grateful roofs of our mouths. Also, unlike my unfortunate father, I need not grumble that at first I do not taste curry at all and then go on tasting it long after I want to.

Taste buds in different parts of the mouth have different structures, and the different kinds of information that these provide are delivered to the medulla, a system in the brainstem, by three different nerves. Spatial distributions and temporal sequences of excitations of taste receptors are differentiated even at this higher level of the system. This same brain system also sends, and probably receives, information through nerve pathways that link it with receptors in the oesophagus, intestine and liver. This useful design-feature allows tastes and smells of available, imminent or inserted food to initiate preparatory secretions by the stomach, pancreas and even the liver. Its existence also testifies to the strong link between taste, smell and appetite, loss of which may, in old age, lead to eating disorders. It is the mechanism that underlies our inconveniently powerful stomach memory for smells and tastes of substances that have once made us feel sick, or which have accidentally been associated with quite different triggers of nausea. Like the heart, the gut has its reasons.

It was once thought that the tongue and mouth receptors, even with help from the nose receptors, could distinguish only between four basic taste sensations: sweet, sour, salty and bitter; four instruments in a quartet playing all the taste-melodies that we experience. More recent work has found that we, and monkeys and rats, also differentiate other tastes such as "metallic" and "chalky", together with the umami taste (famously of monosodium glutamate strongly detectable in Parmesan Cheese and also in Worcestershire sauce) [6]. This is an interesting example of how clumsily our conscious experiences of sensations are abridged by the limited repertoires of adjectives and adverbs in our languages. Our paltry set of verbal tags: sweet, salty, sour, bitter metallic, chalky and umami are economical for rough communication but, even when combined, into "sweet and sour" or "bitter-sweet" sadly constrain our experiences of the world. We can distinguish far more different possible tastes than these few labels suggest but, if we need to go beyond single taste words we must invent similes such as "blackcurrant", "fresh", "grassy", "tropical", "smoky" or, as in the case of some whiskies, "cat". The question whether and how broadening our vocabularies of labels might expand our range of distinct experiences is a different fascinating issue. An idea that my mind clutches to avoid drowning in metaphysics is that we can easily tell whether two or more complex tastes, for which we have no specific names, are the same or different if we experience them one after another. To hold tastes in memory so we can evoke and recognise them we

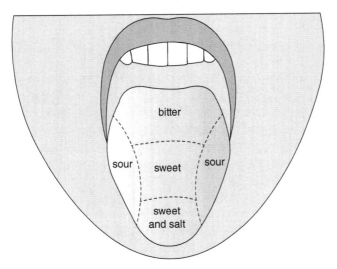

FIGURE 14.1 The tongue and areas of the different taste receptors.

have to label them. These labels become our internal index for remembered smells and tastes.

Whatever the precise number of instruments that play in them, our little tongue and palate bands are impoverished by old age and the intensity and range of tastes that we can distinguish diminishes accordingly. Teaching texts in sensory psychology attribute most losses to "normal aging", usually citing natural losses of receptors, of the nerve cells that transmit information from them to the brain and of neurones in the brain systems that interpret this information. It seems likely that unnatural losses caused by exposure to noxious substances, some medications, physical damage and some diseases, is much greater and increases throughout the lifetime. The result is not only a rise in the threshold levels of the weakest concentrations of chemicals that we can detect, but also a blurring of the precision with which we can distinguish between the relative strengths of much stronger concentrations. This leads to changes in food preferences that have been intensively researched because of interest by the food industry. Also, because some clinicians argue that blunting of taste sensitivity becomes a significant problem for older people because changes in their food preferences and losses of relish may reduce appetite and eventually cause malnutrition [2].

As Figure 14.2 shows, the nose and mouth share the same air and smell sharpens taste sensitivity. Nearly all studies show that age muffles both taste and smell.

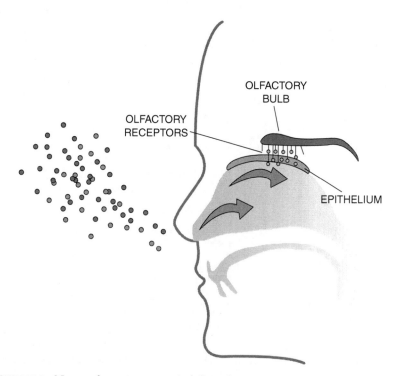

FIGURE 14.2 Nose and tongue anatomical dissection.

It seems that while older people can use the remnants of both senses they can still make as sensitive judgements as the young, but they manage less well when they are prevented from using smell by a nose clip. As we have noticed, much of the sensation that we perceive as taste is, in fact, contributed by the nose which has to be blocked out so that experimenters can control which system they are studying.

It is clear that there are losses of sensations but not yet whether, and how far, these may result in losses of appetite. Even while we are young, most of us are not good at recognising differences between complex tastes. A Swedish study [7] cheerily titled "Magic at the Marketplace", reports that, in the real-life setting of a supermarket, transient shoppers were persuaded to sample two different varieties of jam and tea and choose which of each pair they preferred. They were then asked to taste their preferred tea or jam again and explain why they had chosen it. Unknown to them the experimenters surreptitiously switched containers so that they re-tasted, sniffed and discussed the teas or jams that they had earlier rejected. The deftly deceptive authors report that "No more than a third of the manipulated trials were detected. Even for remarkably different tastes like Cinnamon-Apple and bitter Grapefruit, or the smell of Mango and Pernod no more than half of the exchanges were detected." Their deadpan conclusion is that this suggests "considerable levels of choice blindness for the taste and smell of two different consumer goods".

This is disquieting, but not yet completely damning evidence that food manufacturers can get away with gross crimes against good taste. It shows that, especially when distracted and diffident in a public setting, what we expect can strongly determine our judgements of taste and lead us to confuse flavours. People recollecting tastes in tranquillity would surely be likely to detect that they have opened the wrong packet or bottle. The supermarket experiment also nicely illustrates that taste discrimination and memory for taste are two different things. Shoppers did make confident and reliable distinctions when two teas or jams could be immediately compared, but not when, after an interval and confused by misinformation, they had to compare a current against a remembered taste. It also fits in with evidence that people find common and familiar foods difficult to identify when they have been given unexpected colours by flavourless dyes. The Swedish study does not report age differences, but we may be confident that older individuals who have lost sensitivity of smell and taste would be even easier to dupe. We may even speculate that as we grow older we may increase our enjoyment of life at very small cost by persuading those who truly care for us to stick prestigious labels on our supermarket wine bottles without telling us.

Many studies of losses of taste in old age have tested sensitivity for single chemical compounds to discover both what is the weakest concentration that we can detect and, above this threshold level, what are the smallest differences that we can notice: the just noticeable differences (jnds) that are the grist of studies in sensory psychophysics. Other issues are the relative sizes of differences that we can detect when a particular chemical is presented on its own, in water or is masked by other flavours in a compound of other substances.

The answers people give vary with the precise questions that we ask them. Jnds in intensity for common salt, potassium chloride, sucrose, aspartamene, acetic acid, caffeine, quinine and monosodium glutamate were measured in small groups of young and old people. Chemicals were tasted either when dissolved in distilled water or when added to a complex "product" (it seems likely that this study was funded by the food industry). Age did not much affect relative judgements as to which of two concentrations was stronger but it did affect absolute judgements of levels of concentration, especially when the taste of the chemical was partly masked by the taste of the product. This means that tests of discrimination for pure substances dissolved in water give us rather limited information about the extents of age changes or their implications for our everyday experience. Another point is that both the tastes and the strengths of concentrations of chemicals are effectively masked when they are added to a product. This is not good news for older people who need to control high blood pressure or diabetes by avoiding food with high levels of substances such as salt and sugar.

This issue has been widely recognised and explored. A different question is how far the taste of salt is disguised when other strong flavours are also present. In a useful study, volunteers were asked to detect salt flavouring in tomato soup [8]. The background tomato taste increased the thresholds for detecting salt for both older and younger tasters by seven to ten times but a telling factor is that older volunteers still needed twice as much salt as the young to "just barely detect its presence" in soup. This makes us concerned that elderly people may be more vulnerable to damage by prepared food products loaded with undesirably high levels of salt and sugar.

From the point of view of keeping healthy, an equally useful question is whether and how preferences between tastes change in old age. Because taste sensitivity declines we might suppose that as we grow old we would prefer stronger flavours, and that to achieve any sensation we have to blitz our fewer and failing receptors with extreme concentrations of the tastes we enjoy. It seems plausible that the elderly do begin to need stronger flavours, but I have not been able to find clear reports of this in the literature. For example, older people seem just as sensitive as the young to the taste of capsaicin, the substance that makes chillies taste hot. Some papers suggest the contrary. A convincing study asked (rather small) groups of 24 young (20 to 30) and older (60 to 75) people to assess the relative salt content of eight samples of chicken broth [9]. They found that the old could judge differences in concentrations of salt as accurately as the young, but that they preferred slightly less salty soups. The accuracy and consistency of judgements of people of all ages were not related to their individual taste preferences or to the habitual salt intakes recorded in their diet diaries. We might guess that there is a link between how accurately we can detect traces of particular flavours and our preferences among them. It would be a useful adaptation to become more sensitive to substances that we like and which are good for us and there is a deal of anecdotal evidence that we can do this. It is not an accident that mice, monkeys and men are fond of sugar, which, in the wide world beyond supermarkets, is a scarce and premium source of calories. A genetic predisposition to savour salt is also adaptive because we grow ill if deprived of it. Nevertheless, laboratory experiments testing our degrees of sensitivity to and relish for substances like salt, sugar or caffeine have found little evidence that we are particularly sensitive or insensitive to tastes that we like or would rather avoid. These are well-conducted studies but I am not clear whether the results are consistent for all tastes.

Slight disagreements between studies are likely to occur because volunteers had to make slightly different ranges of comparisons. It is also possible that comparisons between small groups may miss wide individual variations between individuals, both in taste sensitivities and in taste preferences. Other experiments suggest that individual differences in sensitivity and in preference may be large and characteristic of particular sub-groups. For example, a number of studies report that Arab and Sub-Saharan African volunteers have higher thresholds for detecting bitter tastes than Europeans and North Americans. Some researchers have speculated that this is genetically determined by evolutionary selection for taste preferences for locally common and nutritious foods. It is certainly true that the ability to taste one bitter chemical, phenylthiocarbamide (PTC) is genetically determined and a number of studies have speculated that inherited taste blindness to PTC is more common in Africans than in white Caucasians. On the other hand, a study using improved statistical methods found no reliable differences in incidence of genes causing failures to taste PTC in large numbers of Africans, Asians, Europeans and North Americans [10]. Preferences may be learned as much as inherited.

Most studies suggest that women are more sensitive to tastes than men and that they have slightly different preferences. When tested on simple tastes they have sometimes been found to have stronger preferences for sweet tastes. For more complex foods, men prefer robust tastes such as steak and casseroles while women prefer lighter ranges of flavour. Some authors suggest that this is because of women's "guilt", presumably at higher calorie intake. If this is so, I am sorry, but for me it still does not eliminate the possibility that, as perhaps in the case of different racial preferences, while taste sensitivity is probably wired in and may not be easily alterable, preferences are learned during a lifetime. This may explain why, while there is ample evidence that our senses of taste and smell become slightly less sensitive as we grow old, our taste preferences seem to remain quite stable.

Note

1 "When nothing else subsists from the past, after the people are dead, after the things are broken and scattered…the smell and taste of things remain poised a long time, like souls…bearing resiliently, on tiny and almost impalpable drops of their essence, the immense edifice of memory" – Marcel Proust.

References

[1] Hoffman, H. J., Ishii, E. K. and Macturk, R. H. (1998). Age-related changes in the prevalence of smell/taste problems among the United States adult population: Results of the 1994 Disability Supplement to the National Health Interview Survey (NHIS). *Annals of the New York Academy of Sciences, Vol 85 Olfaction and Taste, an International Symposium*, 716–722.

[2] Schiffman, S. S. and Wedral E. (1996). Contribution of taste and smell losses to the wasting syndrome. *Age Nutr.*, 7, 106–120.

[3] Duffy, V. B., Backstrand, J. R. and Ferris, A. M. (1995). Olfactory dysfunction and related nutritional risk in free-living elderly women. *Journal of the American Dietetic Association*, 95, 879–886.

[4] Schiffman, S. S. (1997). Taste and smell losses in normal aging and disease. *Journal of the American Medical Association*, 278, 1357–1362.

[5] Corwin, J., Loury, M. and Gilbert, M. (1995). Workplace, age and sex as mediators of olfactory function: Data from the National Geographic smell survey. *Journals of Gerontology, B*, 50B, 179–186.

[6] Mojet, J., Christ-Hazelhof, E. and Heidema, J. (2001). Taste perception with age: Generic or specific losses in threshold sensitivity to the five basic tastes? *Life Sciences and Medicine*, 25, 331–337.

[7] Hall, L., Johansson, P., Tarning, B., Sikstrom, S. and Deutgen, T. (2010). Magic at the marketplace: Choice blindness for the taste of tea and the smell of jam. *Cognition*, 117, 54–61.

[8] Stevens, J. C., Cain, W. S., Demarque, A. and Ruthruff, A. M. (1991). On the discrimination of missing ingredients: Aging and Salt Flavour. *Appetite*, 16, 129–140.

[9] Drewnowski, A., Henderson, S. A., Driscoll, A. and Rolls, B. J. (1996). Salt taste perceptions and preferences are unrelated to sodium consumption in healthy older adults. *Journal of the American Dietetic Association*, 96, 471–474.

[10] Wooding, S., Kim, Un-kyung, Bamshad, M. J., Larsen, J., Jorde, L. B. and Drayna, D. (2004). Natural selection and molecular evolution in *PTC,* a bitter-taste receptor gene. *American Journal of Human Genetics*, 74, 637–646.

15

FUMBLING AND STUMBLING

One of the most evocative lines of the great Alexandrian poet, Constantine Cavafy is "The lips and the skin remember". For my generation this may be just as well because impressively large polls show that, in all countries, elderly people of both sexes, but especially men, touch, and are touched by others much less than when they were young adults, and far, far less than when they were infants. This is sad because it is not only infants who need physical contact with other humans to thrive. The need for mutual huddling and grooming was wet-wired into the brains of our hominid ancestors and is still central to our emotional lives. When lost it is sadly missed.

Touch is not a simple, single sensation but a complex experience synthesised from the combinations of messages sent by a variety of quite different receptor organs lodged in or just beneath our skins. Each tells us something different about what is happening at our interfaces with the world. To detect light contact and slight roughness, we have tiny embedded bulbs called Meissner's corpuscles that distinguish between slight irregularities and smoothness of surfaces and pick up the faint, slow vibrations and tremors of peacefully living human bodies, purring cats or smoothly running engines. To feel deeper pressures essential for maximum appreciation of vigorous and satisfying back-rubs we have Pacinian corpuscles. For sustained touch and pressure, as distinct from light and heavy stroking, we have Merkel's discs. Even the tiniest of our body hairs, scarcely qualifying as down, have at their roots follicle-receptors that detect minute displacements by hungry insects or tender friends and which, at the bases of our grotesquely flourishing nostril hairs, are a torment to old men. We also have free nerve endings that do not end in specialised receptors and that give us sensations of pain as well as light touch. We register warmth at the skin surface with A and C receptor fibres. All of these subtle devices, severally and together, contribute to the complex of our skin sensations and they are all steadily depleted as we age.

We may not notice our gradual progressive losses of skin sensations because our receptors are unevenly distributed over our body surfaces and the resulting enormous differences in sensitivity between different skin areas may sometimes confuse what we have lost and where. Sense receptors of all kinds are most densely present on our lips, tongues, faces, hands and fingers and feet but there are more than a hundred times fewer of them for each unit of skin surface on our upper arms, backs, buttocks and lower legs. This unequal distribution of receptors is mirrored by the areas of the brain dedicated to receiving and interpreting skin sensations. Figure 15.1 shows a map of the relative sizes of these plotted as a "homunculus" on the brain surface based on an original by Oliver Zangwill [1].[1]

As old age trundles on, losses of receptors blunt sensitivity. Changes can be measured in different ways: thresholds for detecting light touches with the ends of fine hairs; for sensing the minimum gap between adjacent prongs of divider-like instruments (two-point threshold); and for the ability to tell the orientations and the lengths of short lines drawn on the skin surface with a single point. On our very sensitive fingertips, sensory thresholds measured by all these methods consistently decline by about 1 per cent a year between the ages of 20 and 80 [2, 3]. These losses have obvious consequences for skills requiring fine tactile sensitivity – for example reading Braille. Elderly Braille readers who are already limited by visual impairments discover that dulling of the fingertips is a new handicap [4].

Declines of touch sensitivity begin in late middle age, but before age 65 they do not seem to have much effect on highly practised manual skills. An optimistic idea was that losses of touch sensitivity in old age may be checked or even reversed by

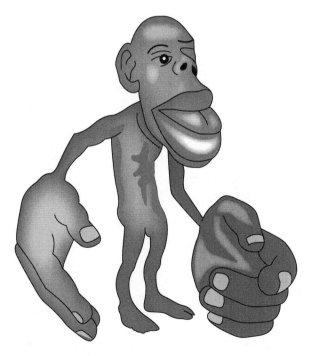

FIGURE 15.1 Homunculus.

long practice so that, for example, skilled and persistent Braille reading might preserve fingertip sensitivity [4] but this turns out to be debatable. This is discouraging
for people who would like to believe that continued heavy use of sensory systems
can maintain their sensitivity in old age. Two-point thresholds are much lower
for children than for young adults, and men have higher thresholds than women.
Age affects two-point thresholds to different extents on different parts of the body,
reducing sensitivity relatively more on the most sensitive areas, the lips, tongue and
fingertips, than on the less sensitive back and abdomen [3].

The picture is similar for other sensations. Sensitivity to warmth and cold is 100
times greater on some parts of the body than others. Our faces, particularly around
our lips and eyes, are very sensitive. Our hands (except for the fingertips) and feet
much less so, and other areas of our body surfaces are somewhere in between. The
more sensitive an area is at detecting cold the better it is at detecting warmth. As
we age, we suffer greater losses of sensitivity of our hands and feet. Especially the
feet, where losses are sometimes too great to safely measure [5].

Detection thresholds for changes in temperature – warming and cooling – fall with
age in people aged from 18 to 88 years. These findings have been plotted to give temperature maps – homunculi that turn out to be very similar to the touch homunculus
shown in Figure 15.1. Temperature sensitivity varies over the body surface by a factor
of 100 or more. As for touch, the face is particularly sensitive. All skin surfaces are
more sensitive at detecting cold than heat. In all areas, sensitivity declines with age,
but very much less in the most sensitive areas such as the face than in the less sensitive,
such as the feet. In old age, feet can become remarkably insensitive to abrupt increases
in warmth and even to pain. Those who care for frail elderly people should be keenly
aware of this, as should free-range elderly people who must bear in mind that a tradi-
tional technique of assessing bath temperature by standing in a tub as it fills with water
may be convenient for the young but risks scalds for the elderly [6].

Estimates that sensitivity thresholds increase by about 1 per cent per year of life
are based on averages. Individuals differ widely. For example, Jain and his colleagues
[7] measured the sensitivity of the hands and feet of a large number of people and
found, like previous authors, that touch thresholds for the feet are from three to
seven times higher than for the hands, and that both hand and foot thresholds
markedly rise with age. Women had lower thresholds than men. It is relevant that
the sample tested were rural dwelling South Asians because their thresholds were
significantly higher than have been found for samples in more prosperous urbanites
in Europe and North America. Evidently, thresholds are markedly affected by sex
and lifestyle as well as by age.

Increases in thresholds in healthy old age are not just due to losses of skin receptors. A comparison of sensory thresholds for the detection of time gaps between two
immediately successive stimuli in hearing, vision and touch found that for all these
sensory systems the accuracy of time-gap detection fell with age. The amounts of losses
in sensitivity of vision, hearing and touch were correlated with each other and also
with scores on intelligence tests [8]. As we noticed when discussing biological markers
for changes in intelligence and information processing speed in Chapter 4, consistently

strong relationships between losses of sensory acuity and mental abilities suggest that changes in sensitivity are not just due to parallel losses of efficiency in our sense receptors for sound, light and touch but are also markers for changes in the brain that affect all our perceptions and also our intelligence and the speed with which we can process information. Losses of touch sensitivity and of the ability to tell which of two touches occurred before the other are due to changes in our brains as well as in our skins.

Losses of receptors in our hands and feet occur in "normal" healthy old age but are dangerously accelerated by diseases such as diabetes or by prolonged excessive alcohol consumption, both of which may cause massive losses in receptors in the hands and feet resulting in glove and stocking anaesthesia. This is not a jolly condition, and increases the risk of unnoticed accidents and wounds and consequent dangerous infections. This is particularly hazardous for those who are most likely to suffer from it, such as diabetics and people with poor circulation. It also results in almost permanent sensations of pins and needles, particularly when standing barefoot on a cold bathroom floor in winter.

Losing sensation in our feet and hands also causes other problems. Loss of skin receptor sensitivity in our feet contributes to unsteadiness when walking on irregular surfaces [9]. This adds to the more serious risks of tripping and falling caused by failures of other systems. Knowing precisely where our hands and feet are in three-dimensional space and moving them about appropriately is a tricky and complicated business. To manage this we need to know the exact state of tension in our muscles and the angles at which our joints are bent. We also need to know about changes in loading and pressure on our arms, legs, hands and feet, how our bodies are oriented in space and how gravity is acting upon them. In addition, we need some degree of peripheral vision. To manage our bodies in space and gravity requires intensive co-operation between many different receptor systems, all of which are degraded by increasing age.

As we age, we lose cells from our muscles and they become weaker. By our sixties, losses of muscle units mean that there have been quite marked declines both in the strength and speed with which our muscles can contract [10]. This means that we balance less securely and are slower to adjust to sudden changes and to recover from trips and stumbles. Controlling our hands to manipulate things skillfully also requires precise information from muscle and joint receptors. It is not enough to be able to hold and handle objects. To avoid dropping or crushing them we must also adjust to their relative weights and degrees of solidity. This means being able to exert low levels of force continuously over quite long periods of time. The sensitivity with which we can make these fine adjustments to grip delicately declines with age [11].

To know whether, and by how much our muscles are tensed or relaxed, we rely on spindle-shaped receptors that are embedded in them and that stretch and relax as they do. We progressively lose muscle spindles as we grow old, particularly if we take little exercise and use our muscles less. This means that the information that we can receive about muscle tension becomes less accurate and we are less able to finely control our movements or judge the positions of our limbs and body in space. These problems are increased by losses of the receptors in our joints that tell us by how much they are bent and this makes us less sensitively aware of the extents and the speeds of the movements that we make, the positions of our limbs and our body posture.

Diminished skin sensitivity, loss of information from muscles and joints with consequent awkwardness of movements and problems with balance and stability are not just due to losses of receptors. We noticed in Chapter 4 that difficulties in balance are associated with aging of the brain that result in losses of brain volume, poorer brain blood supply and increases in the number of white matter lesions – the scars left by the deaths of neurones. This means that losses of balance, limb coordination and difficulties in maintaining posture are also caused by increasing inefficiency of the particular systems in the motor cortex of the brain that control these complicated activities.

To keep our balance, we must combine information from many different sources. Skin receptors in our feet play a relatively minor but important part in telling us the nature of the surface on which we are standing; our muscle and joint receptors provide the information that we need to make small, necessary adjustments to our limbs and information from our vestibular system, the balance receptors in our inner ears, respond to slight changes in posture, body-sway and head position. Our eyes, particularly in peripheral vision, detect slight movements and changes in the vertical orientation of our heads. As information from all of these different sources becomes increasingly sparse and degraded, we become less able to solve the enormously difficult problems of combining information from all our sensors to allow us to work out the positions of our bodies in space and how and what bits of ourselves we must move to adjust our posture and avoid falling over. The complexity of the computations needed to do this means that the gradual degradation of our ability to balance and to adjust our posture is a sensitive marker for our general state of health and so also of the current status of our brains and our life expectancy. An example is a study that tested balance in a large sample of people in Sweden, Denmark and Finland when they were all aged 75 and again when they reached 80 [12]. Those who survived to take the second test showed significant declines even on very simple tests of postural balance such as remaining stable while standing with their eyes open and eyes closed. Those who had died before they reached 80 had, when they were earlier tested at 75, lower balance scores than those who survived. Even very simple tests of balance are predictors of levels of general health and so of risk of earlier death and loss of mental abilities between 75 and 80 years.

We rarely appreciate the triumph of bio-engineering that our species has achieved to keep balanced while standing still on two multi-jointed props. Balancing on one leg is an even more marvellous achievement and managing to do this while also deftly inserting the other leg into the correct tube in a pair of trousers *without hanging on to something* is a morning miracle. Anyone over 75 who can still do this with confident grace can congratulate herself that, as far as balance goes, omens for survival and lasting mental competence are good. Stable posture is a great accomplishment but managing a fluent and confident walk is even more impressive.

The trouser test reveals that we can use another subtle source of information from the world that allows us to keep our balance and manage our bodies in space. To avoid tumbling over, snagged in one's trousers, it is not necessary to grip a chair or doorframe as grimly as a wrecked mariner clutching flotsam. Even very gentle contact of a single finger on a stable object does the trick. We do not use this touch as support but as a reliable reference point from which we can compute where our hand and arm currently are and so also work out the orientation or our entire body in relation to them. This mastery allows us to know where our limbs are, and confidently saunter up and down stairs. We need banisters for spatial reference and balance rather than for support and heavy hauling.

All the sensory changes that we have discussed affect our confidence and stability while walking. Losses of skin-pressure-receptors on the soles of our feet make us less sensitive to small changes in pressure caused by slights shifts of balance. Degradation of information from our vestibular system, the balance organs mounted next to our inner ears, makes our judgements of the vertical less accurate and our appreciation of accelerations and decelerations coarser. Some textbooks, possibly to attempt consolation, genially comment that because seasickness is caused by the mismatch between the information that we get from our vestibular organs of balance and from our eyes, loss of vestibular information means that we increasingly rely only on our eyes and muscle receptors alone. Mismatches do not occur and freedom from seasickness becomes one of the sparse advantages of old age. I only wish that my personal experience bore this out. The vestibular system provides information about forward and backward acceleration, and changes in body position when climbing and descending slopes and stairs. In all these endeavours, vestibular information co-operates with vision, particularly peripheral vision that monitors the peripheral flow of the streaming world as we move forward or backward. As aging progresses, losses of peripheral vision make this less reliable. We also rely on information from our joints and muscles, which, as we have seen, we gradually lose. All these factors make walking precarious, and bones made brittle by osteoporosis make falls a main cause of serious injuries and even of deaths. A key problem causing falls is that it becomes hard to recover from trips and stumbles. This is not only because we lose leg-muscle strength, so that our limbs may collapse as we try to use them to prop ourselves up. A key issue is that we take much longer to notice that we have lost balance and we have also become much slower at processing information so that we are well into a fall before we begin to try to correct it. Then, when at last we realise our danger, we are too slow to make a rapid forward step to counteract a stumble and are sluggish and awkward in initiating other movements to recover balance [13].

Falls are serious, so it is worth spending some time analysing how they occur, what they imply for the ways in which our brains and our limbs interact to maintain mobility and what we can do to make them less likely. An analysis of case histories from women aged 75 years and over found that 50.5 per cent reported falls and their medical histories showed that the risk factors for outdoor falls and indoor falls were different [14]. A strong risk factor for both indoor and outdoor falls was having suffered a previous fall. The most important risk factors for outdoor falls were having some degree of visual impairment, feeling depressed and, paradoxically, having a relatively fast comfortable walking speed and being able to cope with steps as high as 40 cm. This suggests that individuals who avoid challenges by reducing their walking speeds, reduce their risk of falls relative to the more adventurous and confident who sometimes push themselves beyond even their safe limits. For indoor falls, risk factors were having a slower maximum comfortable walking speed (to shuffle, even indoors, is not a good sign), being unable to cope with high steps, poor performance on a simple clinical mobility test, having less good general health and experiencing some cognitive difficulties. Although the authors remark that they adjusted for differences in time spent outdoors, their results can be interpreted as showing that people who were more healthy and mobile are at risk in slightly more challenging outdoor environments, while those who have health difficulties and restricted mobility were at greater risk of falls even in the sheltered indoor environments in which they now spend most of their time. Illness and weakness are risk factors for falls even in lenient surroundings.

The relationship between risk of falls and cognitive losses is interesting because it highlights the unexpected point that walking does take up substantial amounts of our mental capacity. This was shown by Sal Connolly while collecting data for a PhD thesis in Manchester. In what she called her "Gerry Ford Experiment"[2] she gave older people easy tasks such as simple mental arithmetic while they were guided through a short, easy, safe, indoor path. Doing an additional task caused many of them to walk more slowly and some to trip and stumble. On further investigating those whose walking was most affected by these additional mental tasks, she found that they had previously suffered and recovered from strokes which had, at the time, only slightly affected their gait. Their difficulties were not apparent unless they were distracted by simple mental tasks. Excellent studies at the Berlin Max Planck Developmental Psychology headed by Ulman Lindenberger and colleagues [15, 16] have since confirmed and extended Sal's results by showing that not only recovered stroke patients but also normal, healthy elderly people have difficulties in combining mental tasks with walking.

There are things that we can do to rehabilitate ourselves and keep spry. For example, an article in the *Journal of the Academy of Nurse Practitioners* reports the experience of elderly patients who were enrolled in a nine-week course in jazz dance [17]. Within three weeks of joining, and throughout the rest of the course, volunteers experienced significant improvements in balance and stability, cognitive ability and a more positive mood. Many studies of elderly Chinese practitioners of Tai-Chi show that this discipline preserves balance and flexibility. A heroic experiment also found that regular Tai-Chi practice allows even older practitioners to preserve their balance in spite of disorienting stimulation of their vestibular systems [18]. Again, we see that although the reprieves gained by making more effort must, of course, delay rather than abolish losses, they can be large, and real, and greatly add to the ease, safety, duration and pleasure of long lives, keeping us sprightly, supple and stable to the end.

Notes

1 While I was an undergraduate in the Cambridge Department of Psychology, a legend was that data for the first of these homunculus-maps were collected by the then Professor, Oliver Zangwill, from the extremely nude body of an amiable lecturer, the lapsed physicist G.C. Grindley. This is probably true. I am less sure of the apocryphal addition that this investigation was interrupted by a forceful cleaning lady who could not be persuaded that this was a clinical and dispassionate research project. The (edited) map of "C" Grindley's skin is said to be the one in Oliver's fine little book *An Introduction to Modern Psychology* [2].
2 After the alleged remark by Lyndon Johnson that his successor, Gerry Ford, "couldn't walk and chew gum at the same time". He does not merit recognition for an early insight in understanding a relationship between cognition and movement because his actual, far more pungent comment was that the unfortunate Ford "Could not fart and chew gum at the same time". This was the LBJ famous for other brutal comments such as "If you have them by the balls their hearts and minds will follow". I mention this only for sake of historical accuracy. Please do not think too long about it.

References

[1] Zangwill, O. L. (1951). *An Introduction to Modern Psychology*. London, Methuen.
[2] Stevens, J. C. and Cruz, L. A. (1996). Spatial acuity of touch: ubiquitous decline revealed by repeated threshold testing. *Experimental Brain Research*, 216, 287–297.
[3] Stevens, J. C. and Choo, K. K. (1996). Spatial acuity of the body surface over the life span. *Somatosensory and Motor Research*, 13, 153–166.
[4] Reuter, E-M. and Voelker-Rehage, C. (2012). Touch perception throughout working life: effects of age and expertise. *Experimental Brain Research*, 216, 287–297.
[5] Stevens, J. C. and Choo, K. K. (1998). Temperature sensitivity of the body surface over the life span. *Somatosensory and Motor Research*, 15, 13–28.
[6] Dyck, P. J., Zimmerman, M. S. E. E., Gillen, L. P. N., Johnson, D., Karnes, J. L. and O'Brien, P. C.. (1993). Cool, warm and heat pain detection thresholds. *Neurology*, 43(8), 1500–1508.
[7] Jain, S., Muzzafurallah, S., Peri, S., Eilanti, R., Moorthy, K. and Nath, I. (2008). Lower touch sensibility in the extremities of healthy Indians: further deterioration with age. *Journal of the Peripheral Nervous System*, 13, 47–53.
[8] Humes, L. E., Busey, T. A., Craig, J. C. and Kewley-Port, D. (2009). The effects of age on sensory thresholds and temporal gap detection in hearing, vision and touch. *Attention, Perception and Psychophysics*, 71(4), 860–871.
[9] Lord, S. R. and Ward, J. A. (1994). Age-associated differences in sensori-motor function and balance in community dwelling women. *Age and Ageing*, 23, 452–460.
[10] Doherty, T. J., Vandervoort, A. A. and Brown, W. F. (1993). Effects of ageing on the motor unit: a brief review. *Canadian Journal of Applied Physiology*, 18, 331–358.
[11] Galganski, M. E., Fuglevand, A. J. and Enoka, R. M. (1993). Reduced control of motor output in a human hand muscle of elderly subjects during submaximal contractions *Journal of Neurophysiology*, 69, 2018–2115.
[12] Heikkinen, E. P., Gause-Nilsson, I. and Schroll, M. (2002). Postural balance in elderly people: changes over a five-year follow-up and its predictive value for survival. *Aging and Clinical and Experimental Research*, 14, 37–46.
[13] van Dieen, J. H., Pijnapples, M. and Bobbert, M. F. (2005). Age-related intrinsic limitations in preventing a trip and in regaining balance after a trip. *Safety Science*, 43, 437–453.

[14] Bergland, A., Jamio, G. B. and Laake, K. (2003). Predictors of falls in the elderly by location. *Aging Clinical and Experimental Research*, 15, 43–50.

[15] Lindenberger, U., Marsiske, M. and Baltes, P. B. (2000). Memorizing while walking: Increase in dual-task costs from young adulthood to old age. *Psychology and Aging*, 15(3), 417–436.

[16] Verrel, J., Lövdén, M., Schellenbach, M., Schaefer, S. and Lindenberger, U. (2009). Interacting effects of cognitive load and adult age on the regularity of whole-body motion during treadmill walking. *Psychology and Aging*, 24(1), 75–81.

[17] Allpert, P. T., Miller, S. K., Wallman, H., Havey, R., Cross, C., Chevalia, T., Gillis, C. B. and Kodandapari, K. (2009). The effect of modified jazz dance on balance, cognition, and mood in older adults. *Journal of the Academy of Nurse Practitioners*, 21, 108–115.

[18] Tsang, W. W. and Hui-Chan, C. W. (2006). Standing balance after vestibular stimulation in Tai Chi-practicing and nonpracticing healthy older adults. *Archives of Physical Medicine and Rehabilitation*, 87, 546–553.

PART IV

Intelligence, Skills and Wisdom

16

GENERAL SMARTS

When we acknowledge that we have become middle aged, we begin to worry that changes in our brains may already have started to degrade our intelligence and make us more boring in company and less competent at coping with our jobs and everyday lives. In public, we cover inevitable trivial mistakes with nervous jokes about imminent brain death. We are less flippant when we are alone.

In fact, very few of us have any reason for anxiety. Small lapses are common at any age. Questionnaires show that trivial everyday lapses are rarely warnings of rapid and marked decline and are reported as often by overtaxed young adults as by those in their forties and fifties. We need objective evidence to tell us how long we can remain at the very peak of our game and whether we are still as sharp as ever or are almost imperceptibly becoming slower to get the point of a remark, to rapidly understand the issues that it raises and find a quick and adequate reply.

Psychologists have not yet found more sensitive measures of our general mental abilities than our scores on sets of apparently quite trivial problems that they describe as "intelligence tests". When these tests are given to very large groups of people of different ages we invariably find that group-average scores decline slightly, but significantly, between the twenties and thirties, this slight fall continues through the forties, fifties and sixties and accelerates during the seventies and eighties. I cannot find a positive spin for this news, but it is crucial to recognise that, in absolute terms, the declines are very small. For example, during the 20-year University of Manchester study we repeatedly gave all the Manchester and Newcastle volunteers three different, very reliable and well-standardised tests: Alice Heim's AH4 1 and AH4 2 tests [1] and the Cattell Culture Fair test [2]. People's scores on all these tests closely agreed with each other and on all of them the differences between the average scores for people aged between 40 and 59 and those aged from 80 to 89 were only 9 to 13 points or, looked at another way, about 30 per cent of their middle-aged performance.

We must remember that since these are average scores this means that half of all volunteers changed less. Of course, it is not encouraging that this also means that many changed by a little more. This apparently uncomfortable finding is actually reassuring. The amount of change that each of us can expect to experience is not a fixed number, perhaps set by our genes, but is, actually a probability estimate. It is only a rough guide to the *odds* of expected change within quite a narrow range. Those interested will find that David Spiegelhalter's mathematical explorations of how to make the best sense of such comparisons are brilliantly and cheerfully illuminating and are wittily described in his book with Michael Blastland, *The Norm Chronicles*, [3], which I urge you to read. They point out that demographic counts of deaths at different ages associated with dangerous habits such as such as skydiving, smoking or immoderate consumption of coffee, alcohol or nitrate-rich sausages do not actually give us a prediction of the time of our death but estimates of the probability of risks of death that can be computed in units called "micromorts". A micromort is a one in a millionth chance of death during weeks, months or years. A companion index is the "microlife" – one millionth of your adult lifespan – which they estimate at about 30 minutes. These useful words let us discuss the probable effects of cigarettes (estimated cost 1 microlife), two pints of strong beer (1 microlife) or an inch on the waistline (cost 1 microlife a day seven days a week, the same as two hours a day watching TV).

It is useful to think of our population average losses of intelligence test scores of 13 points between 60 and 89 in terms of a similar measure, a "bright", a single unit of AH4 [1] test score. On average, Manchester/Newcastle citizens lost 13/10150 or 0.0013 brights per day. This allows us an index for the effects of lifestyle factors such as poverty, cigarettes, alcohol and sausage consumption in terms of average increases in losses of microbrights, millibrights, centibrights or decibrights per day, year or decade and fixes our minds on the crucial point that we are talking about changes in probability of losses, or of increases in rates of loss, that are alterable by changing our lifestyles, rather than in terms of inevitable daily losses in our store of remaining brights.

If we lead ideal lives, we can expect to change very little and the most important thing is that we can take useful steps to nudge the odds in our favour.

Data from the Newcastle and Manchester samples emphasise this point. As we followed individuals over periods of 10 to 20 years, it became clear that some individuals' intelligence test scores remained almost constant while for others, particularly those with pathologies such as cardiovascular problems or diabetes, there were clear declines. It is good news that some of us experience minimal and almost undetectable changes because by learning more about these lucky individuals we can hope to find out how to share their fortune. Because we have no more sensitive tools than intelligence test scores to detect changes in mental ability, it is worthwhile to consider just what it is that these tests measure. What is this quality or capacity that we call intelligence? Do intelligence test scores also predict performance on tests of other abilities such as memory or mental speed, or do they test something different and much more general?

What *do* intelligence tests measure?

When asked "What is intelligence?" many psychologists reply "What intelligence tests measure". This seems evasively jokey but is actually honest and useful. It makes the point that the word intelligence was once a useful term in everyday language meaning something similar to general cleverness. A hundred and thirty years of efforts to devise some practical way to predict how people will cope with the problems that they encounter in their everyday lives has given it a narrower and more precise meaning. Research on intelligence did not begin as a theoretical quest to identify some basic characteristic of human minds. Creative researchers such as Robert Sternberg have tried to analyse the wider, common language assumptions about what intelligence is by asking people randomly accosted in streets or railway stations what they understood by this vague but widely used word. Most people avoided any formal definition and gave concrete illustrations of the sorts of things that clever people can do better such as solving novel hard problems fast, doing complicated mathematics, succeeding at school or business or just "knowing a lot". Some made a distinction between success at urban or business survival, the acquisition of "street smarts", and the ability to solve abstract problems. Some distinguished between a specific ability to solve particular kinds of problem, in business, science or medicine, or to write excellent books or poems, and general smartness that might allow people to do well in all of these and also many other fields. Some rejected the idea that an intelligent person can brilliantly turn her brain to anything and enjoyed finding examples of people who excelled only in a single limited field such as mathematics, music, drawing or chess but were remarkably incompetent in all others. In other words most persons-in-the street do not believe that intelligence is a single general ability that can be applied to any problem or subject. They tend to think that there may be many different, sometimes very specialised, kinds of intelligence and that having one skill does not necessarily imply having others. They also believed that good strategies for dealing with the world, "street smarts", are learned rather than innate. Many distinguished between the slow acquisition of specialised knowledge that allows people, after long effort, to reach pre-eminence in a particular field such as chess or accountancy and the "basic smarts" that make a person a "fast study" who can rapidly acquire new information of any kind. In fact, these lay-people very precisely and comprehensively described all the issues about "intelligence" that psychologists had raised during the previous century and still continue to debate. We can use these examples of effective folk wisdom to guide our discussion of whether intelligence changes as we age, and what these changes may mean for our abilities to successfully manage our lives.

Testing times

The first intelligence tests were Alfred Binet's [3] best attempts to predict how well young children were likely to cope with the nineteenth-century French school system. He gave them sets of simple problems to solve within a short, fixed time and found that the number of problems that they correctly answered under this time pressure closely agreed with their teachers' rankings of their current levels of achievement in their school subjects and, much more usefully, predicted their future progress at school subjects. Scores on such tests often predicted children's future progress better than teachers did. Over the next two decades, speculation into what, precisely, "intelligence" is, was driven by practical research into test design and validation than by theoretical discussions.

At the end of the nineteenth century, the powerful and original mind of Francis Galton hatched a bad idea that measures of mental ability such as intelligence test scores or speeds of reaction times could be a way to classify mankind into the more or less genetically fit specimens of the human race. This added to his theoretical rationale for eugenics: a loose compendium of theories that mankind could be improved by sterilising or killing unfit persons such as those with Down's syndrome and other genetically transmitted disabilities or even entire "lesser" races such as Jews or Blacks. We all know how these ideas became part of Hitler's justification for the millions of murders of the holocaust, but have lost awareness that between 1930 and the early 1970s legal sterilisations of the mentally challenged in the USA (approximately 60,000) with proportionally similar numbers in Norway and in many other enlightened nations were carried out on premises based on Galton's extremely simplistic understanding of Darwin's theory of evolution. Almost all my colleagues regard these ideas as morally outrageous and crude misunderstandings of the evidence they cite but they still find passionate followers. One late twentieth-century attempt to borrow from Galton and to couple intelligence more tightly to biology was a suggestion by Arthur Jensen and others that the word intelligence could be given a neurophysiological underpinning by being, in association with "mental speed", an inheritable quality of human and animal brains and central nervous systems.

During World War I, these considerations were by-passed by a pressing and practical need to predict what levels of intellectual demands new military recruits would be able to meet. Interviews with selection panels and letters from families, schoolteachers, employers, clergymen, doctors or influential friends were found undependable. Very much against the conviction of Armed Services Selection Boards, who felt that they could infallibly detect by a brief interview whether or not a chap had the right stuff, intelligence test scores predicted people's performance so much more accurately than personal impressions that a minor industry of psychometrics was developed to develop and improve them. During World War II, test development and what had become known as psychometric theory were again boosted by the same urgencies. The test scores of thousands of men and women now constitute a huge database that can be explored to test theories about just how, in what ways and why some people are cleverer and more successful than others. Research also focussed on whether intelligence is a single quality affecting all aspects of mental performance or whether there are different, relatively separate kinds of intelligence, such as verbal, mathematical and spatial abilities, or emotional intelligence and empathy that each of us may have in different combinations and to different degrees.

Until brain scanning became cheap and easy, there were few data to relate intelligence test scores to neurophysiology. The only way was to test predictions from scores on existing and newly developed tests as to how well people can cope with different kinds of mental challenge. For example, during the 1940s Louis Terman [5, 6] published studies showing that scores on tests taken in childhood and adolescence not only predict future success in school and university but also, many years later, in middle-aged careers in business and the professions. By the late 1940s, intelligence testing had become a rather too dominant tool in educational research. Psychologists such as a liberal and loveable British eccentric, Alice Heim [7], reacted against the use of scores, even on the excellent tests she developed, to channel people's lives by excluding them from particular possibilities. The reaction against 11-plus grammar school entrance examination, which is still used in some parts of the UK, was the most widely discussed of many examples. Alice cautioned against using intelligence tests as yardsticks for humans. However, a lively literature still presses dubious claims that small differences in average intelligence test scores "prove" that some races of mankind such as Chinese and Japanese are more clever and others such as Africans and Mexicans are less clever than white Caucasian Americans (see for example *The Bell Curve* [8]). I believe that, for similar reasons, we should also be sceptical when we discuss the social and ethical implications of findings that older people tend to perform less well on intelligence tests than young adults.

We now recognise that intelligence test scores have sometimes been put to dubious uses but also that the rank orders of people's intelligence test scores do modestly predict their relative degrees of success in coping with the mental demands of complicated everyday lives. To repeat an essential warning: this does not mean that a *particular person's individual score* will accurately predict her success in life. An intelligence test score is only a clue to odds of achievement. When we have reliable data from large groups of people, we generally find that more of those with higher than those with lower scores are likely to succeed at whatever they undertake. For those of us elderly who may be uneasy about our mental futures, there are also different issues: whether some kinds of intelligence may be more age-resistant than others so that aging changes the pattern, rather than just the average level of our mental abilities; what it is that intelligence test scores measure, other than higher odds of successful survival in industrialised societies; how early in our lives our test scores begin to change and how fast these changes continue; and whether we all change at similar or at very different rates.

When told our score on any intelligence test, we should hold back from elation or depression. We must bear in mind that these tests are approximate and imperfectly reliable. That is, any person's score may vary by as much as plus or minus five points between successive assessments, even if these are only a few days apart. We notice that this variation between people is as large as some of the estimates of declines in test scores between 50 and 80 years. Although average scores for groups do significantly decline, for any particular person this fall may often be smaller than the measurement error of the test.

If intelligence tests are such imprecise instruments, how much can they really tell us about declines in all our other mental abilities? At first glance, they seem ineffective at predicting scores on tests of other aspects of mental ability such as memory, planning and decision speed. For example, in our Manchester/Newcastle samples, differences in volunteers' intelligence test scores accounted for only 4 per cent of the differences between them in memory test scores; for about 16 per cent of the differences in decision speeds; and for about 9 per cent of differences in scores on tests of making and updating plans. These last tests were tests of frontal and executive function, developed by clinical neurologists to detect mental changes that result from damage to the frontal lobes of our brains. Since scores on tests of memory, speed and planning also drop with age, the next question is whether differences in people's intelligence test scores predict *those particular proportions of the differences between them in memory, speed and planning that are associated with the differences in their ages*. Put another way, how sensitively can any intelligence test pick up just these *specifically age-related* changes in speed, memory and planning? Using the same methods as for the effects of illnesses on changes in abilities with age that we discussed in Chapter 3 (an adaptation of statistical regression analysis developed by Lindenberger and Potter [9]), we found, in the Manchester/Newcastle samples, values of 70 per cent, for both memory tests and frontal lobe tests but an impressive 90–98 per cent for tests of decision speed. To avoid being astonished by these numbers, we must remind ourselves again that differences between people associated with differences in their ages between 45 and 92 accounted for only 4 per cent of all the many factors that make them different from each other on memory tests; for only 9 per cent of all the things that made them different from each other on planning tests; and for only 16 per cent of all the things that make their decision speeds different. So, in the strongest prediction that they could make, intelligence test scores accounted for 90–98 per cent of that small amount (i.e. 16 per cent) of those particular differences in decision speed between people that are associated with differences in their ages between 41 and 92. In other words, intelligence test scores are not particularly good at picking up differences in memory, decision speed and planning between people of the same ages. But they are very good indeed at picking up *just those particular differences in ability between people that have occurred because of up to 40 years of differences in their ages*.

These links between the effects of aging on intelligence test scores, decision speed, memory and the ability to make and carry through plans are clues to how brain aging affects the mind. As we age, many of our brain cells die and this process eventually causes our brains to measurably shrink. Scars left by cell-deaths are visible on brain scans. They are known as white matter lesions. The rate at which we lose brain cells strongly depends on how well the blood supply to our brains is maintained as we grow old. Brain images allow us to compare estimates of the extents of the gross, overall changes such as brain shrinkage, numbers of white matter lesions and current efficiency of brain/blood circulation that people have suffered. It is possible to relate these estimates to people's ages and to their scores on tests of intelligence, decision speed, planning and memory. When we do this, we find that differences in their levels of brain shrinkage, brain circulation and white matter lesions account for *all* the *age-related* differences between individuals in decision speed; *for much but not all* the *age-related* differences in intelligence; and for much less of the *age-related* differences in memory [10, 11].

Investigators such as Salthouse and Jensen discuss their results in terms suggesting they believe that neurophysiological changes cause general slowing of information processing speed which, in turn, causes losses of intelligence, memory and frontal and executive planning and control.

A different interpretation comes from evidence that gross neurophysiological changes, such as those marked by losses of brain volume, increases in white matter lesions and falls in cerebral blood flow, have independent effects on speed, memory, intelligence and frontal abilities and that changes in these four measures also affect each other [10, 11, 12].

Many studies have found that intelligence, planning and memory are not only affected by the general health of the brain but even more by the integrity of particular, small and local brain structures. For example, Brenda Milner, a remarkable scientist working in Montreal, was the first to show how closely memory for all kinds of material depends on the integrity of a structure known as the hippocampus and the medial temporal lobes [13]. Much more recently, John Duncan and others have found that intelligence test scores depend on the integrity of areas of the pre-frontal lobes [14, 15]. Nearly a century of work with brain-injured patients had already shown that planning and control of information briefly held in memory depends on the integrity of the frontal lobes.

Aging affects the integrity of the whole brain, but it seems to affect some particular areas, such as the frontal lobes, earlier and more severely than others [16]. The relative extents to which it affects both the entire brain and local parts of the brain seems to depend on the efficiency of brain blood circulation and the pattern of its decline with age. So, the effects of brain aging are both general and local. The close dependence of specific abilities, such as memory, on specific brain areas, such as the hippocampus and medial temporal lobes, of language with Broca's area

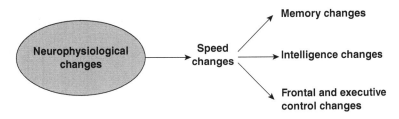

FIGURE 16.1   On this hypothesis, age-related changes in brain anatomy and physiology, such as are indexed by increases in white matter lesions, loss of brain volume and poorer brain blood circulation, slow speed and, because of this, affect memory, intelligence and ability on frontal lobe tasks.

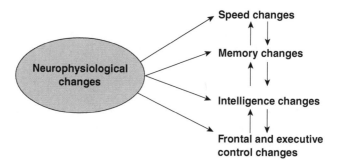

FIGURE 16.2 On this hypothesis, age-related changes in brain physiology and anatomy, such as are indexed by increases in white matter lesions, loss of brain volume and poorer brain blood circulation, slow speed and also, independently of this, affect intelligence, memory and frontal lobe function. But changes in speed, memory, intelligence and frontal lobe function also affect each other.

and Wernicke's area, of vision with the striate cortex and the parietal lobes have all become clear during the last 150 years. In contrast to these systems, there seems to be no comparable specific or local brain area for decision speed. Rather, how fast we can make simple decisions seems to be a particularly sensitive measure of the extent to which cell losses have affected the efficiency of the entire brain. In other words, measures of decision speed, such as reaction times to simple signals, may be the best *behavioural* measurement that we can make to assess *general* or *global* brain health (of course direct neurological information obtained from brain images are probably much better guides to what is going on).

We may not be greatly cheered to learn that as we grow old our brains are damaged by illnesses and by changes that accumulate over our lifetimes, but at least these are factors over which we have some control. A main cause of losses of brain cells seems to be a decline in the efficiency of brain blood circulation. Taking more aerobic exercise reduces risks of heart disease and diabetes, improves brain blood circulation and so maintains intelligence. Even for those like me, whose jogging years hardly began, and are now long past, taking our wits for long pleasant walks still makes a useful difference.

References

[1] Heim, A. (1970). *The AH4 Test Batteries.* Slough, NFER/Nelson.

[2] Cattell, R. B. and Cattell, A. K. S. (1960). *The Individual or Group Culture Fair Intelligence Test.* Champaign, IL, IPAT.

[3] Blastland M. and Spiegelhalter, D. (2013). *The Norm Chronicles: Stories and numbers about danger.* London, Profile Books.

[4] Binet, A. and Simon, T. (1915). *A Method of Measuring the Development of the Intelligence of Young Children* (C. H. Town, Trans.). Chicago, Chicago Medical Book.

[5] Terman, L. M. and Oden, M. H. (1947). *Genetic Studies of Genius. Vol. 4. The gifted child grows up.* Stanford, CA, Stanford University Press.

[6] Terman, L. M. and Oden, M. H. (1959). *Genetic Studies of Genius. Vol. 5. The gifted group at mid life.* Stanford, CA, Stanford University Press.

[7] Heim, A. W. (1975) *Psychological Testing.* London, Oxford University Press.

[8] Herrnstein, R. J. and Murray, C. (1994). *The Bell Curve: Intelligence and Class Structure in American Life.* Georgetown VA, The Bio-ethics Research Library.

[9] Lindenberger, U. and Potter, U. (1998). The complex nature of unique and shared effects in hierarchical linear regression: Implications for developmental psychology. *Psychological Methods*, 3, 218–230.

[10] Rabbitt, P., Scott, M., Thacker, N., Lowe, C., Jackson, A., Horan, M. and Pendleton, N. (2006). Losses in gross brain volume and cerebral blood flow account for age-related differences in speed but not in fluid intelligence. *Neuropsychology*, 20, 549–557.

[11] Rabbitt, P., Scott, M., Lunn, M. and Thacker, N. (2007). White matter lesions account for all age-related declines in speed but not in intelligence. *Neuropsychology*, 21 363–370.

[12] Rabbitt, P., Mogapi, O., Scott, M., Thacker, N., Lowe, C., Horan, M., Pendleton, N., Jackson, A. and Lunn, D. (2007). Effects of global atrophy, white matter lesions, and cerebral blood flow on age-related changes in speed, memory, intelligence, vocabulary, and frontal function. *Neuropsychology*, 21(6), 684–695.

[13] Scoville, W. B. and Milner, B. (2000). Loss of recent memory after bilateral hippocampal lesions. *The Journal of Neuropsychiatry and Clinical Neurosciences*, 12, 103-a-113. (reprinted "Classic Article").

[14] Duncan, J., Rudiger, J. S., Kolodny, J., Bor, D., Herzog, H., Ahmed, A., Newell, F. N. and Emslie, H. (2000) A neural basis for general intelligence. Science, 289, 457–460.

[15] Duncan, J. (2011). *How Intelligence Happens.* New Haven and London, Yale University Press.

[16] Rabbitt, P. M. A. (1997). Methodologies and models in the study of executive function. In Patrick Rabbitt, (Ed.), pp. 1–38, *Methodology of Frontal and Executive Function.* Hove UK, Psychology Press.

17

KEEPING THE SKILLS WE HAVE LEARNED

When Robert Sternberg asked randomly selected American citizens to define "intelligence" he found that all accepted that some of us are "natural fast studies" who can learn new information faster than most, but also thought that "intelligence" was a learned capital of "smarts": useful skills that we have mastered to better manage our daily lives and professions. Since smarts are a bonus that we can only earn by experience, we might expect them to become an increasingly important toolkit as we grow older. Even the most able of us find it hard to learn, let alone invent a new skill. Even if all the separate components of the new knowledge are very simple, we will make embarrassing mistakes until we have mastered all of them and understood how they work together. Initial bewilderments are overcome and turn into barely conscious routines which we can use to effortlessly cope with problems that even the cleverest beginners find impossible. This is not just true for our individual lives but also for our species.

The smarts that species acquire bring huge survival advantages. Our great-great-great-grand-ancestor tree-shrews would have been deleted from the gene pool if they paused to work out how to cope with every emergency from first principles. A hazard survived and remembered could improve competence in the next emergency and useful inventions, such as the technique of extracting termites from their mounds by fishing with twigs, were noticed by our fellow primates and became part of the accumulated forest smarts of our species. Archived solutions to problems are a main driver of our intellectual progress as a species. Two of the most talented mathematicians who ever lived, Leibniz and Newton, needed years of hard thinking to develop calculus that average schoolchildren can now learn within a few weeks.

For those who like computer analogies, speed, memory and central processer size can be compared to the "benchmark performance characteristics" that determine the maximum processing speed of a machine. However, these "brain operating characteristics" represent only unused potential power until we have stored and run programs. A computer program that is ideal for one task is usually useless for any other. This seems to be true for animal brains as well as computers. Finches' remarkable skill at remembering and finding nuts that they have stored to survive winter is a powerful survival aid but no help in the dodge-the-predator game. Like a computer benchmark characteristic, "general intelligence" is a convenient term for the level of efficiency that determines how fast and accurately we can solve any new problems and learn any new skills. However, once learned, particular skills can be intensely specialised, and mastering one may give little or no advantage in others.

A study of exceptional pianists by Krampe and Ericcson [1] showed that although natural talent is a crucial entry qualification for a distinguished career as a musician, the great gap in achievement between excellent music teachers and internationally distinguished concert pianists is brought about by a difference of thousands of hours of deliberate practice maintained over decades. Similarly, although our scores on intelligence tests do predict how fast we can find and learn solutions to new problems, truly outstanding mental achievements owe as much to sustained effort as innate flair. Genius needs perspiration.

We have to ruefully admit that our scores on tests that measure speed, flexibility and competence at solving unfamiliar problems decline as we age. An obvious next question is whether we also gradually lose the mental toolkit of skills that we have acquired or whether this can last us to the ends of our lives. To compare how old age affects "raw" intellectual potential and learned skills, John Horn [2] gave volunteers tests of intelligence, information processing speed and memory, which he termed "fluid abilities"; and tests of acquired information, such as vocabulary and social competence, that are, clearly, learned skills. Fluid abilities declined with age but acquired skills declined less or not at all. Horn called such age-resistant acquired capabilities "crystallised intelligence", perhaps on the analogy that the residues of skills developed by using "fluid intelligence" gradually "crystallise" into durable and unchanging gems of competence. Fluid intelligence limits the quality of the solutions that we can achieve for any new problems that we encounter, and how well we remember them. Once learned, these solutions seem to become functionally independent of fluid intelligence and better survive the effects of age on the brain.

Studies of maintaining high competence in real-life professions make the same point. A study of 43 financial experts aged from 24 to 59 found that while the older had slightly lower intelligence test scores than their juniors, their longer experience seemed to compensate for this in work-related decisions [3]. A similar study also included a questionnaire of "tacit", often unexpressed and un-codified knowledge relating to work problems and found that more experienced older managers performed quite well on this [4]. Just as John Horn had found in laboratory experiments, real-life experience remains available into late middle and early old age and can compensate for gradual losses in fluid abilities.

We would expect our stock of useful crystallised intelligence to grow as we age because the longer we live the longer we have to discover and practice new mental skills. One problem, as Chaucer pointed out, is that omni-competence is a distant and elusive hope "The life so short, the craft so long to learn" (Chaucer, *Parlement of Foules*). Another is that the distinction between fluid abilities that leak away with age and crystallised abilities that can stay grittily resistant to time is not as clear cut as once thought. We may forget what we have learned and though losses in learned knowledge, such as vocabulary, are quite slight they do occur. John Horn found little or no change in people's performance on vocabulary tests, but over two decades of repeated assessments, many of our Manchester/Newcastle volunteers forgot a few of the rarest and so least frequently used words in their vocabularies. Such losses were smaller for people who initially had larger vocabularies and, indeed, some exceptionally articulate volunteers slightly improved their vocabulary scores during the 20 years that we studied them. One encouraging, and potentially sufficient explanation is that clever people who have large vocabularies have built these up by continually using a wide range of words and continue adding to them even in old age. Unfortunately, we also found evidence for a sneakier scenario. Some who prided themselves on their exceptional vocabularies were upset if they did not recognise a few of the most difficult words on which we had tested them. They remembered to look them up when they got home, possibly began to use them more frequently in their daily lives, and triumphantly produced them on their next visit four years later. Nevertheless, their dodge also makes the encouraging point that, even in old age, we can maintain and even expand a vocabulary or any other body of information if we keep working on it.

A limitation to the usefulness of acquired or crystallised smarts is the difference between having information and being able to use it. Practice will maintain our knowledge of individual words, but this does not mean that we continue to use them as dexterously as ever. Susan Kemper [5] showed this by analysing a remarkable collection of diaries written by citizens of Kansas during the late nineteenth and early twentieth centuries and preserved by the enlightened public library system of that fine state. Many covered 40 or 50 years of their authors' lives. Sue, a distinguished linguist and psychologist, analysed how their use of language changed as they aged. The range of words that they used only slightly reduced, but a much larger and more interesting change occurred. While they were young, diarists often used long and complex sentences and deftly handled multiply embedded subordinate clauses but, as they aged, their sentence structures became much shorter and simpler. Producing, and indeed decoding, complicated grammatical constructions requires an efficient working memory. For example, when we have to hold a tortuously unwinding sentence in mind until we reach a word that retrospectively makes sense of the rest.[1] Retaining a large crystallised vocabulary is one thing, but retaining the efficiency of the computational apparatus that allows us to assemble these words into meaningful orders is another. Another example is that because of a lifetime's practice at games such as chess or Go, we may correctly remember deep strategies and sharp tactical manoeuvres but we need working memory to carry these out. For me, a greater daily irritation than my failures at chess is that, although I can remember most of the recipes I need, and have a small but adequate range of kitchen skills, I forget to include ingredients that I have remembered to find and keep to hand, and I often lose the order in which I should do things. Having the necessary crystallised knowledge, in the sense that one can correctly write it all down is one thing; having the computing power and working memory capacity to use it under time pressure is something else.

This prompts the question of whether all acquired mental skills are equally resistant to aging and whether we tend to lose only those, like using complex grammatical structures, crafty chess opening strategies or complicated recipes, that also require active, "on line" computation.

It may seem obvious that the best way to learn how well our mental tool-kits of crystallised knowledge survive into old age, and how effectively we can maintain them, is to study what people achieve during successive decades of their working lifetimes. In 1936, H. C. Lehman published a study of the ages at which people who had made exceptional contributions to mathematics, science, literature, history, the visual arts [6, 7] and music [8] had made their most and their most remarkable contributions. He found differences between the age-trajectories of peak performance in different professions. Both the total number of achievements and the most notable achievements of mathematicians, physicists and chemists were greatest in their twenties and thirties, after which they steadily declined. Historians and philosophers published their best work in their forties and fifties. Novelists and essayists made some striking contributions in their twenties and thirties, but more often in their forties and fifties and sometimes even in their sixties and seventies. Interestingly, poets tended to peak in their thirties, much earlier than novelists and other literary figures. We may argue that poetry is somewhat like mathematics because it requires the use of the fewest and best possible symbols (words) in the most effective combinations. Writing novels and essays is more leisurely and discursive, and so perhaps less demanding. Lehman suggested that graphic artists, such as Titian could still produce remarkable work in their seventies or even their eighties, as could musicians, particularly executants such as Pablo Casals, but also conductors such as Arturo Toscanini.[2] One interpretation might be that great new discoveries in mathematics and science depend on original and innovative thought that may not be based on a very wide and detailed knowledge of a field while, in contrast, in history and literature years of study are necessary to master huge bodies of information before original new interpretations become possible. As we have noticed from the study of pianists, outstanding skill at music requires long, continuous and deliberate practice [1]. This is probably equally true for writing, painting, etching and sculpture.

Lehman's analyses of career trajectories made two different points: one is that even the most able of us become less productive as we grow old. The second, and more interesting, is that age begins to affect some kinds of intellectual activity earlier than others.

The first point is unsurprising because we know that we must all eventually die and that we will probably not be in the best intellectual shape for some time before this event. As we have noticed, volunteers in the Newcastle and Manchester samples showed declines in scores on intelligence and memory tests up to 11 years before death and the amount and rate of their declines differed with the pathologies that were recorded as causes on their death certificates. Research confirms expectation that our final years are unlikely to be our most productive. A study of published correspondence by eminent literary figures found, perhaps unsurprisingly, that the quality of their work began to wane up to 10 years before they died [9]. We gradually lose even skills that we have performed outstandingly well and practised to the end of our lives. A different way in which mortality statistics may affect surveys of career trajectories is suggested by a disconcerting report that 2102 exceptionally creative or "versatile" literary figures and scientists died, on average, from 2.7 to 8.2 years before their less high-achieving peers [10]. I know of no convincing explanation for this apparently well-documented fact, but shorter lives of the great and the good must also tip statistical counts in favour of the "early achievement" hypothesis.

A different and more interesting question is whether there are differences in the survival of different mental skills so that high achievement in philosophy, painting and music remain possible after aging has degraded excellence at mathematics, hard science and poetry. It is hard to find convincing data to use for such comparisons. For example, there is the question, perhaps particularly in the liberal arts, of the difference between a person's age when she first had a remarkable new insight and when she eventually got round to publishing it, perhaps after many years of analysis and checking. Authors and philosophers have spent decades re-writing their major works. Perhaps achievements in the humanities are also less immediately based on competition of ideas than in science because they do not require accepted theories to be challenged and refuted before they are replaced. In science, there is also fierce competition to be the first to solve problems that have long been identified as crucial goals for research. In literature, people compete in different ways and usually not against such time pressure. Other problems are those of perspective. Particularly for writers, painters and composers, but also perhaps for historians and philosophers, general recognition of the value of their most distinguished productions may take many years.

Lehman himself pointed out that his data were not ideal because some of the careers that he documented took place during the nineteenth and even the eighteenth century when short life expectancy brutally curtailed productivity. As we have noticed, even in the young and middle aged, illnesses that terminate in death will accelerate trajectories of cognitive decline, even over periods of eight to eleven years. A different and powerful factor is the marked change in the economically feasible career trajectories of academics over the historical periods that have been surveyed. For example, during the early nineteenth century in the UK, brilliant young men might achieve College Fellowships in Oxford or Cambridge and, while supported by these, could produce distinguished academic work. If they wished to marry, they had to leave their colleges to earn a living in some other profession, often the Anglican Church, in which their intellectual lives were channelled by different demands. Particularly in science even twentieth and twenty-first century career trajectories may favour youthful productivity. Those who make remarkable discoveries when they are young may be rapidly tempted into heavy administration either by promotion within institutions or by pressures to compete for grants to support bigger research teams that become managerial burdens. The funding structure of contemporary science has other aspects that also confuse post hoc analyses of lifetime productivity. The recent increase in publications by successful older scientists partly reflects the talent and energy of their outstanding young professional dependents rather than their sustained personal brilliance.

Recent studies confirm that declines in scientific productivity do, of course, occur but also suggest that they now happen much later than data available from the 1930s to the 1950s suggested. All recent studies of academics report some decline in the number and quality of publications. For example, a study of British psychologists in the 1970s and 1980s [11]; a study of the careers of large groups of less eminent physicists, geologists, physiologists and biochemists published in 1989 [12]; and a study of the careers of economists in 1998 [13] all found that academics do publish less, and in less prestigious journals, as they grow older. Nevertheless, in recent studies of average or slightly above average academic scientists, plateaus of greatest productivity now seem to last more than a decade longer than in Lehman's day and to have become less different from those in the arts. The data on arts practitioners also differs from Lehman's. A 1999 analysis of the number of paintings produced by 739 graphic artists, works by 719 musicians and books by 229 authors found that, like most contemporary scientists, their periods of maximum output were in their thirties and forties [14]. There are also hints of sex differences because the time of greatest productivity for female writers was in their fifties. This may reflect either the longer cognitive preservation of women or their late release from family pressures or, of course, both.

Professional ability is found to decline with age but, for recent generations, the changes are much smaller and slower than early surveys suggested. The contrast between "early flowering and early decline" in the hard sciences and "late flowering and late decline" in the humanities and visual arts now seems less clear-cut. One problem is finding comparable standards across different disciplines. Assessments of quality in the arts are much more contentious and differ sharply between various kinds of achievement, with standards of comparison and even with changes in fashion. For example, a tally of the year 2000 market value of paintings by 51 modern US artists found that for painters born before 1920 the average peak age for the valuation of their paintings was 50.6 but for those born after 1920 it was only 28.8. Changes from a cautious to a speculative market account for similar discrepancies, so that if estimates of quality of productions over an artist's lifetime are taken at face value, this confuses identification of the age at which personal creativity peaks [15]. If we only compared data for current sale prices, we might conclude that artists who are now elderly are painting much better (or at least much more profitably) than their young contemporaries now do or, indeed, than they themselves did when they were young.

It is an intriguing idea that, like their lifespans, periods of peak production are longer for women than for men. Such comparisons as have been made are questionable. Because women live longer, we might expect that they will also keep their talents later in life but there are confounding socio-economic factors. Rearing children may postpone even attempts at achievements until middle age. Women are under-represented in science and mathematics and, perhaps, are now over-represented in literature. The few analyses that I have found do not settle the issue so completely as to make it useless as a provocative dinner party topic. A study of 1367 faculty at the University of Helsinki found that Professors published more than junior staff but, "when other scholarly characteristics were controlled", men published more than women [15]. Since the surplus of men to women in senior positions is notorious, this seems to me to make no clear point. Studies of Finnish academics, including audits of some universities abroad, conclude that age affects productivity in both men and women, but that the effects of marriage and children have very similar effects on both. Since data for women who abandoned promising careers to raise families are not available, the point is, once again, obscure [16, 17].

Ideal data would be details of the achievements of large numbers of extremely gifted people all of whom practise an identical, difficult mental skill and who can be compared against each other in terms of the same, objective standard. Perhaps the careers of Chess Masters are as close to this as we get. Chess is particularly interesting because it requires high levels of both fluid abilities, such as working memory and intelligence, and crystallised knowledge. Like innovative mathematics and, indeed, like solving the spatial problems included in many intelligence tests, chess requires an ability to simultaneously hold many variables in mind and to recognise as fast as possible how patterns of relationships between them will alter if particular changes occur and how the possible outcomes of these changes will compare with each other. The best evidence that we have suggests that there are indeed "natural" chess players who play at a remarkably high standard at ages as early as 6 to 12 or 14 years. On the other hand, chess-play has been so exhaustively researched and documented, and strategies and counter-strategies change so rapidly, and are now so widely available, that even for young prodigies success at the highest levels needs continuous and intensive study. At any age, world-class professional chess players have little time to do anything other than research and study this vast body of information. A study by Charness and colleagues found that even maintaining success at far lower levels requires 5000 or more hours of deliberate practice over 10 years [18]. In terms of John Horn's dichotomy, chess mastery requires both considerable fluid and a formidable body of learned crystallised ability.

A creative statistician, Arpad Elo, provided a tool for research on chess by devising an internationally used ranking scheme for chess players that is now named after him. This is based on gains or losses of points from wins and defeats against other players whose rankings at the times of encounters have also been computed. Since the playing careers of individual grandmasters can span decades, from their twenties through to their sixties, Elo was able to track improvements and declines of individual players over their long lives [19]. He found that nearly all the players gradually improved until their thirties or forties, maintained their highest levels of play until their late fifties or, in some few cases early sixties, and then began to decline. This inverted U-shaped trajectory of achievement is certainly formed by changes in health and so in stamina and mental ability but other factors also contribute. Elo's survey covered a period during which high-level chess was evolving very rapidly and demands on players continually increased as an already vast body of information on opening and endgame theory, and on chess strategy and tactics rapidly expanded. The number of top tournaments also increased, so that the physical strains of travel as well as of competition became much greater. As chess success became involved with national ambitions, state and private sponsorship gave promising young players intensive, elaborate and successful training that had not been available to their seniors. Top-level chess became not only much more demanding but also a larger and better-funded industry that could recruit, train and support many more outstanding natural talents. As top-level chess became an increasingly demanding and insecure profession, many middle-aged masters prudently increased the time they gave to other sources of income. In spite of this, it is cheering to find that gifted individuals can, though perhaps with gradually increasing effort, remain at the very peak of an extraordinarily demanding profession until well into their seventh decade. It is also important that these comparisons show that acquired knowledge and ceaseless practice of many hours a day can support even a skill that is, essentially, computational and very demanding of fluid intelligence until late in life. We must also remember that long after they had retired from competitive chess, these remarkable people could still play at a level that most humans cannot hope to reach at any age.

Chess play illustrates that people can maintain intellectual skills at the uttermost human limits into their fifties and sixties. Unlike chess grandmasters, most of us never need or wish to push ourselves to our personal limits in any skill or profession. Like the averagely talented bank managers we discussed above, we can also supplement our fluid abilities by continually practising and refurbishing our toolkit of acquired skills. Useful sources of information on the lifetime performance of humbler, but nevertheless well-functioning, individuals are surveys of productivity with changing age in industry, business and commerce. As usual, these are also not straightforward to interpret. Jobs require very different skills and make demands that are more or less stressful for older workers. The criteria used to assess older and younger workers are often different, and organisational cultures may selectively favour particular age groups for cryptic reasons.

For example, productivity at heavy manual work markedly declines between 18 and 50 and individuals older than 50 must change jobs or retire. Partly for this reason, most of the data available for the middle aged have been collected on middle- and upper-level managers. A major determinant of the timelines of these people's careers has been the rate and extent of technological changes in their profession. Rapid and radical changes decrease productivity in older employees who learn more slowly. John Rybash argues that older workers manage best when it is possible for them to "encapsulate" their jobs, effectively deploying learned skills while avoiding unfamiliar demands. Because the amount of experience needed to attain peak performance at a job obviously varies with its demands, it is unsurprising that estimates of periods required to gain the necessary crystallised intelligence have varied from two to ten years, with general agreement that as jobs demand increasingly complex analysis this learning time prolongs. An important issue is the way in which performance is assessed. When productivity is rated by colleagues, such as senior managers, assessments for older workers tend to be favourable. There is also good evidence that older workers tend to be more poorly rated in organisations in which the average age is young than those in which it is older. Comparisons of salaries tend to favour older workers, but salary is a questionable index because most studies show that job productivity and salary are only weakly linked. Allowing for these and for other obfuscating factors, the general picture seems to be just what common sense would suggest: learning necessary skills takes time proportional to how difficult they are to acquire. More intelligent and younger people can acquire skills faster; older people take longer. Once learned, and particularly if they are continually practised, skills can remain relatively stable well into late middle age. So, if job demands do not radically change, productivity can also be maintained through the fifties and sixties and, even at this later time of life, new knowledge and competencies can be acquired, albeit more slowly and with greater effort but, hopefully, also with greater personal satisfaction.

The broader point is that, as in all aspects of mental life, the changes that age brings about in our everyday efficiency are not only due to changes in our brains that impose new limits on our mental performance. They are also due to shifts in the resources of time and opportunity that our changing lives allow, and in the particular challenges that our lives impose on us. It is not news to any of us that, in the current state of medical science, we will, most likely, eventually experience illnesses that affect our mental abilities. A more interesting point is what steps we can take to delay this process so that the inevitable final period of mental decline is as short as possible.

The essential thing is to stay well and so to live long and, while we enjoy this good fortune, to continue to practise and refurbish the skills that we have acquired throughout our lifetimes. This does becomes harder as we age but, if we can bear with this, it offsets declines in fluid ability and we can continue to enjoy doing the things that we most like as well as we possibly can.

Notes

1 Recall the legendary simultaneous translator who screamed in anguish during a particularly long and tortuous German sentence – "a Verb,. . .a Verb. . .For God's Sweet Sake give me a verb.").

2 A very entertaining and encouraging book, "Tolstoy's Bicycle", by Jeremy Baker, lists striking achievements of remarkable people aged from 60 to 90+ when they made them. (The title commemorates that Tolstoy first learned to ride a bicycle when he was 67).

References

[1] Krampe, R. T. and Ericcson, K. A. (1996). Maintaining excellence: Deliberate practice and elite performance in young and older pianists. *Journal of Experimental Psychology, General*, 125, 331–359.

[2] Horn, J. (1982). The theory of fluid and crystallised intelligence in relation to concepts of cognitive psychology and aging in adulthood. In F. I. M. Craik and S. Trehub, (Eds), pp. 237–278, *Aging and Cognitive Processes*. New York, Plenum Press.

[3] Colonia-Willner, R. (1998). Practical intelligence at work: Relationship between aging and cognitive efficiency among managers in a bank environment. *Psychology and Aging*, 13, 45–47.

[4] Colonia-Wilner, R. (1999). Investing in practical intelligence: Aging and cognitive efficiency among executives. *International Journal of Behavioural Development*. 23. 591–604.

[5] Kemper, S. (1990). Adults' diaries: Changes made to written narratives across the lifespan. *Discourse Processes*, 13, 207–223.

[6] Lehman, H. C. (1935). The chronological years of greatest productivity; chemists, inventors, poets et altera. *Psychological Bulletin*, 32, 676–693.

[7] Lehman, H. C. (1942). The creative years; oil paintings, etchings, and architectural works. *Psychological Review*, 49, 19–42.

[8] Lehman, H. C. and Ingerham, D. W. (1939). Man's creative years in music. *Science Monthly, N.Y.*, 48, 431–443.

[9] Suedfeld, P. and Piedrahita, L. E. (1984). Intimations of mortality: Integrative simplification as a precursor of death. *Journal of Personality and Social Psychology*, 47, 848–852.

[10] Cassandro, V. J. (1998). Explaining premature mortality across fields of creative endeavour. *Journal of Personality*, 66, 805–833.

[11] Over, R. (1982). Does research productivity decline with age? *Higher Education*, 11, 511–520.

[12] Cohen. L. E. (1991). Size, age and productivity of scientific and technical research groups. *Scientometrics*, 20, 395–416.

[13] Levin, S. G. and Stephan, P. E. (1989). Age and research productivity of academic scientists. *Research in Higher Education*, 30, 531–549.

[14] Bayer, A. E. and Dutton, J. E. (1977). Career age and research-professional activities of academic scientists. *The Journal of Higher Education*, 48, 259–283.

[15] Galenson, D. W. and Weinberg, B. A. (2000). Age and the quality of work: The case of modern American painters, *Journal of Political Economy*, 108(4), 761–777.

[16] Puuska, H-M. (2010). Effects of scholar's gender and professional position on publishing productivity in different publication types: Analysis of a Finnish university. *Scientometrics*, 82, 419–437.

[17] Saxe, L. J., Hagedom, L. S., Arredondo, M. and Dicrisi, F. J. (2002). Faculty research productivity: Exploring the role of gender and family – related factors. *Research in Higher Education*, 43, 423–446.

[18] Charness, N., Tuffiash, M., Krampe, R., Reingold, E. and Vasyukova, E. (2005). The role of deliberate practice in chess expertise. *Applied Cognitive Psychology*, 19(2), 151–165.

[19] Elo, A. E. (1965). Age changes in master chess performances. *Journal of Gerontology*, 20, 289–299.

18

READING OTHERS' MINDS

Because we are an intensely social species, one of the most important skills that we have is the ability to "read" other people. When we talk to others, we use many other things than their words to interpret them correctly. Their facial expressions, tones of voice, and "tells" of body-movements and posture convey more, and sometimes quite different, information to what they say. To resolve these conflicts of evidence and to communicate or disguise our own feelings, we must develop what psychologists call "theories of minds". Since we can assume that others' thought processes resemble our own, we can guess what they know and do not know and something of their motivations and emotions. As we grow old, does our longer experience make us better at this or do we gradually become less perceptive and work with increasingly unreliable ideas of what others really mean and feel?

As young children we are puzzled that what others say is not always what they mean; we gradually learn that what is said must be interpreted in terms of context and soon recognise that to pass as acceptable humans we must learn to offer, as well as to understand, non-verbal cues. People of any age differ widely in their grasp of these complexities. Incurably candid souls cannot help being transparent in all situations, while great actors attain magical subtlety of communicating states of mind that they do not feel. Theatre would have no advantage over poetry or novels if all that is going on in characters' minds could be completely conveyed just by the words in their scripts.

Discrepancies between people's words and their facial expressions, tones of voice and body language are not necessarily signs of dissimulation. We have to interpret and convey unspoken emotions well enough to reassure others that we are not disabled in empathy and that we really understand them because we pick up their unexpressed feelings. This affirms that we are fellow humans.

Like chimpanzees and gorillas, our faces are our main display-boards for threats, interest or indifference. Accurately reading faces and using our own to convey, disguise or simulate feelings are such important skills for primates living in small co-operative groups that they have become wired into particular areas of our brains. When deprived of this reassurance by hoods, veils or masks we become uncomfortable.

Most expressions that our faces can convey are now so well mapped that we can write computer programs that can decide, more accurately than many humans, whether or not faces are smiling and whether these smiles are genuine or feigned. This distinction depends on differences between cues from the lower half of the face, especially the mouth, which are unreliable, and from the upper half, especially the eyes and their surrounding muscles which are much more trustworthy indicators of sincerity. Age reduces the range of different expressions that we can produce, partly because our facial muscles atrophy and our expressions become more fixed, but also because we become less able to coordinate them to signal our feelings. One suggestion has been that we become less able to recognise expressions that we cannot ourselves project.

Dialects of the face

We have suggested that recognition of facial expressions is "wired in" to the brain, but it seems that more subtle cues have to be learned from experience. The ranges and details of facial expressions that people use do differ between human cultures but not by so much as to make us mutually incomprehensible. A study compared the accuracy with which Africans and Chinese, living in either their own country or the USA, could recognise expressions used by people from different races. All were more confident and accurate with faces of their own race but could also correctly interpret expressions of other races. Chinese and African Americans living embedded in a predominantly white Caucasian culture could read Caucasian facial expressions more accurately than their mono-cultural peers [1]. Humans seem to have a basic, perhaps biologically determined, common language of expression that is overlaid by local dialects of the face.

Recognising faces and expressions as we grow old

Other issues are how old age affects the accuracy with which we can recognise facial expressions, whether older people find some particular expressions harder to recognise than others and whether our life experiences affect our sensitivity to expressions of some emotions more than others. All studies agree that, even after their poorer vision has been taken into account, older people are less able to distinguish between unfamiliar faces and between different facial expressions. Both young and old recognise happiness faster and more accurately than fear, anger or disgust. Apart from these apparently wired-in differences in sensitivities to emotions, we are fine-tuned by personal experiences. A pitiful example is that abused children are less able to distinguish between any kinds of facial expression than children brought up in happier environments, but they are particularly sensitive to and vigilant for angry faces [2]. Selective sensitisation to different expressions of emotions may be fleeting or long-lasting. A study in Bologna [3] found that individuals' sensitivities not only varied with their lifelong personal predispositions for anxiety or happiness but also with momentary shifts in their moods. They recognised anxious and fearful expressions better when they themselves were anxious and were more sensitive to projected happiness when merry. Context biases sensitivities so that happy or hostile environments selectively sensitise us to expressions of pleasure or threat. The cues that bias sensitivity can be so subtle that they escape conscious analysis. For example, some experiments suggest that, just as lush advertisements for perfumes would have us believe, even mildly pleasant smells can help to promote affectionate rapport.

In old age we find it harder to identify faces or voices irrespective of their expressions. Studies of eye-witness testimony find that older individuals can accurately report what went on during an encounter but are less reliable at remembering who did what and to whom. A possible explanation was that older people find it harder to recognise subtle distinctions of any kind. Vasiliki Orgeta and Louise Phillips [4] found that this was not the core of the problem, because dramatic exaggeration makes facial expressions easier for people of all ages to read but, nevertheless, helps the old less than the young.

Older people recognise happiness much more quickly and easily than sadness, anger, fear or disgust. Young people also find sadness, anger, fear and disgust slightly harder to read than happiness, probably because these expressions involve subtle and ambiguous facial cues. As a general rule, the harder any task becomes, the greater will be the performance gap between young and old. I suspect that part of the age problem is difficulty in reading subtle cues. Accurate recognition of expressions requires information from the upper face, especially the eyes. Adults who have been trained to spend longer attending to upper faces are correspondingly better at recognising expressions. Untrained older people spend less time than young adults inspecting the eye-regions of faces [5]. It seems that losing sensitivity to facial expressions is partly due to losing efficient scanning strategies that give priority to critical areas – yet another example that even skills that are learned throughout a lifetime and still frequently used can gradually fade. To discover when these changes begin, people aged from 18 to 84 were asked to recognise emotions conveyed by photographs of faces and by tones of voice [6]. Their ages did not affect how well they recognised either faces or voice tones but their ability to recognise sadness and, less strongly, anger declined after age 30. This is unexpected, since the longer we live and the more, and more varied, people we encounter the better we should become at reading faces and voices. This raises the possibility that our surprisingly early decline in recognising expressions must be caused by neurophysiological changes.

Reduced ability to scan for subtle cues is not all the story. People of all ages typically do not attend to specific cues such as the shape of the nose or mouth, but base their decisions on general impressions of familiarity [7]. In particular, older people rely more strongly on overall impressions of faces rather than on their particular features. I think that a weakness of experiments on age-changes in face recognition has been that people have always been asked to judge the expressions of strangers. My family and friends seem to me to have personal and characteristic repertoires of expressions that have taken me many years to correctly pick up and interpret but which I feel that I still decode pretty well. I am not convinced that older people who do not easily recognise the expressions of strangers are necessarily worse than the young at recognising expressions on the faces of close relatives and friends.

When faces, voices and bodies give different messages

Recognising and interpreting expressions is not just a matter of searching through mental check-lists of subtle cues. Non-verbal cues can be over-ridden by other kinds of information. If actors make their facial expressions emotionally discrepant to the words they speak, their audiences tend to take only the message of the spoken words. In some situations, people's faces are treated as the most important clues to what they feel but in others they are treated as unreliable indications of what is going on. Laboratory experiments show that, just as with facial expressions and tones of voice, people become less sensitive to the silent languages of movements and posture as they grow old. As for faces, older people more easily and accurately recognise body language conveying pleasure and happiness than anger, disgust or fear [8]. This is interesting because the body language cues and the facial cues for these states of mind are very different. It begs the question whether older people become more reluctant to recognise or less able to empathise with these unpleasant emotions in other people.

When actors are asked to make their facial expressions, tones of voice and body language express different and contradictory things, many older adults do not notice the disparity and tend to get only the messages conveyed by the words [9]. There are also differences in the sensitivity with which old and young people recognise emotions conveyed by tone of voice and body language. At all ages, women are better at recognising tones of voice than men, but their abilities also decline with age. Studies by Ruffman and colleagues compared how accurately people recognise emotions expressed by tones of voice, body language and posture. Older adults were worse at recognising body language and tone of voice cues of anger, fear and happiness, and found it harder to match tones of voice to facial expressions and body language [10]. They also found it harder to decide whether actors' tones of voice matched their facial or bodily expressions. This was not due to their poorer hearing or vision. A likely explanation is suggested by findings that older people process information more slowly and find it particularly hard to attend to more than one source of information at once. They also need longer to pick up cues from words, faces, tones of voice and posture. They must prioritise decoding the meanings of spoken words because, unless they do, conversations would make no sense. This leaves them less spare information processing bandwidth to read all the other cues available, particularly if these are fleeting facial expressions or brief body twitches.

What goes on in the brain when we recognise non-verbal cues?

An interesting idea is that we recognise facial expressions partly by internal mimicry. Particular clusters of neurones in our brains are triggered by particular movements, actions and facial expressions. The same neurones become active whether we make these ourselves or just see others do so. For this reason these have been termed "mirror neurones". I think of my few surviving mirror neurones as Good Things because they still give me (very) faint sensations of participation in the astounding physical dexterity of athletes I watch on TV. I find myself twitching in sympathy and notice similar sympathetic jerks in other elderly companions. Participation by neural reflection may be a neurological basis for human empathy and sympathy. This suggests the strange idea that it may be hard to recognise emotions that our own faces, and so perhaps also our mirror neurones, can no longer easily display, and that part of our problem in recognising emotions is that we have become less able to externally express and internally reflect them. Findings that older people are less good than the young at imitating facial expressions has been used as evidence for this speculation [11]. It would be interesting to make comparisons between naïve elderly people and elderly actors who may still retain a large, highly practised repertoire of cues.

Accentuating the positive

Whether or not we oldies can more easily recognise those particular expressions that we can still mimic, we are better at recognising expressions of emotions that we are currently experiencing. We are also better at recognising happiness and pleasure than anxiety, pain, anger and distress. We also remember faces with positive or neutral expressions better than faces with negative expressions. A possible reason for this "positivity effect" is that most old people report feeling pretty happy most of the time. A less comfortable idea is that the older we get the more strongly we tend to dislike, and so to suppress and ignore, negative information of any kind. There is some evidence for this "negativity suppression hypothesis" from a study that showed young and elderly people pairs of photos of faces that simultaneously disappeared and were immediately followed by a dot that fell on the previous position of one or the other [12]. They were asked to make the same response to the dot, as quickly as possible, in whatever position it appeared. They responded faster when it fell on a position previously occupied by a neutral rather than by a negative face. The authors suggest that this is because people of all ages, but especially the elderly, have a bias to select positive and suppress negative information.

It would be mean-spirited not to stress the many encouraging findings that, even after differences in their socio-economic opportunities and health have been considered, most people do seem to become happier as they grow old. Elderly volunteers in particular seem to show a Pollyanna bias by judging expressionless faces as being happy and benevolent. Unfortunately, just as we might fear, there is evidence that this bias makes them particularly vulnerable to deception [13]. A dubious compensation is that at least one study suggests that older people are also more likely to get away with it when they try to deceive others [14].

Most reviewers conclude that older people may recognise pleasant expressions more easily not just because they suppress the negative but because they accentuate the positive (and also, perhaps, do not mess with Mr-In-Between). A fantasy test of this idea would be to recruit a particularly vicious group of geriatrics and test whether, unlike genuinely warm and nice old people, they show an enhanced negativity effect or a reduced positivity effect. On the whole, I am happy that this experiment does not yet seem to have been made.

Even if we found that an ugly disposition does reverse the "age positivity effect", this would not tell the whole story. Things are more complicated because of some evidence that age impairs recognition of different expressions in different cultures. Like occidentals, elderly Japanese are less good at recognising sadness than happiness but they are, allegedly, far better at recognising disgust [15].

Back to the brain again

The issues are whether these differences occur because the recognition of emotions, whether these are expressed by faces, tones of voice or body language, is managed by particular parts of the brain that are early affected by brain aging, or whether our ability to sensitively recognise emotions declines as our entire brains are affected by diffuse and global changes. There is evidence for both possibilities. When we control for losses in hearing and vision differences between old and young, people vary with their scores on intelligence tests. Those who maintain high intelligence test scores in old age show no losses of sensitivity. We can interpret this as evidence that weakening of judgements of emotions is due to diffuse changes in the entire brain that tend to reduce general intellectual ability rather than by local changes in specific brain areas.

On the other hand, there is also good evidence that both our feelings and perceptions of emotion are controlled by particular parts of the brain and that our sensitivity to emotional cues is reduced by the effects of age on these particular systems. Recognition of the emotional tone of speech is carried out by the right more than by the left hemisphere of the brain, and age also damages the right hemisphere earlier than the left. Adolphs, Tranel and Damasio [16] compared young and middle-aged adults who had suffered various specific brain injuries on tests of recognition of facial expressions. Damage to the right inferior parietal and right mesial anterior cortex most often impaired recognition of expressions of anger and fear, and less often affected recognition of happiness. In a different study the same authors found that damage to the amygdala, an area in the brain that is involved in both feeling and expressing rage and fear, seemed to selectively impair recognition of these particular emotions. Andy Calder, working in the MRC Cognition and Brain Sciences Unit, found that damage to the ventral striatum selectively impairs recognition of anger [17]. Andy also reported another study [18] in which brave young male volunteers who had agreed to a pharmacological procedure that impaired the efficiency of their dopaminergic neurotransmitter systems became temporarily less sensitive to facial expressions. Dopamine production is critical to feeling and expressing anger. Since dopamine production declines in older brains, this may be a further clue why older people are less sensitive to angry expressions.

There is some evidence that the amygdala, which is directly involved in feeling and expressing anger and rage, is also involved in the recognition of the degree of "trustworthiness" of the faces of strangers and possibly also in recognition of body postures that are signals of threat [19]. An evolutionary explanation might be that trustworthiness is associated with the relative intensity of expressions of menace or aggression, and so of fear, and so also with the decision whether to attack or flee when confronted. These and similar findings suggest that age-related changes in brain chemistry and in specific areas of the brain or that affect our abilities to *feel* particular emotions also affect our abilities to *recognise* them.

Our inner others: modelling minds

We have seen that the ability to recognise expressions, tones of voice and body language depends on learning particular cues, and that our ability to pick up and interpret these cues becomes less efficient and more selectively biased as we grow old. A further and deeper question is how we use the cues that we gather to interpret what others think or feel to build up accurate theories of their minds. One encouraging study suggests that as we grow older we gain wisdom and that part of this gift is acquiring better theories of mind [20]. I would like to believe this, but am discouraged because the data on which it is based seems to have been collected only from unusually intelligent and well-preserved people. Accurately interpreting others' states of mind needs not only considerable experience of them and of the cues they emit, but also vigilance and sensitivity to what they say and do not say. It also requires the ability and interest to relate what we currently pick up about people to what we know about their lives. With great regret, I have come to believe that as we age we begin to do all these things less well. This is not to say that older people become less concerned about others' lives, though this can sometimes be the case. Nor is it to say that they become less benevolent in their attitudes and so, in this sense, have less empathy for others. In fact, the evidence is that, as we age, most of us do become more tolerant and sympathetic and, as far as our situations allow, more nurturing. My point is that as we grow old we understand less about what is going on because we can pick up less of the information that people provide and because our mental engines of interpretation gradually become less efficient.

I believe that it does not matter if, as we age, our insights become less sharp and our interpretations of others' true feelings become correspondingly more fuzzy and unreliable, provided that we develop, instead, a warmer and promiscuously benevolent attitude towards each other. We all swing between awe, astonishment, horror and bleak boredom whenever we confront the certainty that we are brief flickers of self-consciousness in a vast, indifferent Grand Contraption. To cope with this terrifying loneliness, we make up beautiful and terrible stories of omnipotent imaginary beings whom we strive to placate by outrageous flattery chanted in special weird tones of voice and by feigned sympathy with their alleged abominations of particular kinds of sex, seafood, stimulants and charcuterie. Actually, we know very well, in our hearts, and probably also in our amygdalas and right inferior parietal and right mesial anterior cortexes, that in this oblivious universe there is no support other than what we can offer each other. To let old age sap our empathy and sympathy for all of our fellow humans is the worst capitulation of all.

References

[1] Elfenbein, H. A. and Ambady, N. (2003). When familiarity breeds accuracy: Cultural exposure and facial emotion recognition. *Journal of Personality and Social Psychology*, 85, 276–290.

[2] Pollak, S. D., Cicchetti, D., Hornung, K. and Reed, A. (2000) Recognizing emotion in faces: Developmental effects of child abuse and neglect. *Developmental Psychology*, 36, 679–688.

[3] Surcinelli, P., Codispoti, M., Montebarocci, O., Rossi, N. and Baldaro, B. (2006). Facial emotion recognition in trait anxiety. *Journal of Anxiety Disorders*, 20, 110–117.

[4] Orgeta, V. and Phillips, L. H. (2007). Effects of age and emotional intensity on the recognition of facial emotion. *Experimental Aging Research*, 34, 63–79.

[5] Sullivan, S., Ruffman, T. and Hutton, S. B. (2004). Age differences in emotion recognition skills and the visual scanning of emotion faces. *Journal of Gerontology, B*, 62, 53–60.

[6] Mill, A., Alick, J., Realo, A. and Valk, R. (2009). Age-related differences in emotion recognition ability: A cross-sectional study. *Emotion*, 9, 619–630.

[7] Rhodes, M. G., Castell, A. D. and Jacoby, L. L. (2008). Associative recognition of face pairs by younger and older adults: The role of familiarity-based processing. *Psychology and Aging*, 23, 239–249.

[8] Fecteau, S. and Belin, P. (2007). Perception of emotions expressed via speech and nonlinguistic vocalizations. In K. Izdebski (Ed.) p. 137, *Emotions in the Human Voice: Foundations*. San Diego, CA, Plural Publishing Inc.

[9] Montepare, J., Koff, E., Zaitchik, D. and Albert, A. (1999). The use of body movements and gestures as cues to emotions in younger and older adults. *Journal of Nonverbal Behavior*, 23, 133–152.

[10] Ruffman, T., Sullivan, S. and Dittrich, W. (2009). Older adults' recognition of bodily and auditory expressions of emotion. *Psychology and Aging*, 24, 614–622.

[11] Yecker, S. A., Brickman, A. M., Moreno, C. R., Sliwinski, M., Foldi, N. S., Alpert, M. and Welkowitz, J. (2004). Changes in posed facial expression of emotion across the adult life span. *Experimental Aging Research*, 30, 305–331.

[12] Mather, M. and Carstenson, L. (2003). Aging and attentional biases for emotional faces. *Psychological Science*, 14, 409–415.

[13] Stanley, J. T. and Blanchard-Fields, F., (2008). Challenges older adults face in detecting deceit: The role of emotion recognition. *Psychology and Aging* 23(1), 24–32.

[14] Parham, I. A., Feldman, R. S., Oster, G. D. and Popoola, O. (1981). Inter-generational differences in nonverbal disclosure of deception. *Journal of Social Psychology*, 113, 261–269.

[15] Susuki, A., Hoshino, T., Shigematsu, K. and Kawamura, M. (2007). Decline or improvement? Age-related differences in facial expression recognition. *Biological Psychology*, 74, 75–84.

[16] Adolphs, R., Tranel, D. and Damasio, H. (2001) Emotion recognition from faces and prosody following temporal lobectomy. *Neuropsychology*, 15, 396–404.

[17] Calder, A. (1996). Facial emotion recognition after bilateral amygdala damage. *Cognitive Neuropsychology*, 13, 699–745.

[18] Lawrence, A. D., Calder, A. J., McGowan, S. W. and Grasby, P. M. (2002). Selective disruption of the recognition of facial expressions of anger. *Neuroreport*, 13, 881–884.

[19] Todorov, A. (2008) Evaluating faces for trustworthiness. In Kingstone, A. (ed.), *Year in Cognitive Neuroscience 2008*, Ch 11. The New York Academy of Sciences.

[20] Happé, F. G., Winner, E. and Brownell, H. (1998). The getting of wisdom: Theory of mind in old age. *Developmental Psychology*, 34, 358–362.

19

THE GETTING OF WISDOM

Folklores of all nations and races suggest that there is one marvellous bonus of old age: a pinnacle of mental achievement, generically labelled wisdom, that can be earned only by living long enough to gain the necessary experience. In pre-literate societies, human brains were the only archives of all of the useful knowledge about the world that our species gained. The consequent respect that elders enjoyed began to be eroded as soon as we began to make more detailed, accurate and durable records on clay tablets, scrolls and books. The immortalisation of knowledge continued and was refined over the next many thousands of years. Now the World Wide Web holds more instantly available information than any of us can ever hope to scan in a lifetime and our grandchildren are far better at accessing it than we are.

What is wisdom?

For cognitive gerontologists, discussions of wisdom had to begin by framing acceptable definitions for what it is and identifying individuals who have more or less of it. This might reveal what other qualities are included in or associated with wisdom, whether wisdom is a unique gift of old age and whether, even after a lifetime acquiring it, we can still keep and, perhaps, even increase it.

We are offered far too much help from far too many self-appointed experts. These are often confusingly circular or shamelessly imprecise or tell us what wisdom is not rather than what it may be. Jiddu Krisnamurti warns us that "information is not knowledge, knowledge is not wisdom. . .wisdom is when knowledge ends". Frank Zappa remarks that "Wisdom is not truth, truth is not love, love is not music, music is the best." By far my favourite academic institution, the University of Western Australia in Perth, has the motto: "Seek Wisdom". This is splendidly terse and uplifting and would do very well on its own but, as we might expect from this excellent university, we are given further guidance. At one end of a charming reflecting pool, a plinth tells us "Verily it is by Beauty that we come by Wisdom" and at the other, a companion slab reminds us that "Beauty is Truth". Perhaps it was thought tactless to complete the quotation and tell students sweating through difficult courses that "This is all you know and all you need to know". There are scores of such definitions, all inspiring, many unintelligible, most tautologous. None seems to provide a credible launching pad for a research programme. If we need prime examples of Daniel Dennett's wonderful new term "deepities"[1] this is where to look.

Encyclopaedias and dictionaries try to frame less circular definitions. Wikipedia says that wisdom is

> a deep understanding and realization of people, things, events or situations, resulting in the ability to apply perceptions, judgements and actions in keeping with this understanding. It often requires control of one's emotional reactions (the "passions") so that universal principles, reason and knowledge prevail to determine one's actions. Wisdom is also the comprehension of what is true coupled with optimum judgement as to action. Synonyms include: sagacity, discernment, or insight.

Merriam Webster gives:

> **a** : accumulated philosophic or scientific learning : KNOWLEDGE **b** : ability to discern inner qualities and relationships : INSIGHT **c** : good sense : JUDGMENT d : generally accepted belief.

So wisdom is not just useful information about the world and insights into others and oneself. It is not just knowing what is the right thing to do but actually doing it. As we expect this ethical dimension to differ between societies, this inevitably hints that wisdom must be culturally relative. Definitions of wisdom do markedly differ between the cultures that produce them. Some favour Judeo-Christian texts such as the Book of Job that emphasise obedience to an enigmatically capricious and punitive deity ("The fear of the Lord is the beginning of wisdom"). Others from classical Greco-Roman literature are more humane and practical ("Moderation in all things"). Discussions of Confucian ethics stress the desirability of concern for society as a whole over personal wishes. An unusually daring Chinese psychologist, Shih-Ying Yang [1], sought guidance from the people and summarised 220 "wisdom incidents" reported by Taiwanese volunteers into five classes of worthy actions: "Striving for common good by helping others; striving and achieving a satisfactory state of life; deciding and developing life-paths; resolving difficult problems at work and insistence on doing the right thing when facing a problem".

This complexity and variety of definitions makes it clear that everybody agrees that wisdom is a Very Good Thing, that it requires considerable knowledge of the world and particularly of other people that we can gain only by long experience and, even more, through clear understanding and diligent practice of a well-articulated code of ethical behaviour. It is intimidating to try to devise laboratory experiments to unpack such a complicated, diffuse and difficult concept to discover which people have this complex collection of attributes, when they first attain it and how long they can keep it.

Paul Baltes and Ursula Staudinger are perhaps the two most prolific authors in psychological "Wisdom Studies". They set about this by asking volunteers to comment on how people should cope with a variety of imagined dilemmas [2]. Their analyses suggested that the wisest comments fell into five categories: necessary factual knowledge about people and the world; useful factual knowledge and also procedural knowledge of how to get things done; recognition of relativity - that what is best for people to do will differ depending on context and circumstances and particularly on how old they are; ability to recognise that values are relative and not absolute; and perception that life is always uncertain and that plans must be framed accordingly. From these principles, they derived an objective "wisdom rating scale" – a questionnaire that they could use to identify individuals who are wiser than others.

On their wisdom rating scale, people-centred professionals such as health specialists and clinical psychologists scored higher than non-people-centred professionals such as accountants and geologists. Older and younger respondents were rated by the questionnaire as being equally wise. However, each age group could offer more insightful and appropriate guidance for people of their own generation. It seems that wisdom can be acquired young, is most relevant to the particular age and environment of the person who has it and can be effectively maintained in later life – though its content changes to fit the different circumstances of old age. At any age we have much clearer insights into the situations and problems of people living through our own time of life, whose outlooks and feelings we are most likely to share [3, 4]. So we can give our contemporaries good advice – but, if we are truly wise, not often and only if they ask for it.

Another way to find an objective definition of wisdom is to ask volunteers to nominate particular people they think are exceptionally wise and to give reasons for these judgements. A PhD thesis reports a study in which the Baltes's wisdom scale was used to compare 78 men and women whose acquaintances had rated them as being, in general terms, exceptionally wise [5]. Twenty-two had also rated themselves as being wise. A control group was made up of people of the same ages who were not thought to be especially wise, either by others or themselves. Those who had been rated by others as being exceptionally wise gained relatively high wisdom ratings. They were also, on average, relatively better educated, more intelligent, more sensitive to the complexities of the dilemmas they discussed, had fewer dogmatic and inflexible beliefs and were more contented with their own lives. Those who had rated themselves as wise were no different from the control group who were not considered wise, and did not think of themselves as wise. I find this a satisfying empirical validation of intuitions and of the proverb "Knowledge of self is the mother of wisdom".

This study agrees with others that also show that there are particular qualities that, although they have nothing to do with received ideas of wisdom, seem to make wisdom more accessible. People who were identified as wise, whether by their peers or by wisdom rating scales also tend to differ from those identified as less wise in terms of their objective circumstances. They typically had longer educations, were better off and lived in better environments. They also tended to have higher scores on intelligence tests. Their most important characteristic was that they had particularly pleasing personality attributes, tending to be more governed by reason than emotion, to be reflective rather than impulsive and to be emotionally warm and sympathetic. On this last point, it has been argued that an important component of wisdom is having a comprehensive "theory of mind": that is, a clear and accurate idea of how others feel about events in their lives and how they are likely to try to cope with them. Intelligence is necessary for empathy but, unfortunately, the converse does not seem to be true [6].

To summarise, the many attempts to define wisdom suggest that it is as much an attitude to life, people and oneself as a compendium of useful information about how the world, and others in it work, coupled with the ability to predict actions and consequences. Old age is not essential for wisdom nor does it guarantee wisdom. The young can also be wise, but it is likely that they are wise in somewhat different ways and about different things. Both young and old are most insightful about the plights and reactions of their own generations. Wisdom can be learned, as in the caring professions that bring more frequent encounters with distressed people and their problems. A good further question is whether the qualities of mind and heart that make people choose caring professions are also those that encourage empathy and human insight. All definitions of wisdom suggest that, since it implies the ability to correctly make complicated analyses to reach appropriate decisions it must involve intelligence. To the extent that this is true, it must follow that as fluid intelligence declines in old age wisdom will diminish. Nevertheless, what comes through all discussions I have found in the literature is that what matters most are qualities of benevolence of attitude, openness of mind and heart, and sympathy that do not have much to do with how fast we can solve logic problems. This, as we all recognise in others, can gleam through cloudy wits even in extreme old age.

Note

1 See Dennett, D. (2013) *Intuition Pumps and Other Tools for Thinking*. W.W. Norton & Co., NY, 2013; and Penguin Books, UK, 2013. This cannot be too highly recommended.

References

[1] Yang, S. H. (2008). Real-life contextual manifestations of wisdom. *The International Journal of Aging and Human Development*, 67, 273–303.

[2] Staudinger, U. M., Smith, J. and Baltes, P. B. (1992). Wisdom-related knowledge in a life review task: Age differences and the role of professional specialization. *Psychology and Aging*, 7(2), 271–281.

[3] Smith, J., Staudinger, U. M. and Baltes, P. (1994). Occupational settings facilitating wisdom-related knowledge: The sample case of clinical psychologists. *Journal of Consulting and Clinical Psychology*, 62, Oct, 989–999.

[4] Baltes, P. B. and Staudinger, U. M. (2000). Wisdom: A metaheuristic (pragmatic) to orchestrate mind and virtue toward excellence. *American Psychologist*, 55(1), 122–136.

[5] Lyster, T. L. (1996). A nomination approach to the study of wisdom in old age. PhD thesis, Concordia University.

[6] Happé, F. G. E. and Winner, E. (1988). The getting of wisdom: Theory of mind in old age. *Developmental Psychology*, 34, 358–362.

PART V
Living with Aging

20

THOSE OLD BLUES: DEPRESSION AND ANXIETY

Our long-suffering volunteers sometimes wrote to comment on what we were doing, to tell us what they thought we should do instead or to tell us how old age was changing their lives. Most of their letters were cheerful and positive, but one anonymous poem was so articulate and touching that someone pinned it to a notice board in our computer room where I watched it yellow and crinkle for three years. It seemed to be an eloquent act of contrition by a male, retired academic for his hurtful remarks and sarcasm to others throughout his entire life. He now desperately regretted that he could not forget, forgive himself or make amends. If he had not chosen anonymity, there were things we might have said to him: the most banal is that as the view ahead closes in, backward glances become frequent and for any decent person retrospection without remorse is impossible. Clearly our sad poet was disabled by cycles of repetitive and extremely painful thoughts that he could not suppress. These poisoned his feelings about his current life and his value as a person. He would have been greatly helped by an introduction to a work by Mark Williams, John Teasdale, Jon Kabat-Zinn and others who have researched, clinically validated and published very effective ways to escape from distressing cycles of self-blame and self-disgust that are typical of depression.

"Mindfulness Meditation" is now a thoroughly tested and successful clinical technique. It was first brought to the attention of sceptical clinicians by John Kabat-Zinn, working in Boston Medical School, who taught it as a coping technique for patients suffering otherwise untreatable physical pain. In the UK, Mark Williams, John Teasdale and others found it successful in many clinical trials as a technique for coping with depression and anxiety, especially with repetitive, usually painful, thoughts. It is now a recognised treatment for depression validated by the UK National Health Service. A very large number of guides including CDs, computer and Tablet applications and instructional books are now easily available. I think that *The Mindful Way through Depression* by Mark Williams, John Teasdale,

Zindel Siegel and Jon Kabat-Zinn is the best guide available. It is a clear, humane and precise description of the conditions for which it works, a reliable guide to the background of the objective evidence on which it is based and a clear and humane guide to practice.

Our very clever, articulate, good hearted and sad poet's predicament seems to support young adults' view of old age as a drab tail-end of life, embittered by regret for opportunities missed, for things better not said or done, for missed opportunities and for losses of competence, loved ones and health. To the young, any happiness still accessible in old age seems rather thin. Perhaps especially to 20-year-old rock stars like Pete Townsend who remarked 50 years ago, that the things that oldies do look awfully cold and that he hoped to die before age happened to him. No subsequent comments are recorded. Do the rich joys of youth inevitably dilute into insipid pleasures? Or, worse, does old age release a trickle of what Kurt Vonnegut called "bad chemicals in the brain" bringing causeless depression to even the most comfortable lives?

A central theme in geriatric psychiatry has been whether depression becomes more common in old age. Some clinicians comment that depression may be a realistic response to life at any age, and that depressed patients are in closer touch with uncomfortable realities than the naïvely optimistic "normal". Depression and anxiety may indeed be apt responses to inevitable changes. As we lose youth and the illusions that once gift-wrapped our lives, does realistic depression become the penalty for keeping our wits?

A direct test is to ask people to tell us how they feel about their lives. People of my generation do not feel that old age is a sad time. While I do not notice that many of us caper lustily like the bronzed geriatrics advertising life-transforming

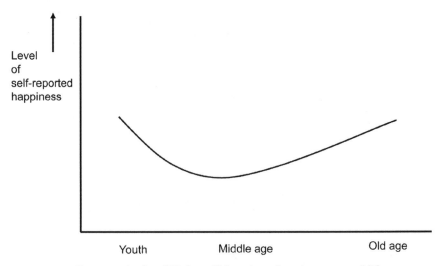

FIGURE 20.1 Some results fit a "U-shaped" happiness function: reported life satisfaction is greatest in young adults, lower in the middle aged but rises to a new peak in old age.

glucosamine sulphate, stair lifts, things for getting into and out of baths, trousers with stretchable waistbands and especially comfortable shoes, most of us still manage amused contentment. Comprehensive literature reviews [1] suggest that we may be only slightly smug. In lucky Australia, the first reports from a 1997 National Survey of Mental Health suggested that depression and anxiety declined throughout youth and middle age and continued to do so after 65. An analysis of reports by half a million randomly sampled North Americans and West Europeans concluded that the lifespan profile of happiness is U-shaped so that the young and the elderly are more contented than the careworn middle aged [2] (see Figure 20.1).

Other analyses conclude that these findings result from mistakes in methodology. For example, that the data from the Australian National Survey were not properly analysed [3] or that the lifetime trajectory of happiness is more "wave-shaped" than "U-shaped", dropping slightly from an early high in youth to a shallow low in middle age, followed by a rise in the early sixties that falls to a deeper low in the seventies and beyond [4] (see Figure 20.2).

The authors of a large, thorough and well-analysed Dutch survey makes the sensible point that if we find an increase in sadness in older samples, we must bear in mind that people's lives radically change as they age - and not always for the better. Before we decide what the true lifetime trajectories of happiness or disaffection are, we must consider that people have very different life-opportunities that will obviously affect their reports of themselves [5]. A recent search of voluminous web-based

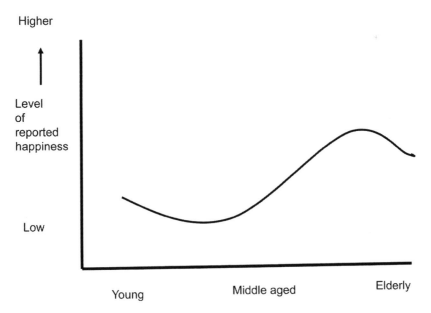

FIGURE 20.2 Other results fit a "wave-shaped" happiness function: reported life satisfaction is high for young adults, lower for the middle age, increases in early old age and then, again, somewhat declines.

data-archives of self-reports from elderly Caucasians found that, as common sense suggests, the frequency and severity of depression is strongly linked to quality of life and, most particularly, to health and mobility. Depression is more often reported by women than men and varies with personal circumstances and degree of independence. It is also relatively rare. Depression is reported by 0.9 to 9.4 per cent of elderly people living in private households and this rises to between 14 and 42 per cent for those living in institutions [6]. If we ignore this variability, and only consider averages from groups of people living in very different circumstances we get a misleading picture of what has been termed the life-trajectory of happiness.

We all know that the risks of unpleasant changes and events increase as we age. In early old age, retirement may bring loss of status, self-respect, comradeship and a less comfortable income. If we live long enough, bereavements become inevitable and worsening health curtails cherished activities and raises anxieties about the future. Even if we bear this in mind, we must interpret questionnaire data cautiously because the connections between the kind of things that happen to people, how these affect them and what they can, or care to, tell others about them are not straightforward. For example, young adults are more depressed by experience of pain and illness than the middle aged and elderly, perhaps because, for them, bad health is a rare and resented misfortune, shared with few acquaintances, curtailing opportunities and ambitions. Other studies agree that older people are both more reticent and more stoical in their attitudes to chronic pain [7]. The findings of differences between attitudes to pain and illness between people aged under and over 70 suggest to me that that these attitudes may develop gradually as people become accustomed to new difficulties that aging brings [8].

Gerontologists do their best to find ways to document and quantify problems of health, social support, income and demographics and to take these into account when analysing changes in people's reports of their levels of happiness during different times of their lives. When this is done, the evidence for increases in depression and unhappiness in old age seems much weaker. Some analyses even find that happiness steadily increases throughout old age. The common-sense intuition that much of the sadness that people report in old age is due to unpleasant life circumstances has been objectively documented. The next issue is how well older people can adjust their attitudes to cope with the new bad stuff that they experience.

We explored this by analysing responses that 2025 Manchester and Newcastle volunteers aged from 50 to 89 made to a questionnaire on which they rated the number of times that they had encountered each of 50 different potentially stressful events during the past year. Volunteers over 70 reported fewer stressful events. This was partly because the amount and kinds of their involvement had gradually changed. For example, people often reported retirement as a stress in their late fifties and sixties but not in their seventies. Those with higher intelligence test scores and who were better off reported fewer stressful events. They experienced the same problems as their less lucky age-peers but less often and they were less affected by them. In the Newcastle sample, as usual, affluence and intelligence are strongly associated. This opens the question of whether clever volunteers avoided or overcame difficulties more deftly or whether they were better protected by their higher income and status. There was some evidence for the second interpretation because even less intelligent volunteers in their seventies or eighties who also happened to be well off reported fewer stressful events and lower levels of stress from identical events than did the socio-economically deprived. Even after differences in age, ability and affluence had been taken into account, women reported more stressful events and also reported greater stress from similar experiences. The message is that people in their sixties, seventies and eighties, and men and women not only have somewhat different kinds of stressful experience, but are also affected in different ways and to different extents by similar problems. I realise that this is not a novel conclusion, but I think that psychologists should be relieved rather than diffident when their findings agree with the collective recorded experiences of the human race over many thousands of years.

In Newcastle, women of all ages reported sadness and depression more often and more strongly than men. This agrees with nearly all findings from many different countries. There are, of course, good objective reasons for this. Even in affluent and liberal societies women are, in many respects, second-class citizens who have to struggle much harder to gain status and incomes. The hardships faced by single mothers are notorious and, even within marriages, childcare is an unequal burden. Men and women also gain different levels of advantages from their marriages and partnerships. At all ages, partnered men and women are happier than lifelong singles and, perhaps less surprisingly, than the widowed or divorced. Nevertheless, it is interesting that men seem to gain more from marriage than women do. Differences in longevity suggest some explanations. During the twentieth and early twenty-first centuries, studies consistently reported that although marriage prolongs the lives of both sexes, men gain more extra years from marriage. One interpretation was that wives may support husbands more effectively than husbands support wives. Another interpretation, popular among evolutionary anthropologists, is that women consciously or unconsciously tend to choose healthy spouses and leave less robust suitors to wilt on their shelves. The longevity of married men reflects the accuracy of their partners' initial assessments of their durability. Things may be changing. In contrast to other male animals that shorten their lives by exhausting competition to demonstrate higher survival potential, advantages of wealth and status in humans are often unrelated to physical health, and may even be linked to greater age. This "Edward Casaubon Syndrome" allows less healthy and older males to inveigle commitments from robust women to be their caring props. Some more recent twenty-first century surveys suggest that the survival benefits from marriage persist for both sexes but are now becoming more equal between women and men. I have not found convincing explanations for this desirable trend.

A different reason why women might complain of sadness more often is that most studies show that they are more willing to talk about their feelings, are better at scrutinising and evaluating their own emotions and those of others and can describe their insights more sensitively and accurately. Men typically give sparse, stereotyped and uninformative descriptions of themselves (and of others).

Older men and women are also less forthcoming and articulate about their feelings than young people. Possibly this is because they have overcome so many difficulties during their longer lives that they have gained perspective, have learned to take misfortunes more stoically and have come to believe that it is foolish and socially inept to dwell on unpleasant realities that they cannot alter. A tendency to ignore or to understate depression may explain why older volunteers' descriptions of their emotional lives remain positive in spite of increasing hardships such as bereavement, poor health and lower income. Intelligence and articulacy also decline in old age and, for some older people, this blunts the ability to express, but also, possibly, to define one's feelings to oneself and so better recognise them. When we use answers to questionnaires to infer the effects of age and sex on the incidence and severity of depression we must remember that what happens to people is one matter, what they feel about this is quite another and how well they can, or are willing to, define and share their feelings is something different again.

How feelings of depression are related to objective hardship is not straightforward. Sadness makes problems seem more overwhelming than they actually are and undermines our belief that we can cope with them. Less intellectually able people are also more vulnerable because they may be less aware of possibilities for help with anxiety and depression and so less likely to mention them, to seek help from others or to discuss them with doctors or counsellors.

Because sadness impairs intelligence and memory, it also makes it harder to resolve even minor problems that may have caused it. The links between depression and losses of intelligence and memory are very well established. Sad young adults have lower scores on intelligence and memory tests than the normally robust. The same is true of older people. We found this even within sub-groups of volunteers whose range of scores on depression questionnaires were so low and positive that they reflected differences in degrees of above-average cheerfulness rather than tinges of even mild sadness [9].

Mary Lunn and Kate Hunter have explored an explanation for this. They took the analysis a stage further and looked at relationships between scores on the Yesavage Geriatric Depression inventory and sex, cardiovascular and circulatory problems, diabetes and intelligence in the entire Newcastle volunteer panel. Because these robust Geordies were atypically cheerful and more than averagely healthy, it was not surprising that their average scores on depression questionnaires were significantly lower and their average intelligence test scores were significantly higher than those for the entire UK population. This allowed Mary and Kate to compare relationships between depression scores, sex, cardiovascular illnesses and diabetes and intelligence test scores within different large groups of people who were much happier, somewhat happier, slightly less happy and very much more unhappy than most other citizens of the UK.

Even among volunteers whose extremely low depression scores suggested that they were much happier than most of us, increases of only three points on depression scores were associated with significant drops of intelligence test scores. Mary and Kate showed that this happened only because even in the most atypically happy group, those individuals who suffered cardiovascular disease and diabetes had slightly higher depression scores than their healthy contemporaries. Although their depression scores were increased by illness, they were significantly lower than the average for the entire UK population. There is convincing evidence that cardiovascular disease and diabetes reduce intelligence. Mary and Kate concluded that health problems that make people slightly less contented also affect their intelligence. Among people who did not have either cardiovascular disease or diabetes there was no relationship between their levels of intelligence and happiness. These relationships contrasted with those found in the most severely depressed group. For individuals whose high depression scores suggested that they should seek clinical help, scores on tests of intelligence and depression were also strongly related to each other but not at all related to cardiovascular disease or diabetes. This again suggests that lower levels of everyday unhappiness can often be due to objective health problems that also affect our intelligence. In contrast, severe depression is caused by biochemical changes in the brain that can occur quite independently of changes in other aspects of health and lifestyle, and these brain changes degrade our intelligence as well as our ability to enjoy life.

Because depression is associated with poor health, it is unsurprising that it is also associated with earlier death. Many other large studies have shown that depression is linked to earlier death from a wide variety of different illnesses, particularly from the major killers of the elderly, cardiovascular problems [10] and cancer [11]. The sick are more likely to be depressed, have shorter lives and lose mental ability earlier than the healthy.

The risk of severe depression markedly increases in that small minority of unfortunate elderly people who suffer dementias. So, when making clinical diagnoses, finding that a patient is depressed should suggest a need to further check the possibility of dementia. Bearing this association between depression and dementia in mind, I have not yet found any convincing evidence that depression or anxiety *cause* dementia. It seems that we, quite understandably, become depressed after dementia has begun but there seems to be no good evidence that being depressed increases the risk of dementing. Depression and anxiety do impair our intelligence and memory, but the changes they cause are very slight compared to the massive effects of dementias.

A fair summary seems to be that for most elderly people mild depression and sadness are most typically caused by objective hardships such as illness, bereavements, lack of social support, poverty and the anxieties that these entail. This gives us a different insight into why some surveys have found that some people report experiencing less depression as they age from 60 through 80 and beyond. We have discussed the possibility that this is because people who survive into very old age must have experienced and transcended many difficulties and so gained perspective and resilience. A slightly different explanation is that because depression is often associated with the slow progress of pathologies that will eventually kill us, those who are depressed tend to die relatively young and, during their last years, also experience faster mental decline. The progressive culling of the depressed means that in any survey the oldest responders are a select group of lucky survivors who have been both kept alive and protected from sadness by their unusually good health, socio-economic advantages and social support and perhaps also by temperaments that allow them to continue to relish their lives to the end.

Various shades of blues

A different issue in discussing morale in old age is that everyday terms such as "depression", "anxiety" and "sadness" do not precisely capture different shades of feelings. Novelists and poets find these single-word descriptions so inadequate that they have to invent metaphors to convey subtle differences between complicated emotions. Most psychologists are unfitted to do this, both by personality and training. Some of us have licences to practice as clinicians, but none could qualify for a poetic licence to coin rich and exact descriptions of emotional life. We have to do the best we can by asking how consistently people use words like anxiety or depression to describe different shades of feelings, and how well our questionnaires can distinguish between their different emotional states.

Beekman and his colleagues gave 3056 elderly Dutch volunteers one questionnaire designed to identify depression and another designed to identify anxiety [12]. Among those that the first questionnaire defined as being "depressed", 45 per cent were also identified by the second questionnaire as "anxious". This large overlap between questionnaires might mean that depression and anxiety are such similar emotional states, or are so closely related in terms of their neurophysiology and neurochemistry, that we cannot easily tell them apart. Or that they are different states but we can feel both at the same time. Or that the questionnaires are not particularly valid measures. The authors suggest a fourth possibility, that the questionnaires ask people how they feel about particular situations, attitudes and problems. Because the questionnaires remind them of unpleasant situations they provoke images of predicaments and states of mind for which the words "anxious" or "depressed" are only arbitrary labels. From this point of view, the words "depression" and "anxiety" are fuzzy terms that try to make broad distinctions between different kinds of objective situation that people may encounter rather than precisely distinguishing the precise qualities of the subjective emotions that these situations provoke.

Other studies support this last suggestion. A survey of 622 Germans aged over 60 found that 7.6 per cent had clinically significant anxiety and 27.5 per cent had clinically significant depression [13]. The incidence of depression did increase with age but, as usual, this could be explained by increases in their objective miseries such as health problems, socio-economic disadvantages and loss of autonomy and personal control. Reports of anxiety significantly and strongly correlated with reports of depression with nearly 50 per cent overlap between cases. Negative feelings were also strongly associated with the chronic fatigue familiarly known to General Practitioners as TATT (Tired All The Time). Again, this suggests that our everyday vocabularies only very coarsely distinguish shades of our experiences.

For lack of easy alternatives, people of different ages may use the same word, "depression" for states of mind with quite different objective causes and emotional colourings. Elderly people who suffer from the enervating effects of no exercise at all, or from physical illnesses, or from loneliness, or from a sense of anomie that leads to chronic apathy are experiencing qualitatively different shades of blues than young adults who are equally miserable because they are thwarted in pursuit of success or love. These predicaments may be felt to be equally emotionally unpleasant but their causes, effects and remedies, and also their subjective emotional qualities may be quite different. Everyday language has few single words to distinguish them. To define them for ourselves or convey them to others we need metaphors and complicated explanations. This raises the unresolved question of whether we can distinguish between emotional feelings without having language to do this. Our ability to find exact verbal descriptions of our feelings must diminish with age and, lacking precise categorisations for our experiences, we lose the ability to define what we are feeling to others and even ourselves.

Lynn McInnes's analysis the of stressful life events experienced by Newcastle volunteers gives some support to the idea that counts of different kinds of objective life event can tell us more than comparisons based on fuzzy labels for emotional states. Lynn found that, as we would expect, the number of people reporting bereavements and deaths of close friends increased from age 50 to 85. However, she also found that the older volunteers were, the greater was the stress that such losses caused. Money worries and relationship problems declined with age, as did ratings of the intensity of their emotional impacts. As we grow old, the things that most trouble us also alter. In our seventies and eighties we have usually given up caring about some things like failures to achieve different kinds of "success" with which we may have been obsessed in our fifties and sixties, but we can be badly thrown by events that once had little effect on us. For instance, the death of a pet becomes a more significant grief as age advances. We must recognise that greater age not only changes the relative likelihood of different kinds of unpleasantness but also the contexts in which these occur, their impacts on our lives and also our sensitivities to them. These are further explanations for the apparent contradictions between studies that find that we do and those that find that we do not grow sadder as we grow old.

The final stress

A good example of the effects of context on stress is how our attitudes to death change as we grow older. In 2007, the *Journal of Death Studies* published an analysis of answers on the "Colbert Leiter Fear of Death" questionnaire given to 304 people aged from 18 to 87 [14]. Anxiety about eventual death was greatest early in life, between the ages of 20 and 30 and, after this, steadily declined. Women experienced a second peak of death-anxiety in their fifties. Intrigued by this difference, the authors questioned a second sample of 113 women aged from 18 to 85 and, once again, found that a gradual decline in death-anxiety as age increased was interrupted by a second peak in the fifties. They suggest an association with menopause that brings to focus losses of potentiality and inevitability of further, undesired changes. Studies from many different countries and cultures all report the same gradual reduction in fear and anxiety about death as age advances and also that, in general, women are more anxious about death than men. A possible explanation is that the longer people live the accumulating losses of family and friends and deaths of public figures accustom them to this inevitability. A different and sadder possibility is that, for many of us, if living becomes less rewarding death seems less important.

A sage aphorism is that people think very seldom about death until about the age of 40 but, after this, remember it every day. Impertinent enquiries, for which I have been rightly derided by acquaintances, suggest that this may be true – at least for those who will give me any polite response. This also suggests that becoming accustomed to the inevitability of death removes most of our apprehension, leaving only reasonable practical concerns about planning for dependents and the best use of remaining time. Most of my acquaintances agree and add that, in our seventies, we no longer entice ourselves with plans or ambitions that can only mature two or more years ahead. Those who appear the most contented seem to live in tighter boundaries of the present.

To summarise, most studies suggest that any increases in sadness, depression and anxiety in old age are mainly due to inevitable objective difficulties. A good aspect of this news is that we are not doomed to inevitable sadness in old age by neurochemical changes that we cannot avoid or control. We are mainly distressed by objective predicaments that we can understand, and that may be resolved by advances in medicine, social engineering and economic equality or by self-training in techniques such as mindful meditation. In our old age, as throughout our entire lives, we will have to confront many unpleasant things that we cannot do anything about. We must deal with these with what grace, dignity and stoicism we can manage. The approach of death is one of these unpleasant inevitabilities, but even this last stress does not seem to be a particularly powerful downer. One strategy to keep our spirit level as we grow old is to develop a relentless curiosity about what is happening to us and to explore, with all the intelligence and humour that we can manage, this fascinating condition in which we find ourselves.

References

[1] Jorm, A. F. (2000). Does old age reduce the risk of anxiety and depression? A review of epidemiological studies across the lifespan. *Psychological Medicine*, 30, 11–22.

[2] Blanchflower, D. G. and Oswald, A. J. (2008). Is well-being U-shaped over the life cycle? *Social Science & Medicine*, 66(8), 1733–1749.

[3] O'Connor, D. (2006). Do older Australians truly have low rates of anxiety and depression? A critique of the 1997 National Survey of Mental Health and Wellbeing. *Australian and New Zealand Journal of Psychiatry*, 40, 623–631.

[4] Frijters, P. and Beatton, T. (2012). The mystery of the U-shaped relationship between happiness and age. *Journal of Economic Behaviour and Organisation*, 82, 525–542.

[5] Beekman, A. T., Bremmer, M. A., Deeg, D. J., van Balkom, A. J., Smit, J. H., de Beurs, E., van Dyck, R. and van Tilburg, W. (1998). Anxiety disorders in later life: A report from the Longitudinal Aging Study Amsterdam. *International Journal of Geriatric Psychiatry*, 13, 717–726.

[6] Diernes, J. K. (2006). Prevalence and predictors of depression in populations of the elderly: A review. *Acta Psychiatrica Scandinavica*, 113, 372–387.

[7] Yong, H-H., Gibson, S. J., Horne, D. J. and Helme, R. D. (2001). Development of a Pain Attitudes Questionnaire to assess stoicism and cautiousness for possible age differences. *Journal of Gerontology, B*, 56, 279–284.

[8] Turk, D. C., Okifuji, A. and Schaff, L. (1996). Chronic pain and depression: Role of perceived impact and perceived control in different age-cohorts. *Pain*, 61, 93–101.

[9] Rabbitt, P., Donlan, C., Watson, P., McInnes, L. and Bent, N. (1995). Unique and interactive effects of depression, age, socioeconomic advantage, and gender on cognitive performance of normal healthy older people. *Psychology and Aging*, 10, 307–313.

[10] Schultz, R., Beach, S. R., Ives, D. G., Martire, L. M., Ariyo, A. A. and Kop, W. J. (2000). Association between depression and mortality in older adults. *The Cardiovascular Health Study Arch Intern Me*, 160, 1761–1768.

[11] Pinquart, M. and Duberstein, P. R. (2010). Depression and cancer mortality, a meta-analysis. *Psychological Medicine*, 40, 1797–1810.

[12] Beekman, A. T. F., de Beurs, E., van Balkom, A. J. L. M., Deeg, D. J. H., van Dyck, R. and van Tilburg, W. (2000). Anxiety and depression in later life: Co-ocurrence and commonality of risk factors. *American Journal of Psychiatry*, 157, 89–95.

[13] Schwarz, R., Gunzelmann, T., Hinz, A. and Brahler, E. (2001). Anxiety and depression in the general population over 60 years old. *Deutsche Medizinische Wochenschrift*, 126, 611–615.

[14] Russac, R. J., Gatliffe, C., Reece, M. and Spottswood, D. (2007). Death anxiety across the adult years: An examination of age and gender effects. *Death Studies*, 31, 549–561.

21

THE SPEED OF THOUGHT

In 1796, Nevil Maskelyne, the fifth Astronomer Royal of Great Britain, sacked his experienced assistant David Kinnebrook because Kinnebrook's measurements of the precise moments when stars crossed fixed reference points were consistently slower than his own. Maskelyne is now remembered for his attempts to suppress and undermine the achievement of John Harrison whose innovative clocks were the first practical solution to the problem of determining longitude: a problem that Maskelyne also had a strong vested interest in solving.[1] This discreditable episode suggests that Maskelyne was obstinate and self-centred, but he was also a capable observer and a dedicated scientist and, through the Royal Society, in touch with the wider science of his time. His harsh treatment of Kinnebrook could be justified in terms of the little then known about human minds. It was not then understood that there might be individual differences in decision speed that even diligent practice, effort and attention cannot alter. The story of how we came to discover why these ideas are mistaken neatly illustrates that science progresses, not only through abrupt brilliant insights but far more often, by a gradual realisation that widely accepted ideas must be wrong.

Twenty years later, the problem was resolved by another illustrious Astronomer Royal, this time to the court of Prussia. Friedrich Wilhelm Bessel working in Königsberg was aware of the wide inconsistencies between astronomers' timings of the same observations. When he checked Maskelyne's and Kinnebrook's data, he noticed that although Kinnebrook's observations were, on average, eight-tenths of a second slower than Maskelyne's, each was very consistent when compared against himself.

Bessel realised that the point is not to discover who is the most accurate "ideal observer" in absolute terms but to recognise that individual differences do occur and are considerable but, because they are also highly consistent over time, differences between individuals can be taken into account. Comparing records between individual astronomers, he calculated for each a personal correction factor, the "personal equation" that could be added to or subtracted from his observations to resolve inevitable differences between observers. Too late for poor Kinnebrook who never regained his prestigious job at the Royal Observatory and had to make a living as a schoolmaster.

It is odd that it took until the early 1800s for humans to verify that they consistently differ in the maximum speeds with which they can make decisions of any kind. Much older phrases such as "quick-witted" or "slow" show that people realised that we differ in how fast we can recognise things and do something about them. Nevertheless, we failed to take the next step to realise that this might mean that individuals' brains and nervous systems work at different speeds. Part of the problem was that even when physiologists and anatomists became aware that nerve cells communicate with each other by initiating and transmitting electrical impulses, these events were too fast for their limited technology to measure. If the speed of thought is immeasurably fast, disparities between individuals that are as large as eight-tenths of a second must be due to slackness or perversity rather than to biological limitations. In 1849, once again at Königsberg, another eminent German Professor, Hermann von Helmholtz, arranged the recording needle of a galvanometer to reflect a light beam across a room so that its tiny movements were sufficiently amplified to be observed. This allowed him to estimate the time between the initiation of an electrical impulse in the sciatic nerve of a frog and its later arrival at its calf-muscle. He calculated the speed of nerve transmission as between 24.6 and 38.4 metres a second. These results encouraged him to make further experiments to test differences in the times that his colleagues took to respond by moving a hand in response to touches on their feet and cheeks. He assumed that times to react to foot-touches would be measurably longer than to cheek-touches because nerve impulses from the foot had further to travel to reach the brain. This was so, and dividing the differences between reaction times to cheek- and foot-touches by the body lengths of his volunteers gave estimates that agreed quite well with his earlier, direct, frog observations and, surprisingly, also with modern observations made with very much more precise equipment. I have many times made a fool of myself by trying to replicate Helmholtz's gentle experiment in laboratory classes with undergraduate students. All of us always tried our best but produced only impossible results. Helmholtz was, of course, a wonderfully gifted experimenter and a very great scientist.

The question "Old and Slow?" became an obvious topic for research into mental changes in old age. In the mid-1950s, Jim Birren, another of my extraordinarily warm and generous personal mentors, made this a main theme of a long and distinguished research career. He noted that age differences in nerve transmission rates are so tiny that they cannot account for consistent differences of 50 milliseconds or more between the average reaction times of old and young adults [1]. His further experiments showed that age hardly affects the movement speed of short hand movements so that these differences cannot just reflect lags in muscles and joints but must be evidence of slowing of the time that the brain needs to recognise that something has happened and to trigger a response to do something about it. Many subsequent experiments have also discounted the other possibility that people's reaction times become slower as they age only because they become more cautious. When older people are forced to respond as fast as the young, they make errors. Differences in central decision time are real, they increase from 50 milliseconds in very easy tasks to 500 milliseconds or much more in difficult tasks, and they do not disappear with practice.

It may seem finicky to make such an issue of differences of a few thousandths of a second, but this does lead to at least two interesting thoughts. One was first suggested to me by a frighteningly clever Oxford colleague, Michel Treisman, who pointed out some surprising arithmetic. When a flash of light falls on the retina it takes at least 40 milliseconds for the retinal cells to generate nerve impulses that travel to the particular parts of my brain that correctly decide that this is not a meaningless random background event but the signal to which I have agreed to respond. It takes at least another 50 milliseconds for my brain to send a message to the muscles in my forearm and hand to begin and complete the necessary twitches of meat and joints to move my finger to press a key. When I was 26, my simple reaction time was about 150 milliseconds. This must mean that the time that my brain took to register that a flash had occurred and to begin to organise a response to it was only 50 milliseconds. Michel pointed out that because the minimum time that one nerve cell needs to activate another is 1 millisecond, the circuitry in my brain that manages the whole business of recognising signals as relevant or irrelevant, and program and trigger my responses to them, cannot use nerve pathways of more than 50 nerve cells connected in series. At 79.5, my reaction times are now 40 milliseconds slower. This fits quite well with a jokey estimate made by David Madden, working in Virginia, that as we age our reaction times to simple events such as buzzes or flashes of light increase by about 1 millisecond a year. I try not to be depressed and continue to be puzzled because the tiny age lagging of my individual neurones cannot account for such a big difference.

The next important discovery was made by Joseph Brinley, who compared the amounts of slowing of reaction times of older and young adults as the tasks that they were given were made more difficult. As we would expect, the harder the tasks became the slower everybody responded. The increase in reaction times with task difficulty was greater for the old than for the young. This was not surprising. The interesting thing was how extraordinarily regular this difference was across tasks. On every task, easy or difficult, the average reaction times of old volunteers could be exactly estimated just by multiplying the corresponding average for young volunteers by the same constant of about 1.2. John Cerella checked and extended Joe Brinley's findings by analysing published data from more than a hundred studies that had compared reaction times of older and younger adults on different tasks [2]. He found that however easy or difficult the tasks, and whatever were the signals to which they responded, older adults' reaction times could be closely estimated by multiplying younger adults' times by this same "Brinley Constant" of approximately 1.2. Figure 21.1 illustrates this surprising result that has now been replicated many hundreds of times. We now know that the value of the Brinley constant increases with the age gap between the groups of people we compare. For instance, we must multiply averages for 20-year-olds by approximately 1.2 to predict the reaction times of 60-year–olds, but by around 1.3 to estimate times for 70-year-olds and about 1.4 to estimate times for 80-year-olds. So if we measure how long young adults take to make any simple decision we can accurately predict how much longer older people will need to do the same thing.

This intriguing regularity is useful to engineers who have to allow for the effects of human factors on the systems that they design. For theoretical psychologists the Brinley constant has been exciting, but for methodologists like me it has become extremely irritating. On one hand, such a marked regularity must be telling us something important. On the other hand, it has prevented us from using behavioural data to infer physiological changes in aging brains. For example, we have excellent evidence that as our brains age our frontal lobes, the parts of our brains that are responsible for planning, control of attention and working memory, tend to lose volume earlier and more substantially than other areas [3, 4, 5]. So we might expect that even normal, healthy, elderly people will perform poorly on the diagnostic tests that neurologists have developed to identify patients who have damaged frontal lobes. Unfortunately, performance on all these neurological tests must be measured in terms of differences in decision times. Very thorough studies have failed to find that the age lags for frontal and executive tests are greater than for any other kinds of simple decisions [6, 7]. So "age-related general slowing" has been an intriguing puzzle that has provoked scores of useful experiments but it has also become a great nuisance by frustrating all simple-minded attempts to relate

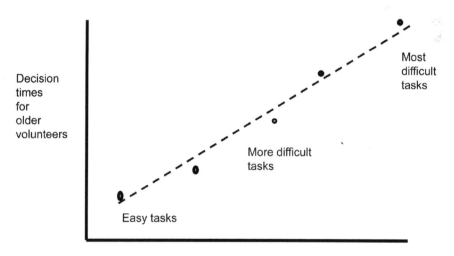

FIGURE 21.1   Joseph Brinley's discovery: as tasks become more difficult both young and older people become slower, but always by a constant ratio of between 1.2 and 1.5.

changes in behaviour to age changes in the brain. A wonderful meta-analysis of all of the scores of experiments showing similar Brinley constants for tasks as different as moving our eyes to focus on a flash of light and complex frontal and executive tasks has just appeared, and points to new ways of understanding this enigma [8].

In another respect, the Brinley constant has raised even wider problems. We find it even when we compare people of the same age on the same simple tasks. Art Jensen, an expert on individual differences in intelligence, repeatedly and convincingly showed that people of all ages who have relatively high scores on intelligence tests make simple decisions faster than others with lower scores [9]. I ignored Jensen's evidence as long as I possibly could but was forced to confront it when I not only consistently replicated his results but also found the same puzzling regularity that Joe Brinley and John Cerella had shown for differences in age also applied to differences in intelligence. Across tasks of different levels of difficulty, average reaction times of low intelligence test scorers can be accurately estimated by multiplying the average times of higher scorers by a constant that varies between 1.2 and 1.5 depending on the difference in the average intelligence test scores of the groups we compare [10]. Are the effects of individual differences in both age and intelligence just due to differences in general brain speed?

In 1985, Tim Salthouse published a radical suggestion that kept me cantankerously busy for the next 20 years [11]. Tim's important discovery was that differences in speed between young and older people largely accounted for differences in all their other mental abilities, even differences on simple memory tests. He took a further step and calculated that after differences in information processing speed have been taken into account, differences in people's ages have no further effect on their scores on memory tests. He decided that this must mean that a general slowing of information processing by the brain is not just a symptom but *the underlying functional cause* of differences in most or even in all mental abilities. On this argument "Old and Slow" is not just a description of a growing trivial inconvenience in late life. As we grow old we also become more forgetful and less clever *because* our brains have become slower.

There are clear and direct links between how fast we can process information and how well we can remember and learn new things. In 1972, Alan Baddeley and Graham Hitch showed that the efficiency of working memory depends on how rapidly we can recognise them and repeat them rapidly to ourselves (to rehearse them) as they are read or shown to us. So if we can rehearse faster we can remember more. In this context, Tim Salthouse's findings of close relationships between slowing of information processing speed and losses of memory efficiency make excellent sense.

It is always a very bad idea to become so irritated by any scientific hypothesis as to become blind to its advantages and abandon more constructive work to try to challenge it. Tim's general slowing hypothesis vexed me, partly because it seemed a premature Theory of Everything because, if age changes in all mental abilities are caused solely by general slowing nothing remains to be explained. This seemed too simplistic to be correct. A more serious issue was the common dilemma in science that a theory is weak if it depends solely on assuming causality from associations. Tim's fine experiments clearly showed that, as we age, the speed with which our brains can process information and the efficiency of memory and intelligence all decline, and that the amounts of these changes in different abilities such as decision speed and memory are correlated. This is just what would happen if information processing speed were indeed a master functional property that supports all or most other mental abilities. However, like circumstantial evidence in a court of law, correlations can only suggest but cannot prove causal relationships. It might be that the amounts and progress of quite separate and unrelated changes in the brain will be correlated only because they occur over the same periods of time. Or that, although information processing speed, loss of memory efficiency and declines in intelligence test scores are indices of the progress of changes in quite different brain systems, they may all change together, although at different rates, because some gross and diffuse change in the brain affects all brain systems to similar extents over the same periods.

Together with Mike Anderson, once a very Scottish student of mine at Oxford, and now an extremely Australian Scot, and a Professor at Murdoch University in Perth, I analysed data from the Manchester/Newcastle longitudinal study to look at the relationships between age, speed, intelligence and memory in 5000 people aged 41 to 92 [12]. Ulman Lindenberger and Ulrich Potter working at the Max Planck Institute for Human Development in Berlin had developed a neat statistical technique that allowed us to ask the question in a different way [13]. It is easy to calculate the total variance in scores on tests of speed, memory and intelligence between our volunteers. This variability between people must, of course, be due to differences in each and all of countless and diverse factors, such as their genes, health, education and everything else that distinguishes them from each other. Ulman and Ulrich's computational method allowed a new step. We could compute how much *that particular part of the difference between people in intelligence that is associated with differences in their ages* is **also** associated with differences in their information processing speeds. This gives us an estimate of the maximum extent to which declines in memory and intelligence in old age can be specifically related to general slowing of information processing speed.

The estimates we got surprised us. The proportion of the differences between volunteers' intelligence test scores that was associated with differences in their ages between 41 and 92 years was 16 per cent. This is a very modest amount but, if we turn it around, we see that it means that up to 84 per cent of the differences in intelligence test scores between members of an elderly sample is **not** associated with differences in their ages but, rather, *with all the other factors apart from growing old,* such as their genetics, lifestyles, experiences and environments, that have made them different from each other throughout their long lives. Although the effects of age on intelligence are real, they are not alarmingly great. The surprise was that of this very modest proportion of only 16 per cent of specifically age-related differences in scores on intelligence tests, between 96 and 100 per cent was associated with differences in scores on speed tests. Relationships between age and speed and memory test scores were quite similar. While only 8.8 to 14.2 per cent of differences in memory scores were associated with differences in age, between 65 and 83 per cent of these proportions were separately associated with differences in speed.

This seemed to be very strong support for Tim's general slowing idea, but there still remained an obstinate logical problem that correlations between variables, even if they are as powerful as those we had found, may strongly suggest, but cannot prove causal relationships. It remained theoretically possible that speed, memory and intelligence are all reduced by some other unidentified factor, such as neurophysiological changes in the brain and central nervous system.

In aging brains, nerve cells continually die and connections between them are lost. Only a very small proportion, are replaced. Individual neurones become less efficient as they age and are invaded by fatty lipids and eventually perish. As a result of these cell deaths, the entire brain gradually shrinks. The scars resulting from cell death can be picked up on brain scans as small white specks indicating areas of damage: lesions in the white matter of the brain. The more of these white matter lesions that appear, the greater is the diffuse damage that has occurred. Many convincing studies in Rotterdam had shown that increases in white matter lesions are strongly associated with slowing of the information processing rate but also, to a smaller degree, with declines in intelligence and memory.

Because of this continual cell death, we gradually lose brain volume. The amount of this loss can be measured by relating the current size of older people's brains to the inner volume of their unchanged skulls. Increases in white matter lesions and reduction in brain volume are associated with declining efficiency of brain blood circulation. This means that measures of brain blood flow, brain volume and white matter lesions are coarse, but easily measured, indices of how far gross brain aging has progressed. It had been known for many decades that an increase in white matter lesions, loss of brain volume and a decline in brain blood circulation are associated with slower information processing speed, and poorer intelligence and memory. To labour this point yet again: to find correlations between measures of gross neurophysiological changes and scores on tests of speed, memory and intelligence is not yet convincing evidence that they *cause* these losses, but it makes it very likely that this is what happens.

Behavioural data alone cannot resolve this logical problem. For this we need the new technology of obtaining images of living brains. Ninety Manchester volunteers had agreed to brain scans. We had found that the amount of brain volume that they had lost over periods of 8 to 20 years closely predicted the declines in their intelligence and information processing speed that we had separately measured over the same periods. This gave us data to which we could apply Lindenberger and Potter's computational method to see whether scores on speed tests continued to account for age-related changes in tests of intelligence and memory with age after the number of white matter lesions, amount of loss in brain volume and level of brain blood circulation were also taken into account. We found that brain volume, blood circulation and white matter lesions accounted for *all* of that particular proportion of the differences between volunteers' information processing speeds that was associated with the differences in their ages. In contrast, these same neurophysiological measures accounted for only some, but by no means all of the differences in their scores on intelligence and in memory tests [14, 15, 16]. Better statistical methods sharpened this picture [17]. They showed that white matter lesions and loss of brain volume and circulation affect memory, intelligence and scores on tests of frontal lobe function and planning not just because they slow information processing. These gross neurophysiological changes also had effects on memory and intelligence that are separate from and additional to their effects on information processing speed. General slowing does not drive *all* the mental changes we experience in old age.

This is not surprising because tests on brain-damaged young adults and stroke patients have shown that while memory and intelligence do depend, to some small extent, on the integrity and efficiency of the entire brain, they depend much more strongly on the integrity and efficiency of particular, quite small local brain areas. For example, since pioneering work by Brenda Milner in Montreal in the early 1980s [18] we have known that damage to the hippocampus, a relatively modest area of the inner brain, causes catastrophic losses of memory. Work in many laboratories, including in our own in Manchester, has shown that brain changes with age are not only diffuse, involving the entire brain, but that in particular individuals they can be local and specific. Older people who, for one reason or another, have suffered an unusually severe loss of volume of their hippocampus have exceptionally poor memories. John Duncan, working at the MRC Cognition and Brain Sciences Unit in Cambridge UK, has shown that performance on intelligence tests is markedly affected by specific damage to the pre-frontal cortex of human and monkey brains. Aging affects the entire brain, and so all of our abilities. It seems that slowing of information processing is the best behavioural index that we have of the progress and amount of these gross and diffuse brain changes, but we must always remember that brain changes in old age are not just general and diffuse but also local and specific. For example, if changes in circulation affect some brain locations, such as the frontal lobes, more than others, they can also be specific, and so affect some abilities more than others. Gross brain aging can not only cause closely comparable changes in all of our mental abilities but local changes, superimposed on these global changes, can also affect some abilities earlier and more than others. Changes with age are not equal over the entire brain but are, to some degree, patterned. We have not yet mapped what are the most frequent patterns of brain changes that occur, or how the effects of these specific and patterned changes are modified by global and general changes. Meanwhile we should acknowledge Jim Birren and Tim Salthouse for being the first to raise the important questions that started this search.

Note

1 See Dava Sobel's excellent book, *Longitude*. Barnes and Noble, New York, 1997.

References

[1] Birren, J. E. and Botwinick, J. (1955). Age differences in finger, jaw, and foot reaction time to auditory stimuli. *Journal of Gerontology*, 429–432.

[2] Cerella, J. (1985). Information processing rates in the elderly. *Psychological Bulletin*, 98, 67–83.

[3] Albert, M. (1993). Neuropsychological and neurophysiological changes in healthy adult humans across the age range. *Neurobiology of Aging*, 14, 623–625.

[4] Haug, H. and Eggers, R. (1991). Morphometry of the human cortex cerebri and cortex striatum during aging. *Neurobiology of Aging*, 12, 336–338.

[5] Rabbitt, P. M. A. (1997). Methodologies and models in the study of executive function. In Patrick Rabbitt (Ed.), pp. 1–38, *Methodology of Frontal and Executive Function*. Hove UK, Psychology Press.

[6] Rabbitt, P. M., Lowe, C. and Shilling, V. (2001). Frontal tests and models for cognitive ageing. *European Journal of Cognitive Psychology*, 13, 1–2, 5–28.

[7] Shilling, V. A., Chetwynd, A. M. and Rabbitt, P. M. A. (2002). Individual inconsistency across measures of inhibition: An investigation of the construct validity of inhibition in older adults. *Neuropsychologia*, 40, 605–619.

[8] Verhaegen, P. (2014). *The Elements of Cognitive Aging. Meta-analyses of Age-Related Differences in Processing Speed and Their Consequences*. Oxford, Oxford University Press.

[9] Jensen, A. R. (1982). Reaction time and psychometric g. In H. J. Eysenck (Ed.), pp. 93–182, *A Model for Intelligence*. Berlin, Springer Verlag.

[10] Rabbitt, P. M. (1966). Do individual differences in speed reflect "global" or "local" differences in mental abilities? *Intelligence*, 22, 69–88.

[11] Salthouse, T. A. (1985). Speed of behaviour and its implications for cognition. In J. E. Birren and K. Werner Schaie (Eds), pp. 400–426, *Handbook of the Psychology of Aging*. New York, Van Nostrand Reinhold.

[12] Rabbitt, P. M. and Anderson, M. (2006). The lacunae of loss? Aging and the differentiation of cognitive abilities. In E. Bialostok and F. I. M. Craik (Eds), Ch. 23, pp. 331–342, *Lifespan Cognition: Mechanisms of Change*. Oxford, Oxford University Press.

[13] Lindenberger, U. and Potter, U. (1998). The complex nature of unique and shared effects in hierarchical linear regression: Implications for developmental psychology. *Psychological Methods*, 3, 218–230.

[14] Rabbitt, P., Ibrahim, S., Lunn, M., Scott, M., Thacker, N., Hutchinson, C., Horan, M., Pendleton, N. and Jackson A. (2008). Age-associated losses of brain volume predict longitudinal cognitive declines over 8 to 20 years. *Neuropsychology*, 22(1), 3–14.

[15] Rabbitt, P., Scott, M., Lunn, M., Thacker, N., Lowe, C., Pendleton, N., Horan, M. and Jackson, A. (2007). White matter lesions account for all age-related declines in speed but not in intelligence. *Neuropsychology*, 21(3), 363–372.

[16] Rabbitt, P., Scott, M., Thacker, N., Lowe, C., Jackson, A., Horan, M. and Pendleton, N. (2006). Losses in gross brain volume and cerebral blood flow account for age-related differences in speed but not in fluid intelligence. *Neuropsychology*, 20(5), 549–556.

[17] Rabbitt, P., Mogapi, O., Scott, M., Thacker, N., Lowe, C., Horan, M., Pendleton, N., Jackson, A. and Lunn, D. (2007). Effects of global atrophy, white matter lesions, and cerebral blood flow on age-related changes in speed, memory, intelligence, vocabulary, and frontal function. *Neuropsychology*, 21(6), 684–695.

[18] Scoville, W. B. and Milner, B. (2000). Loss of recent memory after bilateral hippocampal lesions. *The Journal of Neuropsychiatry and Clinical Neurosciences*, 12(1), 103-a.

22

PAYING ATTENTION

In the great evolutionary arms race, our ancestors had to choose between being quick or dead, but a limit to how fast they could deal with the world was set by the maximum speed with which their nerve cells could transmit information. Helmholtz discovered that this is about 30 metres a second for frogs and humans. Modern recording equipment now shows that the fastest human motor neurones can transmit impulses at up to 120 metres a second – 432 kilometres an hour, which is about the cruising speed of a passenger jet. Flies have even faster neurones that only need to carry messages over the tiny distances within their minuscule bodies, gaining an infuriating advantage over our longer and slower chains of neurones that carry signals from our eyes to our brains to trigger ponderous muscles to try to swat. We should find it impossible to overcome this disadvantage, but tiny brisk flies sometimes lose to gigantic sluggish humans. How do we do it?

To compensate for their sluggishness, our big brains have found ways to predict what will happen and to begin to respond before the critical moment. Our species, and most others, could not have survived if they had not mastered how to live in the immediate future. We keenly realise this when first learning to drive when everything happens too fast until we learn to read the road to anticipate events rather than beginning to brake only when a pedestrian actually steps off a curb. It takes long experience to learn all the critical cues that we need to make such predictions, but our modest accident rates per millions of motorist hours and miles show that we can become rather good at this. As we grow older, our reaction times become slower, but we also have longer experience of the world to guide our predictions. May improving our capability for instant prophecy compensate for increasing slowness in old age?

It is outrageously over-dramatic to illustrate a peaceful discussion of cognitive gerontology by pointing out how infantry learn to crouch instantly and appropriately when they learn the characteristic noise of dangerous missiles and to ignore innocuous incoming fire. But the accuracy to which this skill is developed is remarkable.[1] Thankfully, we cannot study such highly motivating contingencies in (most) universities where we make tame experiments in which volunteers respond, as fast as possible to a signal, such as a flash of light that occurs after a different warning signal, such as a buzz. These simple experiments nevertheless answer interesting questions such as what is the minimum time in which people can reach optimal preparation for an event? Does this minimum preparation time change if we have to choose between different responses to each of several different signals? How effectively do warning signals tell us not just *when* something will happen but also *which* of several different things it is going to be? What happens when we are wrong-footed because what happens is not what we expected? How does old age affect all these different kinds of anticipation?

A different scenario is searching in cluttered environments to find a plausible match to a sock in a drawer or a friend in a crowd. For this, we must construct in our minds search images of the unique sock or acquaintance we seek and compare what we see against these until we get a match. An extension of this scenario is how long we can remain attentive-efficient as the time for which we have to expect events increases from milliseconds to hours. Do we become less efficient as the number of different things that we try to detect increases? Does our ability to detect signals start to decline sooner if they are faint or are in some way perceptually degraded? A different question is how rapidly and efficiently we can switch attention from one aspect of a fast, demanding task to another, and how old age affects our ability to do this.

Preparing

To measure the shortest time in which we can prepare ourselves to recognise and deal with any expected event we vary, from trial to trial, the time between a warning buzzer and a light flash to which a volunteer must respond. Young adults improve by about 50 milliseconds as the period between the warning and the signal changes from 50 to 200 to 300 milliseconds. People aged between 65 and 75 need from 50 to 100 milliseconds more to reach optimal preparation and, even when they are allowed this extra time, do not gain as much as the young. Age not only slows our responses when unexpected events occur but also increases the time that we need to predict and prepare for them.

To compare how well older and younger people can use different cues to anticipate different events we arranged that the same warning signal was followed by one of several different signals that required a different response from the volunteers. We know from daily experience that any kind of advance information allows us to make faster and more accurate responses. By giving volunteers a different warning signal for each of several signals, we can let them know not only when a signal is due but also which of several different signals it is going to be. Now the old gain more than the young from this advance information but they also need longer to use it. Regrettably, if they are wrong-footed because the unexpected happens they are delayed longer and make more impulsive errors than the young [1].

Being prepared

To be able to use some events to predict others that regularly follow them is helpful but, for creatures locked in evolutionary wars, this alone is hardly enough to guarantee survival. We also need to scan our environment to detect things that we need or fear. In laboratories we can mimic this activity by asking volunteers to search pictures of crowds for familiar faces or displays of text for particular words or letters of the alphabet. Humans are very good at this, needing less than a tenth of a second to scan each of a number of faces or words to decide whether it is one that they seek. Chimpanzees not only scan faster than humans but can also remember, after only a 200-millisecond view of a display, all of nine digits that were present and the random positions in which they were located.[2]

So we seem to have lost some of our edge since we came down from the trees to stroll the savannah, but we still have the vital skill of interpreting our environment remarkably fast. Ulrich Neisser asked young volunteers to search displays of random letters for particular target letters and found that they hardly slowed when the number of different letters they had to search for increased from two to ten. He argued that our ability to simultaneously scan a busy visual field for many different things means that our minds can maintain separate independent search processes each checking for the presence of a different one of many possible objects [2, 3]. In an influential paper, "The Multiplicity of Thought", he developed this fine insight further by arguing that the brain can not only run several different search programs simultaneously and in parallel but can also simultaneously follow several different trains of thought, allowing only the one that becomes most relevant to eventually access consciousness [4]. I think that this brilliant insight has been undervalued and is still insufficiently explored. This seems a good explanation for the amazing versatility of sportsmen, athletes, comedians and orators who seem able to switch from one to another pattern of movement or theme of argument so fast and effortlessly that it is difficult to imagine how they can manage to do this unless they concurrently run many separate brain-programs, each anticipating a different contingency. Unfortunately, as we age, unlike Neisser's young volunteers the more different things we search for, the slower we become. One way of thinking about this is that, like wireless servers, we have limited broadband with which we can simultaneously run parallel programs. I believe that it is the gradual loss of the ability to simultaneously run several programs in parallel that causes us to lose the ability to simultaneously hold ready many different associations and connections between arguments and that this is the cause of the duller, single track thinking and conversation to which old age can eventually reduce us. Loss of thought bandwidth makes us less versatile and flexible and, in a word, duller.

While I was a research student in Cambridge UK, I spent much of my time on the problem of how we manage to recognise not only single things but all members of entire classes of things so extraordinarily rapidly and accurately. To test this, I asked people to spend an hour or longer scanning long lists of letters and numbers. Research students in psychological laboratories depend on each other for many things, but most particularly to volunteer for each other's experiments. This mutual aid is far more important than just a companionable exchange that can conveniently be repaid in coffee or beer. Research students learn far more from each other's critical comments and insights than from their official mentors. Unfortunately, my experiments were so outrageously boring that not even offers to repay my colleagues by spending hours testing their least congenial rats persuaded them to help.

I could not replace the insights and advice that I might have obtained, but luckily other brains were available. In the late 1950s the Science Area was overstaffed by middle-aged and elderly porters who were glad, especially on bleak wet days, to sit in a warm room for an hour staring at displays of letters and numbers and scoffing bribes of tea and biscuits. I felt easy about testing older rather than young adults because the received wisdom then was that although older people make decisions more slowly, there was no evidence that they processed information in any qualitatively different way. I was confident that the porters would do the same things in the same ways as my young colleagues, just a bit more slowly. Finding that I was wrong altered the direction of my research and determined that I would spend my next 50 years as a Cognitive Gerontologist. I am still grateful to those kindly and patient porters.

The older porters did not just scan displays of letters and numbers more slowly than Neisser's young adults and my young colleagues. The more targets that I asked them to find, the longer they took. Further experiments found that this was partly because young people can search very economically for unique particular details, such as a single horizontal line or a looped tail that distinguish one letter from others. The older porters seemed not to be able to discover and use only those particular minimum key aspects of a symbol that distinguish it from all the others among which it was embedded. They seemed to check even aspects of targets that were redundant in the sense that they were shared with many or all of the background items that they had to scan and so did not uniquely identify them [5].

It seemed that old age reduces the precision with which we can learn the least, and so the most efficient, cues to distinguish what we are looking for from everything else we can see. We have less precise and efficient search images. We are also less selective and economical in the range of cues that we examine, failing to find and use just those critical cues that distinguish symbols from each other.

Staying prepared

A different question is how long we can efficiently keep on attending? The first experiments that asked this question were made during World War II, driven by the need to discover for how long military personnel can remain competent at watching for brief, and sometimes very rare, faint and blurred signals on radar displays. The first studies were made at the then Medical Research Council Applied Psychology Research Unit in Cambridge UK [6] and, during the 1950s and 1960s, keen interest by military sponsors supported dozens of studies of how well young humans can efficiently remain vigilant. The general conclusion was that young, fit and motivated people can accurately detect all the rare, critical signals that occur during a watch of 15 minutes or less but begin to make increasing numbers of errors as watches become longer. Military sponsors are not much interested in the abilities of elderly people. Industrialists are, because quality control operatives must rapidly and accurately detect small flaws in streams of newly manufactured items, such as ripples in sheets of plate glass or flaws in the weave of fabrics as they rapidly trundle along conveyor lines. This encouraged work by Raja Parasuraman and his colleagues in the USA on whether older people could maintain vigilance as well and as long as young adults.

In these studies, volunteers watched for appearances of simple targets, such as the digit 9, in continuous streams of numbers. As far as I know, these were the first experiments that found no differences between young and older people. Unfortunately, as tasks were made more difficult and volunteers had to meet additional mental demands, such as noticing sequences of two successive digits that added up to nine, the older began to miss signals earlier and more often than the young [7]. The same contrast occurred when old and young were compared on displays on which signals were made harder to see. If all signals could be easily identified, the old were as competent as the young, but if they were difficult to make out, the old began by detecting as many as the young did but as time went on, began to miss many more of them. Age seems to have very little effect on the ability to remain alert for simple signals but the more difficult the task, the sooner the elderly become tired and begin to miss things.

One issue is that as we get older our vision and hearing becomes less efficient so that we have to strain to see or hear signals that once strongly claimed our attention. As a deaf old person, increasing mind wandering during lectures convinces me that this is a problem. I checked this by comparing how long older people who had good hearing and those who were slightly deaf could continue to detect particular designated target phrases like "as I have said" that repeatedly occurred during an unusually boring lecture. Deafer volunteers begin to miss target phrases earlier in a lecture. My personal conviction is that they also began to miss more of the content.

To continuously pay attention costs effort. The harder the task, the more effort is needed. The earliest discussions of vigilance and sustained attention emphasised the gradual ebbing of arousal – the ability to sustain mental effort – as the main cause of increasing numbers of missed signals as a watch drags on. The common language expression "staying alert" is a useful and exact description. Even those of us elderly who do not (yet) find ourselves nodding off suddenly, rudely and often, find that we must make greater efforts to pay attention over long periods.

As far as I have been able to discover, the scientific literature on old age is strangely silent on this problem, but autobiographies written in old age often stress this point. Bertrand Russell complained that in his later years he could not work at a high level for longer than two hours a day. My subjective experiences agree with the comments of lawyers and judges that excusing people aged over 70[3] from jury service is wise and humane, not because they tend to lose the ability to understand and remember complex legal arguments but simply because they find it increasingly hard to sustain attention over long periods of time. On the same theme, the excellent chess-tutor Jeremy Silman blogging on how to beat skilful older opponents recommends that, when one is the younger player one should try to spin things out because "Old Guys get tired very, very quickly". This seems to me to confront a hard reality with which all of my generation must struggle. We become less able to pay attention, particularly to difficult tedious stuff for hours at a time. Loss of mental stamina, ebbing of energy and slow slackening of the muscles of the mind now seem to me to be some of the most important ways in which our abilities change as we grow old. I cannot understand how we have neglected these problems for so long. I should dearly love to set to work on them – If only I could summon the energy.

Notes

1 See Robert Graves, "Goodbye to All That".
2 No, this does not mean that chimpanzees learn to read digits or to count. It just means that lazy psychologists have used convenient digits instead of other patterns equally arbitrary for apes.
3 An official acknowledgement that things are changing and that current generations of septuagenarians are more vibrant than their predecessors is the proposed UK legislation to extend the period of potential service to 75.

References

[1] Rabbitt, P. M. (1964). Set and age in a choice-response task. *Journal of Gerontology*, 19(3), 301–306.
[2] Neisser, U. (1964). Visual search. *Scientific American*, 210(6), 94–102.
[3] Neisser, U. (1963). Decision-time without reaction-time: Experiments in visual scanning. *The American Journal of Psychology*, 76, 376–385.
[4] Neisser, U. (1963). The multiplicity of thought. *British Journal of Psychology*, 54, 1–14.
[5] Rabbitt, P. M. (1967). Learning to ignore irrelevant information. *The American Journal of Psychology*, 80, 1–13.
[6] Mackworth, N. H. (1956). Vigilance. *Nature*, 178, 1375–1377.
[7] Deaton, J. E. and Parasuraman, R. (1993) Sensory and cognitive vigilance: Effects of age on performance and subjective workload. *Human Performance*, 6, 71–97.

23

GOOD TIMES AND BAD TIMES

Like everybody else I have always been convinced that I have good days on which my ideas flow rapidly, my questions are unusually sensible and my answers sometimes to the point. Also bad days on which body and mind are sluggish and even routine tasks get done badly, if at all. Now, in old age, good days seem rarer and when they happen no longer make everything magically easy. Is this just the lethargy of an under-exercised academic no longer paced by brilliant and energetic students and colleagues or just another sign of aging of my mind?

As usual, experimental psychologists have the thankless job of trying to find objective evidence for things that we all intuitively know, in the hope of teasing out deeper explanations for why things are the way they are. Like housekeeping, this is essential, but there is no glory in it.

To decide whether people become more or less variable as they grow older, we must first define the time-scales and contexts in which we study them. We can ask whether age affects variability from moment to moment during any fast, continuous task; whether it affects changes in average performance from session to session and day to day; or whether it alters the way our abilities change with the rhythms of the world we live in such as the 24-hour cycle of day and night or the slow cycle of the seasons. As we shall see, our measures of all of these different kinds of variability are both statistically and biologically related to each other. Let us start with moment-to-moment variability.

Variability from moment to moment

Variability from moment to moment is the easiest to study. We simply ask people to respond as fast and accurately as they can to scores or hundreds of signals that occur one immediately after another, and compare how older and younger people's reaction times vary from trial to trial. Older adults' reaction times always vary more but, because they respond more slowly, this may be an artefact of measurement. So we have to allow for a change in average speed to take this into account.[1] When we do this we find that slowing of responses in old age does not explain this marked increase in variability from moment to moment and so from response to response during a continuous task [1].

The next issue is whether this increase in moment-to-moment variability with age is caused by changes in the brain and central nervous system or whether it is due to changes in our muscles that make us less able to exert a constant force or to make movements at a constant speed. For example, variability of grip strength and muscle tremor increases with age and this can contribute to variability in some tasks that require delicate and precise manual control. Authors such as K. M. Newell [2] suggest that increases in this kind of variability with age represent increases in the random noise in the neurological systems that control movements. This may be so, but muscle tremor and variability in grip and contraction speed cannot explain the entire variability of reaction times in easy continuous tasks because we can separately measure the movement component and the decision component of responses. When we do this, we find that age has little or no effect on movement times but a large effect on decision times. So we have to ask further questions as to how age affects variability in simple, continuous tasks.

Variability from day to day

Brian Stollery's remarkable charm and empathy persuaded Manchester residents to volunteer for one of the longest, most tedious psychological studies ever made. Ninety robust Mancunians came to our laboratory at the same time and on the same weekday for every week in a year to do the same easy and, I am embarrassed to admit, excruciatingly boring sets of six different tasks. We had learned to expect dogged good humour from these fine people, but they were also extraordinarily cheerful and generous. As Christmas approached we enviously watched Brian's testing rooms fill with bright festive cards, small heart-warming bottles of Special Cognac and humorous plastic ducks and cats. For the first 25 weeks, volunteers' striking improvements on all tasks showed that however old we become we can get much better at almost anything, however tedious, if we try long enough. Our gains may be smaller and slower than they once were, we may never again reach levels of performance possible when we were young, but gaining any new skill is always an enduring and encouraging achievement. Their performance after they could no longer improve at any of the tasks that he gave them, could then show whether their ages and intelligence test scores affected how their performance changed from moment to moment and from day to day. Paul Osman [1] used it to show that people who show greater variability during one session of any particular task on one day will also vary more on it from day to day. This is not a matter of differences in their brains or biology but statistical inevitability.

To visualise this, imagine that all the reaction times that a person makes during the year in which he is tested represent a year-pool from which, each week, he draws a sample of a few hundred to oblige Brian Stollery. If all the reaction times in each of these weekly samples are very dissimilar – that is, they have a very loose and sloppy distribution with a large spread (standard deviation about the mean) – this must be because the distribution of times in the volunteer year-pool also has a similarly large spread, (standard deviation). The converse must also be true: that is, if the standard deviation of the reaction-times in the year-pool is large, so must be the standard deviations of the samples drawn from it, and so also will be the standard deviation of the distribution of the means of these many samples. So, if a person's reaction times are more variable within every test session that he experiences so must also be the averages of each of the runs of reaction times that he produces week after week.

Excellent studies at the University of British Columbia (e.g. [3]) confirm that moment-to-moment variability increases with age and with poor health, brain damage and the onset of Alzheimer's dementia. Dementias and brain damage also increase day-to-day variability.

To find an answer to the question that had motivated us required us to test whether individuals' perform better on some days than on others and this proved a quite different and much more challenging problem. We had to find a statistical method that would tell us whether their performance on all of six very similar tasks that we gave them rose and fell together from session to session. Luckily, just because this problem was difficult it interested two Oxford statisticians, Mary and Dan Lunn, who found a solution and used it to show that Brian's volunteers did, indeed, have unusually "good" days on which they scored better and "bad" days on which they scored worse than average on all tests.[2] A paper called (by Dan) the Lunn–Rabbitt–Lunn procedure explains how to do this, and will soon be published. We had not tested enough people to be able to confidently tell whether these rises and falls were more frequent for older individuals and for those who scored lower on intelligence tests. Science does not stand still and a series of papers by Ulman Lindenberger and associates have found no consistency in daily performance across ranges of different tasks [4, 5]. So, although all humans have realised for many thousands of years that we do have relatively good days on which we are better and bad days on which we are worse, there is still no formal evidence for this. It may be that to pick up such changes we need to compare volunteers on very similar tasks, day after day, as Brian Stollery did, or to study people whose general health is marginal so that it fluctuates from day to day and they show large variations in competence over time. My observations of myself and other people of my age, and the elderly Manchester volunteers' comments convince me that this is still a problem worth further research and that alas our bad days may become more frequent as we grow older. If this is so, why might this happen?

The most obvious explanation is that we all have days on which we are physically below par, whether because of minor infections such as colds, loss of sleep, depression or various kinds of over-indulgence. Brian kept careful records of his volunteers' reports of their sleep on nights before test days and of their feelings of general physical well-being during testing, but these did not account for the ups and downs found in their day-to-day performance. Nevertheless, his questionnaires might not have detected small changes in well-being and so efficiency. Older people are more vulnerable than the young to minor health problems that can affect their performance. It also seems likely that, as we age, we gradually lose spare capacity and so always have to perform closer to our limits so that even small perturbations that do not bother the young might significantly affect us.

Regular changes during each day

A different issue is how aging affects our sensitivity to the marked and consistent changes in ability that humans and nearly all other animals experience during the 24–hour cycle of each day. These periods of relative liveliness and lethargy are termed "circadian rhythms" and affect nearly all living creatures from micro-organisms to fish, insects, birds, and ourselves and other mammals. As we note in Chapter 24 on sleep, it is sensible for animals to adjust their cycles of activity to the rotation of our planet. Sense organs and survival strategies ideal for daylight fail in the dark and vice versa. Surprisingly, the same circadian rhythms of activity locked to an invisible day are found even in creatures such as fish, amphibians and arthropods that have lived for many hundreds of generations in the perpetual darkness and unchanging temperature of deep caves and, at least for some millipedes [6], can be re-set if even after generations in darkness they are again exposed to alternating light and dark periods. Most over-ground-dwelling animals' cycles of activity are in step with and calibrated by alternations of light and dark. This re-setting is essential because durations of night and day vary throughout the year particularly in high Northern and low Southern latitudes.

To gratify their scientific curiosity or for strange personal whims, some resolute humans have deliberately lived for months in unchanging environments such as deep caves. They continue to experience the same cyclical patterns. They only gradually slip out of synchrony with surface days and nights because, like many other animals, they seem to be naturally locked to a 23 rather than a 24-hour cycle. Under normal circumstances, this shorter cycle is continually re-set by sunrise and sunset [7]. Very recent data from a simulated Mars Mission shows that patterns of sleep-disturbances in an unchanging environment are not only hazardous to efficient management of tasks, but that their extents and impacts vary much more between individuals than had previously been realised.

Circadian rhythms seem to be wired into human physiology in many subtle ways, many of which we do not yet understand. They are controlled by an area of the brain called the suprachiasmatic nucleus that seems to act as a biological clock co-ordinating activity in most bodily systems. One way it does this is by controlling the secretion of melatonin, a hormone that entrains the activity of diverse body systems including gut movements, blood pressure and the heart and circulatory system. This has implications for our vulnerability at different times of day that are not completely understood. For example, a team of cardiac specialists [8] reported a study of 2250 patients who had suffered cardiac arrests and found that deaths were fewest in those whose episodes occurred between midnight and 6.00am, after which the probability of death increased by up to four times by midday. Men and women of all ages showed the same patterns.

A fascinating back-story to how the suprachiasmatic nucleus is re-set by alternating light and dark is the discovery, by Russell Foster, that among the light receptors in the retinas of our eyes we have ganglion cells that are evidently responsive to light but contribute nothing to our conscious visual experience. Studies of completely retinally blind patients have found that they can tell, with complete accuracy, whether they are in the light or dark, although they angrily protest that they can see no light at all and are simply guessing. This "blindsight" is another good example of how consciousness is by no means the main business of the brain. Nearly all of the brain's computations are done without bothering to keep the conscious mind informed.

One easily measured biological marker that tracks circadian rhythms is body temperature. This increases by about half a degree Celsius from a low at around 2.00 am to reach a high in early afternoon. Another marker is secretion of corticosteroids, hormones that are associated with experience of greater stress and requirements for higher levels of activity. During the mid-1960s, a group working in Cambridge UK examined relationships between body temperature, loss of sleep and performance (see for example [9]). In a series of papers, they reported strong relationships between time of day or night, body temperature, corticosteroid secretions and performance on simpler mental tasks. They also checked the common impression that humankind divides into larks who get up early but fade in the evenings, and owls who rise late and reluctantly, but warm up during the day and can continue to perform until quite late at night (See Chapter 24 on sleep for a more detailed discussion).

These stable differences make it important for us to discover and make the best use of our best times of day, but an annotation by Simon Folkard suggests that different times of day may suit different aspects of our mental performance. He gave young people tests of logical reasoning at six different times of day and found that while all of them became faster from 8.00 am to 2.00 pm and then rapidly slowed down, their accuracy remained constant. Simon suggests that the time of day affects how fast we can work, but our ability to be accurate and to monitor ourselves for errors remains relatively constant.

Does old age affect circadian rhythms in amounts of activity, body temperature and corticosteroid secretions? Studies of age-related changes in cycles of body temperature have not yet found convincing differences between old and young adults. Perhaps this is because such studies are hard to make and so far have used only small, and so possibly unrepresentative, groups [10]. Elderly people are more likely to rate themselves as being morning persons, but it is not clear that measures of differences between them and young adults support this [11]. Studies of animals seem to agree with these intuitions about our human experience. As rats, gerbils and hamsters age, their periods of activity and quiescence became less clear-cut and more fragmented. Beagles have been kept in indoor pens in which only artificial lighting distinguishes their "days" from their "nights" and, when false dawns arrive, older dogs take longer to get themselves together and start moving about. During their "days", old dogs are less active and take more rest. Continuous artificial daylight does not seem to disrupt their activity rhythms, but when they are housed in pens in which they can move at will between indoor and outdoor areas, bright sunlight and alternating light and dark re-synchronised their activity rhythms [12]. The beagle experience seems close to my own and that of my contemporaries. We have, and some of us even use, the option to re-set our rhythms, even in the long nights of the Oxford winters by using brighter and bluer artificial illumination. Confirming my personal responses to the seasons, both older and younger Norwegians living in Tromsø complained of seasonal affective disorders with depression during their long dark winters and manic behaviour in long bright summer days [13]. Similar results are reported for Lapps, Finns and North Japanese, with comments that eating habits, weight fluctuations and sleep patterns all alter in autumn and spring. One review suggests that extreme annual daylight fluctuations in high northern latitudes not only bring about fluctuations in mood, sleep patterns and activity cycles but also in the incidence of eating disorders and some cognitive problems. The middle aged and elderly are particularly vulnerable, but adolescents seem to be little affected [14]. Older humans living in residential facilities, especially those who are cognitively impaired, seem to benefit from emphasised alternations between light and dark to calibrate their increasingly haphazard activity rhythms.

It is still not clear whether fragmentation of the normal cycles of greater and lower arousal in old age is a cause or a symptom of brain changes that bring about cognitive losses. Older animals that are forced to adopt fragmented activity cycles also tend to perform more poorly at simple memory and learning problems. I suspect that the same is true of older humans. Disorientation from altered activity cycles is a problem for 24/7 societies in which shift work is becoming normal. Although young adults can learn to adapt to working patterns involving night shifts, they find this uncomfortable and the disturbances of their normal activity patterns and difficulties in managing to get sufficient sleep does make them more prone to mistakes and accidents. A recent review of the literature concludes that middle-aged and elderly workers have even greater problems in adjusting to night shifts, causing loss of productivity and increased risk of accidents after age 45 [15]. Following a different line of thought, other researchers checked whether body temperature and activity cycles are suppressed if people are kept inactive in a constant environment, and asked younger and older volunteers to spend 36 hours in bed. The body temperature cycles of old and young did not differ but older volunteers' normal sleep patterns were more disrupted and, probably because of this, they began to perform less well on mental tests.

The general story is that as we and other mammals age our circadian rhythms are more likely to become disrupted and the differences between daily peaks and troughs of competence that are clearly marked in the young, gradually become less evident. There is also evidence that the effects of disruptions of our normal 24-hour cycles by forced irregular alternations of light and dark, shift work or jet lag become more severe as we grow older. These difficulties can be eased and our rhythms recalibrated and locked into the cycle that best suits our lifestyle by arranging our living conditions to achieve emphatic alternations of bright light and darkness.

This evidence that old age tends to disrupt our circadian rhythms and so reduces differences between peaks and troughs of competence does not answer the different question of whether it may also systematically alter our activity cycles so as to make us more lively and capable either early or late in the day. In general, elderly rats and humans seem to be most comfortable and competent at the peaks of their activity cycles which tend to occur in the mornings. Further studies found that laboratory rats, housed in facilities that exposed them to the normal day/night cycle, were better at learning and memory tasks in the mornings than later in the day. These reports also suggest that elderly humans strongly prefer to be tested in the mornings than in the afternoons, and that their scores on memory tests vary accordingly [16, 17, 18]. A problem with interpreting evidence of this kind is that not only physiology, but also lifestyle changes in old age. We also noted that UK volunteers preferred to come to morning rather than afternoon testing sessions, but they explained that this was because in both Newcastle and Manchester our laboratories were near the city centres so that they could conveniently have lunch and do their shopping after visiting us. Also public transport is less crowded in mid- and late morning than during the afternoon. In Manchester and Newcastle, volunteers of all ages performed equally well during morning and afternoon sessions. Diaries that our volunteers kept also showed no clear systematic changes in their normal patterns of sleep and other activities. That said, my own personal experience, and that of my tiny poll of my generation, is that while old age has not yet made us splendidly glad and confident morning people it does, sometimes, seem to weigh more heavily on our afternoons.

Notes

1 We do this statistically by calculating the "Coefficient of Variation" (CV), which is simply the standard deviations of people's response times divided by their means.
2 In a recent study Ulman Lindenberger and associates gave volunteers several different tasks on many occasions but did not find that they consistently improved or got worse on all of them on different days. Since I am convinced of Brian's data and Mary's statistics I suspect that a critical difference may be that the Berlin group used many different tasks while Brian used versions of the same reaction-time task. I am looking into this.

References

[1] Rabbitt, P., Osman, P., Stollery, B. and Moore, B. (2001). There are stable individual differences in performance variability both from moment to moment and from day to day. *Quarterly Journal of Experimental Psychology*, 54, 981–1003.
[2] Sosnoff, J. J. and Newell, K. M. (2006). Are age-related increases in force variability due to decrements in strength? *Experimental Brain Research*, 1, 86–94.
[3] Hultsch D., Macdonald, S. W. S. and Dixon, R. A. (2002). Variability in reaction time performance of younger and older adults. *Journal of Gerontology, B*, 57, 101–115.

[4] Schmiedek, F., Lövdén, M. and Lindenberger, U. (2009). On the relation of mean reaction time and intraindividual reaction time variability. *Psychology and Aging*, 24(4), 841–857.

[5] Schmiedek, F., Lövdén, M. and Lindenberger, U. (2013). Keeping it steady: older adults perform more consistently on cognitive tasks than younger adults. *Psychological Science*, 24(9), 1747–1754.

[6] Koltra, A. J., Sharma, V. K., Marimuthu, G and Chandrashakaran, M. K. (2000). Presence of circadian rhythms in the locomotor activity of a cave-dwelling millipede glyphiulus cavernicolis sulu (Cambilidae Spirostreptida). *Chronobiology International*, 6, 757–765.

[7] Lavie, P. (2001). Sleep-wake as a biological rhythm. *Annual Review of Psychology*, 52, 277–303.

[8] Thakur, R. K., Hoffman, R. G., Olsen, D. W., Joshi, R., Tresch, D. D., Aufderheide, T. P. and Ip, J. H. (1996). Circadian variation in sudden cardiac death: Effects of age, sex, and initial cardiac rhythm. *Annals of Emergency Medicine*, 27(1), 29–34.

[9] Blake, M. J. F. (1967). Relationship between circadian rhythm of body temperature and introversion–extraversion. *Nature*, 215, 896–897.

[10] Monk, T. H., Buysse, D. J., Reynolds, C. F., Kupfer, D. J. and Hoiuck, P. R. (1995). Circadian temperature rhythms of older people. *Experimental Gerontology*, 30, 455–474.

[11] Duffy, J. F., Dijk, D. J., Hall, E. F. and Czeisler, C. A. (1999). Relationship of endogenous circadian melatonin and temperature rhythms to self-reported preference for morning or evening activity in young and older people. *Journal of Investigative Medicine*, 47, 141–150.

[12] Siwak, C., Tapp, T., Dwight. P., Zicker, S. C., Murphey, H. L., Muggenburg, B. A., Head, E., Cotman, C.W. and Milgram, N. W. (2003). Locomotor activity rhythms in dogs vary with age and cognitive status. *Behavioral Neuroscience*, 117, 813–824.

[13] Haggag, A., Eklund, B., Linaker, O. and Gotestam, K. G. (2007). Seasonal mood variation: An epidemiological study in northern Norway. *Acta Psychiatrica Scandinavica*, 81, 141–145.

[14] Magnussen, A. (2000). An overview of epidemiological studies on seasonal affective disorder. *Acta Psychiatrica Scandinavica*, 101, 176–184.

[15] Folkard, S. (2008). Shift work, safety and aging. *Chronobiology International*, 25, 183–198.

[16] May, C. P., Hasher, L. and Stolfus, E. R. (1993). Optimal time of day and magnitude of age differences in memory. *Psychological Science*, 4, 326–330.

[17] Winocur, G. and Hasher, L. (1999). Aging and time of day effects on cognition in rats. *Behavioural Neuroscience*, 11, 991–997.

[18] Winocur, G. and Hasher, L. (2004) Age and time-of-day effects on learning and memory in a non-matching-to-sample task. *Neurobiology of Aging*, 25, 1107–1115.

24

SLEEP

Pulp-fiction thrillers regularly exploit the idea that old people need little sleep and that any sleep that they get is shallow. A light-sleeping elderly victim is the first to sense a creeping perpetrator. Psychologists have always had to accept the thankless task of testing folklore. Are the elderly, like Capitoline geese, effective early warning systems against night raiders? Do they need less sleep? Is the sleep that they get really lighter? Do they wake up more often? Do they go to bed later or get up earlier? Do they catch up on missed night-time sleep by daytime napping so that, like Belloc's Uncle Bill "at last [their] sole idea of fun is sitting snoozling in the sun"? Are the changes in sleep patterns that many of us experience in our old age "normal", and so probably benign, or are they signals of impending troubles? How do changes in our sleep patterns relate to the regular circadian rhythms of greater and less alertness that people of all ages experience during the 24-hour cycle? Does the cost of losing sleep become greater in old age? Do we dream more, dream less or dream differently?

Parents know that new-born babies sleep a great deal but also have unpredictable fits of wakefulness that painfully clash with their own cycles. As they grow, infants sleep less but adolescents still seem to need more sleep than adults. Sleep scientists use measurements of changes in the electrical activity of the brain to distinguish different depths of sleep. In shallow sleep, the rhythms of brainwaves, electrically recorded through the scalp, are fast and pronounced and bursts of rapid eye movements (REMs) are frequent. When awakened from shallow sleep, people often report that they have been dreaming. In deep sleep, the electrical activity of their brains is less intense, their brainwaves are shallower and slower, their eye movements become fewer and wakened sleepers seldom report dreams. An analysis of 65 studies published before 2003 [1] found that sleep duration decreased during childhood and adolescence ("but only in studies conducted on School Days"!). After adolescence, the amount of deep sleep declined throughout young adulthood to middle age. People older than 65 took longer to drop off after they had settled down to sleep (increased sleep latency), awoke more often (reduced sleep efficiency) experienced longer and more frequent episodes of REM sleep and less slow wave deep sleep. These changes occurred together with, and were related to, increases in incidence of illnesses and medications and episodes of obstructed breathing accompanied by uproarious snoring (sleep apnoea). Apnoea is especially likely to occur if we get fat. Clinicians are concerned that apart from being a trial to our partners and families, the choking and spluttering of apnoea are warning signs of respiratory and circulatory problems that reduce blood-oxygen supply to the brain and so are a marker for shortened life and so faster fading of mental abilities.

Can we distinguish between the effects of normal aging and those of illnesses, medications and obesity? A survey of exceptionally healthy men aged from 11 to 83 found that the percentage of total sleeping time spent in deep sleep declined from 18.9 per cent between 16 and 23 to only 3.4 per cent between 36 and 50. After 50, proportions of deep sleep did not change, but the average time that people spent awake at night increased by 28 minutes and amounts of shallow REM sleep increased by about 10 minutes per decade [2].

In another study, volunteers aged from 18 to 32 and from 60 to 75 slept fitted with wrist-worn activity-recorders [3]. The older did not spend less time in bed at night but woke up sooner and more often after they had first fallen asleep. Records of their 24-hour activity patterns suggest that they might have made up for any sleep that they lost during the night by napping during the day, particularly during the two hours before going to bed. Up to 42 per cent of the young adults also took daytime naps, but this did not seem to affect how long they slept at night. Those young who napped, typically did so in the early afternoon. Bright illumination in the late evening tended to delay the times that elderly people went to bed and also their first night-time awakenings. For those enduring dark northern winters, lamps that mimic the colour and intensity of sunshine and include ultra-violet radiation did help to maintain a regular sleep/wake cycle. For all elderly people, taking more exercise and losing weight reduced evening napping and delayed the first night-time awakening.

Do older men and women have different sleep patterns? A large Icelandic study found that both men and women aged 61 to 84 spent about the same time, 7.25 hours, in bed [4]. Among both men and women, 9.6 per cent had difficulty getting to sleep and 16 per cent awakened earlier than they would have preferred. Reports of insomnia increased with age. Men reported more frequent night-time awakenings (an average of 1.2 times) than women (0.8 times). The wretchedness of male prostate problems probably account for this.

Are these changes in sleep-style natural and harmless or symptoms and by-products of ominous changes? In old age, a main factor associated with disturbed sleep is obesity, which is also linked to high blood pressure and difficulties with breathing (apnoea). Sleep disturbances are also associated with depression. Getting to sleep is miserably difficult when we are afflicted by persistent sad or anxious thoughts, and disturbed sleep can also be a sign of clinically significant depression associated with changes in brain biochemistry.

Research on the effects of loss of sleep and drowsiness on mental competence has been driven by interest in the effects of irregular sleep patterns on relatively young people – military personnel and young workers on rotating shifts. Surveys find that shift workers in their fifties and sixties, who are much younger and fitter than people of my old/old generation, are more debilitated by night work and adapt less completely to difficult shift rotations than their colleagues in their thirties and early forties. Less is known about the effects of forced changes in sleep/wake cycles in old age. Both field [5] and laboratory studies [6] find that older people are less tolerant of changes in their normal sleep/wake patterns. A French government survey found that shift work increased complaints of sleep disturbances and use of sleeping pills until the early fifties, but it is hard to tell from this whether adaptation continues to become less efficient as middle age progresses, because those workers who are most inconvenienced tend to resign. We are all aware of problems of jet lag but, counter-intuitively, the little evidence that we have suggests that, if anything, it may become less stressful in old age. A small study of 85 people travelling eastwards across ten time zones found that the older reported slightly less inconvenience [7]. An even smaller study of airline pilots crossing seven to eight time zones in both directions [8] found that those over 50 were less tired and anxious after travel, but also points out that aging airline pilots have a practical incentive to report low stress and round the clock alertness. A still smaller laboratory study of 14 men found that the few middle-aged volunteers aged from 32 to 52 complained more than those who were older and younger about the effects of a six-hour advance in their schedule [9].

Daily rhythms

Even conspicuously brisk and energetic young adults experience regular fluctuations in physiology and so in mental competence during the 24-hour day/night cycle. Like nearly all other organisms, from bacteria to whales, we are locked into cycles of activity in which we do as little as possible during those periods of day/night alternation when there is less to be done (and possibly more to be afraid of) and concentrate our activities into those periods when we can most effectively, and safely, get on with making our livings. This strategically cyclical activity occurs in night-active as well as in day-active creatures (in reversed form of course) and is accompanied by appropriate physiological changes. We humans increase our body temperatures from a low at around 2.00 am and then warm up steadily through the later morning to reach a peak at about midday, followed by a sharp and brief decline (nicknamed by applied psychologists the "post-lunch dip") in the early afternoon (the "dip" is not actually tied to eating, though there is evidence that lunching increases midday lethargy). This dip is followed by a rapid rise to a new, lower peak followed by a slow decline through the evening and into the night. Those of us who are unlucky enough to live in cold gloomy countries glumly speculate that the early afternoon drop in body temperature with accompanying increased temptation to drop off to sleep, and ease in doing so, is still inappropriately wired into our physiology as a legacy of the tropical suns that our remote ancestors once enjoyed, but preferred to avoid from noon to 3.00 pm.

The effects of very prolonged loss of sleep, for 100 hours or more, has been studied in some extreme laboratory experiments and is still illustrated by the antics of very minor celebrities who, having exhausted all other devices of competitive exhibitionism have voluntarily kept awake for periods of 72 hours or longer. They always experience catastrophic declines in problem solving, memory and decision making and, in many cases, disorientation and hallucinations.

Much of the pioneering work on the effects of modest sleep deprivation was done during the 1950s and 1960s at the Medical Research Council Applied Psychology Research Unit in Cambridge, where fit young sailors, aged from 20 to 35, were kept awake for periods of 24 to 48 hours. They grumbled, but it was surprisingly hard to find any changes in their scores on brief, lively tasks. Quite slight changes in competence were most sensitively detected by simple, repetitive and boring tasks, lasting from 15 to 60 minutes. These simulated paying attention to radar displays on which signals were brief, inconspicuous and rare. Volunteers showed much less change on lively fast-paced tasks in which they responded as rapidly as possible to simple signals for periods up to 30 minutes. The average speed of their responses to signals did not change, but they did begin to make occasional, unusually slow responses taking 1.5 seconds or longer. The number of these "blocks" increased, both as any single session continued and after they had been sleep-deprived. Decades of subsequent research show that the effects of sleep deprivation are greatest on long boring tasks in which the flow of events is slow, regular and dull, and when critical signals seldom appear. Bob Wilkinson's early work suggests that sleep deprivation can impair performance even on mentally challenging and engaging activities like playing chess. It seems possible that this distinction between large effects of sleep deprivation on simple, boring tasks and apparently smaller effects on difficult and engrossing tasks is only apparent. Bob's volunteers were relatively unskilled chess players so changes in the levels of their play were hard to evaluate. More to the point, future investigations of the effects of sleep deprivation on really difficult skills, such as making complicated tactical decisions in military emergencies or playing chess at a high level, may well find that loss of sleep markedly reduces the limits of performance that we can reach.

Michael Blake, a member of the same research team, checked associations between fluctuations in body temperature and mental performance during the 24-hour cycle [10]. He persuaded volunteer (or perhaps that should be "volunteered") sailors to swallow huge pills containing sensors that wirelessly transmitted their body temperatures.[1] Fluctuations in body temperature and in mental ability were linked. Sailors' temperatures and their scores on simple tasks rose from dawn to lunchtime, then fell slightly, (even when illicit midday cold lager consumption had been detected and successfully banned), then rapidly rose and again gradually cooled off until bedtime and beyond.

Larks and owls

An interesting sub-plot was that these sailors, like the rest of us, fell into incompatible sub-groups whose answers to personality questionnaires classify them as "introverts" or "extroverts". Introverts reject suggestions such as "Do you seek thrills" or "Do you hate spending time alone" with which extroverts enthusiastically agree [11]. It seems that these individual differences in sensation avoidance and sensation-seeking signal basic differences in physiological rhythms. People with high introversion scores warm up early in the morning but, being thoroughly decent souls, do not make a nuisance of themselves. They continue to warm and are increasingly active and competent until they experience their own, slightly earlier post-lunch dips and then, after a late afternoon recovery begin to cool off and are ready for bed relatively early. Extroverts begin to warm later than introverts, are relatively sluggish during the morning but take longer to cool down at night, and remain lively until a late bedtime. Many studies suggest that introverts, in general, have higher intelligence test scores than extroverts and also tend to be socio-economically more successful. This may be thought of as a scientific validation of the adage "Early to bed and early to rise, makes a man healthy, wealthy and wise", but extroverts are unimpressed and argue that, whether or not this is true they have much more fun.

Daily fluctuations in body temperature, activity and mental competence are clearly marked in young people. As we age, the same rhythms persist but their peaks and troughs become less pronounced. A study in 2000 compared sleep patterns and body temperature in older and young adults [12]. As age increased, body-temperature cycles shifted slightly towards a lark pattern of early morning arousal and late evening decline. Other studies suggest that age smoothes out fluctuations in physiological indicators, such as blood pressure, that keep step with fluctuations in body temperature and activity and are also associated with changes in arousal and in the need for sleep. Recent reviews agree with this general picture [13, 14] and suggest that these fluctuations are driven by changes in the level of activity of a particular brain location, the suprachiasmatic nucleus, a structure associated with the hippocampus that seems to be the main driver of circadian changes in level of activity and which, in many individuals, suffers tissue loss in old age.

Apart from cyclical changes in body temperature and blood pressure, an important factor controlling the sleep-cycle is production of melatonin, a hormone secreted by the pineal gland. In youth, when our entire physiology is in excellent shape, melatonin production peaks in the evening promoting sleep, and declines through the night to a low in the morning when we need to wake up and become active. Melatonin secretion reduces in old age and we produce less when it is most needed to promote sleep at bedtime and during the night. Some investigators have suggested that disturbances of sleep patterns in old age, with consequent depression and seasonal affective disorder (SAD) can be alleviated by the use of bright illumination with an ultra-violet component to counteract early dusk combined with melatonin replacement therapy. Other reports suggest that the effects of melatonin are temporary and are soon lost when treatment is discontinued. Because there are disadvantages to regularly taking melatonin, it is not a panacea for sleep problems or for re-calibration of disturbed activity cycles in old age.

Is poor sleep a warning signal?

The strong links between loss of sleep quality and survival in old age are well documented but should inform rather than alarm us. Loss of sleep quality and duration are significantly related to high blood pressure, depression and obesity. All these conditions are indicators that other pathologies are probably present and, for this reason, are associated with reduced odds of survival. Obesity, in particular, is a sign of a generally inauspicious lifestyle with overconsumption of food, and possibly also alcohol, low levels of exercise and so higher risks of illnesses such as cardiovascular problems and diabetes. All these factors shorten life and accelerate cognitive decline. Obesity is also directly linked to sleep disturbances because it is strongly associated with snoring and sleep apnoea, with the associated possibility of brain-oxygen-starvation. These links sufficiently explain correlations between reduced sleep quality and earlier death. In short, we are not more likely to get ill and die because of poor sleep quality: it is rather that poor sleep quality is a warning sign that other things are not going well. For example, poor sleep quality is a key symptom associated with depression and anxiety - for which there may be good and objective, but non-physiological causes. Loss of sleep quality is a signal to pay more attention to our general well-being, and possibly to take medical advice, but not a reason to panic. Though these webs of associations between sleep problems and other more serious conditions are statistically significant – in the sense that they are very unlikely indeed to occur only by chance – they are very far from being so strong that insomnia, even if coupled with outrageous snoring, is a death sentence. They just mean that we may have problems that we should address to maximise our chances of enjoying a very long and competent and hopefully nocturnally quieter old age.

In our sleep what dreams may come?

My daytime life is still excellent but night life is dull because my dreams are rubbish. They used to be more exciting. At age seven, most nights I could depend on being chased by wolves around my boarding school; in my twenties I was often in dodgy spaceships that leaked oxygen to vacuum and in my thirties and forties I continually hurried to miss trains and planes. In my fifties and sixties, I turned up, late, to speak at meetings where I had no idea what to say or had brought the wrong PowerPoint. In my seventies, I am relegated to the audience at dull lectures and, last night, the talk was so bad that I dreamt that I was dozing off. Since I am what my profession has made me, I do not puzzle about the metaphysics of dreaming that one is going to sleep but read what my colleagues have to say about dreaming in old age.

A problem is that we can only count and analyse dreams that people remember. While we are dreaming, bursts of electrical activity that can be recorded from our brains through our skulls (EEG) are brief, fast and accompanied by REMs behind closed eyelids. If we are woken during shallow REM sleep, we often report dreams. During periods of deeper sleep, we make few or no eye movements, our slower EEG waves are interrupted by brief bursts of very fast activity ("sleep spindles") and, if woken, we seldom report dreams. Older people have less deep and more shallow sleep, but with fewer REM episodes. They also report fewer dreams in total, so it has been assumed that they may dream less often. I have not found data on a key question whether, over all awakenings from REM, the ratio of reports of dreams to reports of no dreams changes with age. This might give a clue to whether age affects the number of dreams or, rather, memory for dreams.

One report suggests that older people who are more intelligent, and particularly those who have better visual memories, recall more, richer and more complex dreams [15]. Older women also recall more, and more vivid dreams than old men. This can be linked to evidence that keeping memory and intelligence depends on good health and slower brain aging and underlines the fact that women are more durable than men. This could also explain the general agreement that older people remember fewer dreams [16]. If dream-dearth in old age is caused by brain aging, this would explain why those, like women, who live and stay healthy and mentally able to a greater age, experience slower brain aging and keep up their dream productivity. I prefer to believe, like some researchers, that we begin to recall fewer of our dreams from early middle age onward simply because we regard them as irrelevant and tedious [17] or because that is how they become as our lives attenuate. A study of 1,065 men and 1,263 women aged from 17 to 92 and a review of results from this and 174 other experiments report consensus that older women recall more of their dreams than old men [18]. This is apparently not just because they live longer and tend to keep sharper than men of the same age because, even in childhood, there is a small sex difference that reaches a lifetime maximum in adolescence.

As always, there are many possible explanations for sex differences. Women not only recall more of their dreams than men, but report having livelier dreams and pay more attention to them. A small study followed 11 men and 11 women over 20 nights and found that the men's dreams were not more aggressive, but starred more male characters and single characters and included more noise effects but were also, more often, not in colour. Female dreams were more complex and emotionally intense and polychromatic. This makes it understandable that women become more involved with their dreams than men do. Their dreams are better-plotted, stage-managed and produced and directed, and so more entertaining.

The internet opens remarkable new opportunities for researchers to collect huge, rich data-sets. A web study of 19,367 women and 4,634 men (the difference in samples adds to the evidence that women are more interested in discussing their dreams) found that, at all ages younger than 60, women reported more nightmares per month (4.4 as against 3.3). Their average monthly nightmares increased from age 10 to 19 and from 20 to 30 and then declined. Men's nightmare averages were constant from age 10 to 39 and then also reduced [19].

Apart from the differences in their dream quality and frequency, men and women seem to dream of slightly different things. This is unsurprising because when they are awake they are pre-occupied by different things. Our daily lives and our dreams share the same scenery and stage-props. So androids dream of electric sheep and a large study of truck-drivers found that they tend to dream of driving trucks [20]. Much of the difference in the emotional quality of dreams can also be explained by differences in life context. Formal studies find that in both women and men, sex and aggression in dreams diminishes from youth through middle age and later life. Notoriously, physically and emotionally stressful single events and stressful occupations feed their traumatic scenarios into dreams.

Findings that most of our dreams are replays of bits of our daily lives account for observations that, contrary to the stock ideas of romantic fiction, older people do not seem to dream more often of the past than the young do [21]. Although we have a greater proportion of past to present to dream about, the now, whether exciting, disturbing or uneventful, takes control. The cloth of old dreams is woven from the threads of old lives.

To radically change our lives to make our dreams more entertaining does not seem worthwhile but, although the scripts are hard to control, it seems possible that we can at least liven up the production values and the scenery. A persistent theme in dream research has been whether people dream in colour or black and white. At least one study suggests that, for whatever reason, young men are more likely to have monochrome dreams than young women but that colour comes to dominate in old age. The evidence for late colour is debated. At least one study insists that black and white becomes less frequent, but this is to support an argument that black and white and technicolour dreams reflect changing trends in television and cinema. Some of my colleagues claim that this does not just reflect changes in cinema during lifetimes in early affluent societies, but also the more rapid transitions from monochrome to colour television in later developing countries. I am puzzled that while all of us, except the colour blind, see life in vivid colour the tints of our dreams may be strongly determined by the media that we watch. But at least the chance that this may be so offers easy solutions to dream enhancement: buy a huge bright TV set and use it to watch others' exciting lives.

Note

1 The sensitivity of these pills was confirmed by their instant detection of cold lager during the sailors' unscheduled escapes from the laboratory, appropriately to the Volunteer pub on Trumpington Road.

References

[1] Ohayon, M., Carskadon, M. A., Guilleminault, C. and Vitiello, M. V. (2004) Meta-analysis of quantitative sleep parameters from childhood to old age in healthy individuals: developing normative sleep values across the human lifespan. *Sleep*, 27, 1255–1273.

[2] Van Cauter, E., Leproult, R. and Plat, L, (2000). Age-related changes in slow wave sleep and REM sleep and relationship with growth hormone and cortisol levels in healthy men. *Journal of the American Medical Association*, 284(7), 861–868.

[3] Yoon, I-Y., Kripke, D. F., Youngstedt, S. D. and Elliott, J. A. (2003). Actigraphy suggests age-related differences in napping and nocturnal sleep. *Journal of Sleep Research*, 12, 87–93.

[4] Gislason, T., Reynisdottir, H., Kristbjarnason, H. and Benediktsdottir, B. (1993) Sleep habits and sleep disturbances among the elderly—an epidemiological survey. *Journal of Internal Medicine*, 234, 31–39.

[5] Harma, M. I., Hakola, T., Akerstedt, T. and Laitinen, J. T. (1994). Age and adjustment to night work. *Occupational & Environmental Medicine*, 51, 568–573.

[6] Monk, T. H., Buysse, D. J., Carrier, J. and Kupfer, D. J. (2000). Inducing jet-lag in older people: Directional asymmetry. *Journal of Sleep Research*, 9, 101–116.

[7] Waterhouse, J., Edwards, B., Nevill, A., Carvalho, S., Atkinson, G., Buckley, P., Reilly, T., Godfrey, R. and Ramsay, R. (2002). Identifying some determinants of "jet lag" and its symptoms: A study of athletes and other travellers. *British Journal of Sports Medicine*, 36, 54–60.

[8] Tresguerres J. A., Ariznavarreta, C., Granados, B., Martin, M., Villanúa, M. A., Golombek, D. A. and Cardinali, D. P. (2001). Circadian urinary 6-sulphatoxymelatonin, cortisol excretion and locomotor activity in airline pilots during transmeridian flights. *Journal of Pineal Research*, 31, 16–22.

[9] Moline, M. L., Pollak, C. P., Monk, T. H., Lester, L. S., Wagner, D. R., Zendell, S. M., Graeber, R. C., Salter, C. A. and Hirsch, E. (1992). Age-related differences in recovery from simulated jet lag. *Sleep*, 15, 28–40.

[10] Blake, M. J. (1967). Time of day performance in a range of tasks. *Psychonomic Science*, 9(6), 349–350.

[11] Blake, M. J. F. (1967). Relationship between circadian rhythm of body temperature and introversion–extraversion. *Nature*, 215, 896–897.

[12] Dijk, D-J., Duffy, J. F. and Czeisler, C. A. (2000). Contribution of circadian physiology and sleep homeostasis to age-related changes in human sleep. *Chronobiology International*, 17, 285–311.

[13] Czeisler, C. A., Dumont, M., Duffy, J. F., Steinberg, J. D., Richardson, G. S., Brown, E. N., Sánchez, R., Ríos, C. D. and Ronda, J. M. (1992). Association of sleep-wake habits in older people with changes in output of circadian pacemaker. *The Lancet*, 340, 933–936.

[14] Hofman, M. A. and Swaab, D. F. (2006). Living by the clock: The circadian pacemaker in older people. *Ageing Research Reviews*, 5, 33-61.

[15] Waterman, D. (1991). Aging and memory for dreams. *Perceptual and Motor Skills*, 75, 355–365.

[16] Giambra, L. M., Jung, R. E. and Grodsky, A. (1996). Age changes in dream recall in adulthood. *Dreaming*, 6 17–31.

[17] Schredl, M. and Reinhard, I. (2008). Gender differences in dream recall: A meta-analysis. *Journal of Sleep Research*, 17, 125–131.

[18] Herman, S. and Shows, W. D. (1984). How often do adults recall their dreams ? *International Journal of Aging and Human Development*, 18, 343–254.

[19] Nielsen, T. A., Stenstrom, P. and Levin, R. (2001). Nightmare frequency as a function of age, gender, and September 11 2001: Findings from an internet questionnaire. *Dreaming*, 16, 145–158.

[20] Schredl, M., Funkhauser, A. and Arn, N. (2006). Dreams of truck-drivers: A test of the continuity hypothesis. *Imagination and Personality*, 25, 179–186.

[21] Giambra, L. M. (2006). Daydreaming about the past: The time setting of spontaneous thought intrusions. *The Gerontologist*, 17, 36–38.

[22] Schwitzgebel, E., Huang, C. and Zhou, Y. (2006). Do we dream in colour? Cultural variations and scepticism. *Dreaming*, 16, 36–42.

25

TIME PASSING

About once every five years, my ex-teacher and later friend, Richard Gregory, used to ring me up to ask some slightly odd but interesting questions. I miss these contacts greatly and am sad that this can no longer happen. He was extraordinarily brilliant and genial, his great intelligence, amiability and sense of fun warmed lecture rooms and the halls of the "Science Exploratoriums" that he set up in Bristol and elsewhere. Because I had revered him while I was an undergraduate, it was still deeply flattering when I reached my seventies for him to hint that I might know something that he did not. His last question arose because, in his eighties, he had become uncomfortable that his personal time now seemed to be passing much faster.

Richard knew that we do not have sense organs to directly perceive time, as we have for light, sound or touch. Time is not registered; only events are. We only know time from successions of different things, whether movements of the sun and moon or our own heartbeats. We cannot directly perceive time but we notice and remember changes. As Einstein remarked "Time is what prevents everything happening at once".

Richard asked whether I thought that, if we begin to process information more slowly as we grow old, we must surely also feel that the world is speeding up. As usual, he also had a second agenda. He had read some comments that I had once made on findings that people who have higher scores on intelligence tests process information faster. He thought, in his typical phrase, that it would be "jolly" if very high intelligence (he never, throughout his long life, had any reason to learn modesty) meant that although he might now be running out of years he might still pack an exceptionally large number of rich experiences into those he had left.

His arithmetic seems plausible. Over the last 50 years, my reaction times on a particular two-choice reaction time task have slowed from 220 to 250 milliseconds just a little less than the average of 1 millisecond a year. On Richard's theory, this might slow my subjective time by 15 per cent. This seems to agree quite well with my subjective feeling about how far I am now slipping behind the world, but I do not think that it completely explains my existential predicament.

Judging very short periods of time

A more direct test than comparing older and younger peoples' reaction times is to ask them to estimate durations of brief time intervals. The Junior Time Lord of British Psychology, John Wearden,[1] with Alison Wearden and I did this [1] and found no support for Richard Gregory's intuitions or, indeed, for the general complaint by older people that time now passes much faster for them. Average estimates of durations of periods of around 500 milliseconds did not change between 60 and 80. Older volunteers did not consistently underestimate time intervals, but they were more variable in their judgements. Those with higher intelligence test scores also gave us less variable estimates, but were no more accurate on average. Richard's sustained zest for new experiences in his eighties was probably due to other enviable aspects of his psychology than fast information processing speed.

In psychology, what goes around comes around. In 2013, anyone planning any behavioural experiment can be certain that they are not the first. John, Alison and I were late riders on this magic roundabout. Wilhelm Wundt was the first scientist to call himself a "psychologist" and set up the first Psychological Laboratory in Leipzig in 1879, where his associate Munir tested how accurately people could estimate and compare brief time intervals varying from a few tenths of a second to several seconds. Like Richard 100 years later, Munir was curious to discover how the rates of events that we might notice during intervals of time affect our judgements of how long these intervals have been. He also compared the effects of different kinds of noise during the intervals that volunteers judged: music, but also trains of clicks that were softer or louder and occurred at fast or slow rates. He found that the faster the trains of clicks, the longer they judged the intervals to be. This might encourage the idea that people use the number of clicks they hear as a rough measure of interval durations and that although they are well aware that the rates of the clicks varied from trial to trial they nevertheless interpret more clicks as occupying a longer time interval. However, counting clicks cannot be a complete explanation for his findings because his volunteers also judged that intervals were longer if the same number of clicks was made louder. Our estimates of brief intervals may be affected by our levels of arousal by louder noises or by other stimulation.

Hour glasses of our lives

A Dutch historian of psychology, Douwe Draaisma [2], has written the most charming and scholarly account of memory, and in particular of time perception in old age, that I have read. To illustrate the difference between two kinds of account of the ways in which age might affect accuracy of time estimation I shamelessly plagiarise his touching image of Ernst Jünger, author of a treatise on time, *Das Sanduhrbuch* – the hourglass [3]. Jünger kept on his desk an antique hourglass given to him by a lost friend. He reflects that as the years pass the hourglass gradually records briefer intervals of time because the sand moving from the upper to the lower bulb slowly wears and widens the pinched funnel between. This is a neat, direct mechanical metaphor for one possible effect of human aging: it may gradually alter the accuracy of any physiological and neurological mechanisms, the "biological clocks", that we may have that allow us to estimate the passage of time independently of what is happening around us. This does not at all exclude the different well-documented fact that changes in time perception are related to changes in the efficiency of our memory because, to judge whether time is speeding up or slowing down, we have to compare our memories of two or more periods. So our perception of the duration of any period of time depends on what and how much happens to us during it, and also on how completely we remember this cluster of events. It follows that the ways in which we make these comparisons, and so our estimates of time passing, depend on the precise questions about the passage of time that we ask.

On the hourglass analogy, we could use our awareness of regularities in our internal processes to serve as clocks. We need not be conscious of doing this. Our bodies continuously go through regular cycles of changes of which we are hardly aware, like heartbeats or breaths or, on a longer scale, digestive processes or regular fluctuations in light and temperature or alternations of sleepiness and wakefulness during the 24-hour cycle. As we noted in Chapter 23 on variability, humans who choose to live in unchanging environments such as deep caves for periods of weeks can still, quite accurately, estimate the number of days they have been there but gradually drift from a 24-hour towards a 23-hour day. Consequently, as their imprisonments grow longer they increasingly overestimate their stays.

The state of our bodies also alters the accuracy of our perceptions of short periods of time. An excellent review of studies on the effects of body temperature on time estimation up to 1994 [4] found general agreement that the higher our body temperature is the faster we feel that time is passing (and the faster also our rates of counting that we might use to estimate time). There are fewer studies of the effects of lowering body temperature. Among these is Alan Baddeley's classic finding [5] that divers in wet-suits counted seconds more slowly while they were chilly underwater at temperatures of four degrees centigrade than when they were warmer ashore (I am not aware of any unambiguous evidence that slight changes in body temperature in old age bias our body clocks in a similar way).

Judging the durations of very brief periods, of the order of seconds or milliseconds, is an unsatisfying way to explore the general elderly experience of a subjectively accelerating world. What we older people usually mean when we say that time has speeded up is that when we remember and compare stretches of our lives, more recent periods seem to have passed more rapidly than more distant days, weeks and months. We compare remembered spans of experience and, since we cannot perceive time directly, this means that we must compare the remembered densities of experiences over different parts of our lives. How we manage to estimate intervals of a second or less is quite a different matter. On the gross scale of hours, days, weeks and years, time perception depends on comparing what we can remember about what went on during these different parts of our life-cycles.

Memories of past times

William James's *Principles of Psychology* [6] is possibly the most intelligent and certainly the most elegantly written account of the philosophical and experiential foundations of our subject. James and his contemporaries were well aware that subjective time speeds up with age and that this must have something to do with our memories of our past lives. When James wrote his "Principles", a common explanation of why the same period should seem longer when remembered by a child than by a geriatric is that both tend to compare any recent period against the span of their total conscious experience. So, for a 10-year-old last year is 10 per cent but for a 70-year-old only 1.4 per cent of an entire remembered existence. James dismisses this as "a description rather than an explanation". Although shrewd commentators such as Douwe Draaisma [2] and Claudia Hammond [7] agree with him, I think that James's dismissal is unfair and that it actually makes an equally interesting, but rather different point that is better remembered because it is expressed in one of the most lushly written paragraphs in the psychological literature:

> [When we are young] apprehension is vivid, the retentiveness strong, and our recollections of that time, like those of a time spent in rapid and interesting travel, are of something intricate, multitudinous and long drawn-out. But as each passing year converts some of this experience into automatic routine which we hardly note at all, the days and weeks smooth themselves out in recollection to contentless units and the years grow hollow and collapse.
>
> [6]

Apart from the wonderful image of the collapsing hollow years of later life, James's addition to the idea of age-relative time is only that we compare the remembered experiential content rather than the duration of times past. The memory of tumults of events experienced during bustling youth and recorded by an efficient young memory system may indeed seem more "multitudinous and long-drawn-out" than records of uses of semi-conscious routines preserved in the sparse and fading archive of an older brain. But both of these explanations of the time-acceleration effect depend on the same logic: to judge the duration or the speed of time we must make comparisons. The unstated corollary is that we can compare periods of time by making whatever comparisons suit us, or are available, and that the answers that we get will differ with the particular contrasts that we make. We can, and sometimes do, compare the past months or years with the entire, long or short, stretches of our lives. We can also make other comparisons and James's luminously expressed insight is that because we can also compare periods of time in terms of the experiences that filled them, our judgements will depend on the number of experiences that we had, how vivid they were and how efficient our brains were and are while they recorded and now retrieve them. If we compare the remembered events of the last year against all the events of our entire lives, the contrast will be much greater for someone aged 10 than for someone aged 70.

Not all events are equally striking or equally well remembered and so equally easy to place in the correct time-sequence. A more important issue is the difference between judging whether time, at this current moment, is passing rapidly or slowly and whether a designated past period of life now seems to have gone by fast or lethargically. This point was eloquently made by Jean-Marie Guyau, whose brief life (1854 to 1888) elapsed during a romantic period of European philosophy. Ornate nineteenth-century prose bedecks some quite simple ideas on the different perspectives of time at different ages:

> Youth is impatient in its desires; it wants to devour time ahead, but *time drags*. Moreover the impressions of youth are fresh and numerous, so that the years are distinguished in thousands of ways and the young man looks back on the previous year as a succession of scenes in space.

> Old age, by contrast, is more like the unchanging scenery of the classic theatre, a simple place, sometimes a true unity of time, place and action that concentrates everything around one dominant activity and expunges the rest; at other times the absence of time, place and action. The weeks resemble each other, the months resemble one another, the monotony of life drags on. All these images fuse into a single image. In the imagination time is abridged. …If you want to lengthen the perspective of time then fill it, if you have the chance, with a thousand new things.…when you look back you will notice that the incidents along the way and the distance you have travelled have heaped up in your imagination, all these fragments of the visible world will form up in a long row and that, as people say so fittingly, presents you with a long stretch of time.

> Quoted in [2].

This anticipates James's reasoning and almost trumps his prose style. The number of events we can recall determines what we might feel as the grain or texture from which we infer the duration of time past. It also introduces the new idea that we can mentally map time as we can map space and that the same simple mental imagery of positions along a continuum can be used for both. Time maps are simpler than space maps because they need only one rather than three dimensions. We can, of course, choose to use more if we wish. As Richard Gregory might well have said on a typically expansive day "Wouldn't it be *jolly* if we could talk about 'East of tomorrow and under yesterday'".

The anecdotage of newly retired academic colleagues suggests a different kind of comparison that persuades them that their times have speeded up. Colleagues who retired some while ago smile at newcomers whose typical comment on their recent self-employment is "Retirement! What Retirement? I just don't have time for all the things I want to do". This returns us to a modified version of Richard Gregory's insight. As we get old we can do fewer things in an hour or a day. If we feel that we are falling behind some actual or self-imposed schedule, perhaps because of growing inertia as well as because we now work more slowly, we are likely to feel that time is rushing by inconveniently fast (though it is also true that if we pause to think about it we may no longer be able to remember how we spent it). If we measure time by the number of things that we would like to do but fail to complete, the world seems to have speeded up alarmingly.

Time at the magic mountain

Novelists' explorations of the subjective experience of time are much more entertaining than dull experimental tests. They provoke enjoyable introspections and mutual sharing, codifying and defining of the minutiae of our subjective experiences. They are not at all a waste of time just because they deal in metaphors rather than numbers, but this does make it hard to bring them to any objective test. (Perhaps the certainty of never reaching any definite conclusion is a defining characteristic of any good topic for a novel or for a conversation in a pub or at a dinner-table.) Arguments tend to be about which metaphors are the most attractive or best catch our personal experience rather than whether and how they can be tested. At any rate, the journey is more entertaining than a time-slowing trudge through the current experimental literature. For example, the staple of all discussions of the elastic properties of subjective time is a fine novel, Thomas Mann's *The Magic Mountain*. At the top of Mann's mountain is a tuberculosis asylum that his hero visited only to discover that he, himself, had contracted the romantic malady and then had to take up residence as a patient. From the new perspective of the summit he is able to compare the deadly slow passage of any current day with the speed-blur of remembered previous weeks and months. At the peak of the magic mountain, time passes achingly slowly because of the impatient wait for something, anything at all, to happen. In contrast, summit time, remembered at the foot of the mountain, seems to have been remarkably brief because there were so few events to mark its passage.

Mann's comparisons illustrate why it does not seem wise to try to check or to improve literary descriptions by tedious attempts at empirical analysis. They show that the answers we get from people will depend on the precise questions that we ask: for example, how fast do you think that time is, currently, passing? How fast did it pass yesterday? How rapidly did it seem to pass in Paris or Beijing? or at different periods of your life? and so on, endlessly. For all these reasons, it is hard to find any experimental methodology that would give us sensible numerical estimates of the degrees of difference in subjective speed of time experienced by younger and older people. Subjective judgements of relative speed of time's passing can tell us whether and when older people feel that time is passing quickly or slow but give us little idea *by how much* old age or other existential circumstances distort time judgements.

How long ago was that?

Another thing to try is to use people's estimations of how much time has passed since a significant event occurred. Sully [8] may have been the first to notice that, after a sensational trial, the convicted criminal spent three years in prison, but on news of his release, there was general surprise that his sentence was already over. In a more recent large formal study Crawley and Pring [9] asked UK residents to remember the month and year of significant and widely publicised events ranging from Elizabeth II's 1977 Silver Jubilee to the 1989 fall of the Berlin Wall and Mrs Thatcher's resignation. Those aged from 35 to 50 gave incorrectly recent dates, but those aged over 50 gave incorrectly early dates. Crawley and Pring argue that this shows that the older we are the faster time seems to pass. To me it seems possible to argue either way. We can either suppose that time has gone by faster for the young because they date events as being more recent or, as Crawley and Pring seem to argue, it goes by faster for the old because they can pack fewer remembered time markers into the actual calendar years and so feel that past events are nearer than they really were.

At this point, obstinate empiricists will be annoyed that there does not seem to be any direct way to decide who is right (or, if I correctly intuit what *really* motivates many of my colleagues, to prove someone is wrong). Again we see that the dilemma is that people can get the subjective feel of quantities of time by making any of a number of different kinds of comparison. We can also get at the relative dates of different events in many different ways. Perhaps we should re-cycle Einstein's aphorism and say that "Memory is what prevents us from thinking that everything happened at once." Time offers no time-markers. The temporal location of events can only be defined in relation to other events. So, in Crawley and Pring's experiment it would be easy to date Thatcher's premiership as being after the Silver Jubilee and during the declaration of the Falklands war. If their volunteers could have examined the entire questionnaire before answering each individual question, I believe that they could have used events as time-marks for each other and, much more accurately, worked out their order and, from this, also a reasonably accurate absolute calendar dating.

Mind maps of space and time

Subjective uncertainty about degrees of separation is not a peculiarity of time. It also works for space. Readers in need of a trivial diversion can check their intuitions about the extent of the world by comparing their subjective impressions of the distances between their capital city and others in the world against actual values.[2] It is very easy to quickly decide, for instance, that Moscow is nearer to London than Shanghai because, in our mental world map we know that Moscow is between the two. To have as accurate a subjective feeling of whether London is nearer to Shangai (5727 miles) than to Los Angeles (5455 miles) or Johannesburg (5616 miles) is much harder. The caricatures of the distorted "mental maps" of the world by citizens of different cities make this point very clearly. They add the point that the presence of locations on our mental maps depends more on our knowledge of something trivial about them than on their geo-political significance.

The point is that we can have mental representations or mental maps of time as well as space, that these can include many different kinds of information other than distance in space or time and that we seem, typically, to mentally represent or map time in spatial terms, as on graphs or dials. Given that we do this, and can choose the display schemes and co-ordinates that we use, we can change our perceptions of time, and possibly also the accuracy with which we estimate the passage of time by altering our mental systems of representation.

Perhaps we should yet again re-cycle Einstein's aphorism as "Space is what prevents everything being in the same place." When everything is data, and all the data are in the same place – such as in a mind – we need to plot some kind of mental map to establish the relative positions of things in space and time. As in spatial navigation, we can interchangeably use the observations of the stars, the position of the sun, the Earth's magnetic field (if we are pigeons) or dead reckoning between known landmarks and measures of our speed and travel time (if we are birds with less advanced biotechnology). Our subjective conscious feelings about our positions in space and time seem to justify this analogy by being easily conflated in clichés that also incorporate the relative significance of events. An event that has become inconsequential and so no longer culpable is long ago and far away or "in another country and besides the wench is dead" [10]. Our minds are devices for representing the world by whatever means they can and in any iconography. We develop that form of representation that allows us to make the most appropriate decisions. We interpret our worlds in terms of mental maps, and this leaves us free to use whatever cartographies we please, introducing as many dimensions of depiction as our minds can handle. In that sense, we can refer to events that are distant in space as well as in time as "Far East of yesterday" and even include probabilities of outcomes in our mental representations by referring to unlikely future outcomes as "Far short of tomorrow".

Notes

1 The Unchallenged Senior Time Lord in the UK is still, at the time of writing in 2013, Michel Treisman.
2 E.g. for London see http://www.timeanddate.com/worldclock/distances.

References

[1] Wearden, J. H., Wearden, A. J. and Rabbitt, P. M. (1997). Age and IQ effects on stimulus and response timing. *Journal of Experimental Psychology: Human Perception and Performance*, 23(4), 962–979.
[2] Draaisma, D. (2004). *Why Life Speeds up as you get Older: How memory shapes our past.* Cambridge, Cambridge University Press.
[3] Jünger, E. (1954). *Das Sandhurbuch*. Frankfurt am Main, Springer Verlag.

[4] Wearden, J. H. and Penton-Voak, I. S. (1995). Feeling the heat: Body temperature and the rate of subjective time, revisited. *The Quarterly Journal of Experimental Psychology*, 48, 129–141.

[5] Baddeley, A. D. (1966). Reduced body temperature and time estimation. *American Journal of Psychology*, 79, 475–479.

[6] James, W. (2011). *The Principles of Psychology*. Digireads.com.

[7] Hammond, C. (2013) *Time Warped: Unlocking the Mysteries of Time Perception*. Edinburgh, Canongate Books.

[8] Sully, J. (1881). *Illusion: A psychological study*. New York, Appleton.

[9] Crawley, S. E. and Pring, L. (2000). When did Mrs Thatcher resign? The effects of ageing on the dating of public events. *Memory*, 8, 111–121.

[10] Marlowe, C. (*c.* 1589). *The Jew of Malta*.

PART VI
Aging Well

26

WHAT CAN WE DO ABOUT ALL THIS?

It is alarming to find how skills we have not used for a while have rusted and that we can no longer do things that we once did well. While we are middle aged we can keep calm and be sure that this is not the beginning of some general mental collapse. We only need to decide whether to spend time rehabilitating our lapsed skills or learning more useful new ones. As we grow even older, unease sharpens into fear that changes may be irreversible. How can we repair our former and preserve our remaining mental talents?

Even late in old age, some of us continue to improve at things that we have done superbly well throughout our lives. In their seventies and eighties, Casals and Segovia still gave masterly performances and Picasso and Titian produced brilliant and original art. The distressingly interminable careers of vicious octogenarian dictators show how less admirable talents also endure. Late achievements by exceptional people make inspirational biographies, but do they mean that all of us can protect our islands of competence from rising tides of mediocrity?

Things that help to preserve our wits

This is probably the most important problem that cognitive gerontologists can tackle but remarkably few have researched it. Convincing surveys show that those who have had a stimulating youth and middle age are healthier, live longer, experience slower mental declines and are less likely to suffer dementias when they become old [1]. People with exceptionally intelligent and lively partners are also more likely to live longer and to stay competent [2]. Interpretations of these demographic data are not straightforward, because all the many factors that contribute to successful aging are tightly intertwined. Clever children are more likely to be born into affluent families and so gain better educations, have intellectually demanding careers, become affluent themselves, attract clever and stimulating partners with similar advantages, remain healthier throughout their lives and into old age and so to live and keep their wits about them for longer. Unequal beginnings shape lives that remain unfair to the end.

We now know that our experiences and the skills that we learn can alter our brains in lasting ways. Rats and monkeys raised in enriched environments with stimulation and playthings learn laboratory tasks faster than others brought up in bleak cages [3]. It was once thought that once neurones die they cannot be replaced and that even prolonged stimulation and practice does not have any effect on brain neurophysiology. We now know that throughout our lives our dwindling stock of aging and ailing neurones is supplemented by new nerve cells, born from endogenous stem cells [4]. There is hope that we will very soon understand this process well enough to repair damaged brains. The brains of rats that have led stimulating lives show fewer of the fatty deposits that are one of the signs of brain aging. As early as the 1960s, we learned that rats that are reared in enriched environments develop richer growths of spines and dendrites on their nerve cells and so more complex connections between them [5]. It is reasonable to assume that to have more, and more richly connected neurones makes a rodent brain a better computer.

There is similar evidence for humans. Widely publicised studies [6, 7] found that when experienced London taxi and bus drivers imagine and describe complex routes they have learned to navigate, they show marked activation of the right hippocampus, an area known to support spatial memory. A later study also found that bus and taxi drivers who had spent many years acquiring and using detailed knowledge of London had increased volumes of grey matter in areas of their brains and that the parts of their brains that were affected become active while they recall familiar routes [8]. On the other hand, brain changes that are associated with practising particular skills seem to be specific and to affect only the particular brain structures that support them. It has proved very difficult to find convincing evidence that practice on any particular task benefits the entire brain and so rehabilitates many different skills. What improvements can we make, how late in life can we make them and how long do they last?

Changing part or all of the brain

In one of the jollier experiments in cognitive gerontology, elderly volunteers were taught three-ball cascade juggling. Brain scans showed that practice was associated with long-lasting changes in grey matter in the middle temporal areas of their visual cortex and with more transient changes in their left hippocampal areas and in both their right and left nucleus accumbens [9]. (Unfortunately, for the less dextrous this happened only in those individuals who actually succeeded in mastering the juggling.) Several studies have found long-lasting increases in cortical thickness in experienced meditators and there is also evidence that learning to meditate improves the ability to concentrate for long periods [10]. These changes are not found in controls who do not meditate. Because of these and many other similar findings it is now accepted that even in elderly brains, stimulation and training can bring about changes in particular brain structures and in patterns of brain activity, and that that these changes may persist for at least 2 years. Unfortunately, bringing about beneficial changes in the entire brain is a different matter.

We should all be happy to realise that even when we become very old we can improve at any skill by dogged practice. It is much less clear whether improvements occur only on the specific tasks that we practice or whether they can also generalise to benefit different tasks on which we have not been trained.

Brain training programs

For over 150 years, neuroscientists have known that some mental abilities are supported by particular, often quite tiny, specialised areas of the brain. A Japanese neuroscientist, Ryuta Kawashima, was not the first to notice that when we carry out particular tasks the blood supply to the particular parts of the brain that support them briefly increases. He was also not the first to speculate that prolonged practice of skills might improve both local and general brain blood circulation and so also improve general brain health and mental competence. However, he was the first to develop a hand-held "Brain Training" games console that guides purchasers through simple tasks involving mental arithmetic, memory and decision speed, and scores their performance in terms of estimated "brain ages". I cannot find any way in which estimates of brain age can sensibly be derived from scores on any behavioural task. When they are calculated from average initial performance, as for the Kawashima tasks, it is unsurprising that middle-aged and elderly purchasers who are unused to hand-held game consoles have initial difficulties and so are shocked by frightening estimates of their current brain ages. Of course, they may soon become elated as their inevitable marked improvement is translated into a gratifyingly younger brain age.

A sad snag is that old and young people improve with practice at different rates and by different amounts. On choice reaction-time tasks, which are probably the simplest possible laboratory tasks, they have to press the correct one of two buttons as fast and accurately as possible to answer the appropriate one of two possible signal lamps. Such tasks are very convenient for studying practice because it takes only a few hundred trials for most of us to become as fast as we are ever going to be. It seems surprising that young adults show much smaller initial improvements in their reaction times than people over 70, but this is only because even on their first few dozen trials they are nearly as fast and accurate as they will become when they are practised to their limits. In contrast, elderly people improve markedly from a much lower initial level to a lower final peak. They just take longer to get to lower performance peaks. Practice always improves performance and, in this sense, does partly reverse some losses in efficiency that occur in old age, but we need more time and effort to reach lower peaks than we could once attain [11]. It may be encouraging for purchasers of the Kawashima device to be told that their prolonged improvements are evidence that their brain ages are steadily becoming more youthful, but I do not think that this is what is happening.

It is important to remember this methodological snag when we assess the claims of a thriving industry that currently markets courses to train elderly brains. Boosts to our morale are always good, and if the tasks we learn are also useful in our daily lives even modest gains may be well worth the effort. It is an excellent idea to devise programmes to re-train older people as fast and pleasantly as possible on any particular skills that make their lives more comfortable. It would be an even greater achievement to develop training programmes that do not just improve their competence on a single task but also on many others that have not been practised. Many of us have tried very hard to do this but I do not think we have yet convincingly succeeded.

An inconvenient reality is that older people only experience rapid improvements on very simple tasks such as choice reaction times or easy mental arithmetic. On more difficult skills, such as languages, mathematics or chess, they not only start from far lower baselines but improve much less and much more slowly than the young. Even after long practice, older people never reach the performance peaks that they could have attained when young. We should remember that the harder the skills are, the greater will be the differences in learning times and peak achievements between older and younger people. Of course, even very modest improvements in life-enhancing skills like languages or mental arithmetic are rewarding and worthwhile, but older people need more time to achieve them.

Sales of Kawashima's "Brain Trainer" exceeded three million units in a market in which sales of one million are exceptional. He was urged to make controlled trials to provide evidence that practice on his brain training tasks also generalised to improve performance on others. Ichiko Fuyuno [12] reviewing Kawashima's work for the prestigious scientific journal *Nature* reports that he declined to do this. Perhaps Kawashima is prudent. Other well-intentioned efforts to evaluate brain-training programs as tools to rehabilitate cognitive performance in older people have provoked surprisingly unpleasant disputes in our placid grey science.

Some disagreements between results

Adrian Owen, with distinguished colleagues based in Cambridge and Manchester took advantage of an offer by the BBC to sponsor a web-based experiment for a TV programme, *Bang Goes the Theory*. In 2010, they collected data from 11,430 mainly young and middle-aged people who had trained themselves for about three sessions a week for six weeks on computer-based tasks that involved memory, planning, spatial skills and selective attention. They published their results as a paper titled "Putting Brain Training to the Test" [13], in which they reported that, as always, people of all ages became much better on all the particular tasks that they practised. They were disappointed to find no evidence that these improvements extended to other, different, unpractised tasks, even when these were quite similar to those in the training battery. Immediately after their paper appeared, the editor of *Nature* received a letter demanding its withdrawal from a very distinguished North American scientist who had reported positive results with a different training program that is currently being marketed by a company for which he is scientific advisor.

In any science, disagreements between experiments are inevitable, frequent and essential for progress. This is because differences between results always identify important differences in assumptions, logic, experiments or analyses. Ceaseless challenging of evidence is the core of the scientific method. Science advances by disagreements and is crippled by attempts to suppress results or opinions.

My own attempts to find something useful to say about brain training taught me how easily conflicts of evidence can occur and why this field is so frustrating that many workers choose to avoid it. Results from the Manchester longitudinal studies show that even the very oldest volunteers' improved on all the tests of intelligence and memory that we gave them, even though they only experienced them once every 4 years. Dramatically, even those who had spent 10 minutes completing a particular intelligence test on their first session and had accidentally missed the next session 4 years later, did significantly better if they came back and did the same intelligence test again after 8 years with no intervening practice [14]. Ted Nettelbeck's students at the University of Adelaide report similar results. I, personally, am delighted and proud for our species to find that even 70 and 80-year-old brains can use 10 minutes experience of a particular intelligence test to do better on it nearly a decade later.

Unfortunately, this is not the only possibility. It is hard to be certain what is going on, because when volunteers first visited our laboratory they needed some time to adapt to a strange environment, to become less shy of us and of their fellow guinea pigs and to be reassured that none of the tasks that they would be given would be embarrassingly difficult and that they were all only moderately tedious. Apart from being less discombobulated when they took the tests again, many had also experienced an interleaved session at which they took a different test battery. Psychologists working with animals have learned that rats and monkeys who have learned one task then learn new tasks faster, not only because they have become more at ease with initially intimidating laboratory surroundings but because they have learned how to learn. Gradually realising what it is that an experimenter actually requires you to do and improving your general learning strategies are also plausible reasons for the long-lasting improvements that we found.

To discover "master tasks" that can also make us much better at everything else is a very old ambition for educationalists. Until the early twentieth century, school and university courses were based on the idea that general intellectual improvement is just what a solid education in classical Greek and Latin achieves. A recent meta-analysis of results from 23 different studies of schoolchildren made to discover training programmes that bring about general and lasting rather than specific and brief improvements in working memory found no evidence that this happens [15]. Many researchers have been frustrated to find that ability on any particular skill is surprisingly specific and often does not generalise even to other quite similar situations. My personal experience of this came from supervising a study by Belinda Winder who based her Manchester MSc thesis on an experiment to test the conviction of many elderly Manchester volunteers that they had preserved their everyday competence by constantly practising cryptic crossword puzzles. Belinda compared fanatical cryptic crossword experts aged between 70 and 85 against non-experts of their own age on memory tests, intelligence tests, vocabulary tests and tests of mental speed. She found that on all these unfamiliar tests, the crossword experts were no better than the non-experts. Tim Salthouse reports similar results [16]. It does seem surprisingly difficult to show that lifelong expertise in one skill necessarily generalises to improve or preserve ability in other, quite similar, skills.

Experiments on brain training have set out to answer several different kinds of question. One is whether practise on any particular task can generalise to improve the rate at which we learn others. Another is whether, even if training on a single task does not do this very well, training on several different tasks that, collectively, make a wider range of demands, may do the trick. A third question is whether and how practice may improve brain physiology, either by boosting local or general brain blood supply, and so improving the general well-being and efficiency of the entire brain. A fourth is whether we can devise mental aids, such as mnemonics or improved memory coding, that people can successfully apply in a variety of different situations. Even if we do find that practice brings about neurophysiological changes, we still have to check that these are actually associated with improvements in task performance and whether old age affects how great these gains are and how long they last.

Like many of us, Brian Stollery was discouraged by attempts to follow the first of these threads. To see whether practising one task affects the rate at which others can be learned, he gave 90 Manchester volunteers aged from 60 to 83 thirteen sessions of practice on nine different tasks involving memory and reaction times. John Bithell and his Oxford students have recently checked how well the rate at which volunteers improved on each of these tasks task predicted the rate at which they improved on any of the others. They found no evidence that rates of learning on different tasks were correlated, as we would expect if learning one of them helped volunteers to learn any of the others. On the other hand, volunteers' scores on each and all of three different tests of general intelligence did significantly predict how rapidly they improved at all these simple tests of memory and decision speed. This suggests that learned skills can be remarkably domain-specific in the sense that the ability to learn one is not related to the ability to learn others. It also suggests that people's levels of "general fluid intelligence", assessed by their scores on intelligence tests, can predict both how much and how quickly they improve in a wide range of different situations. Can we design training programmes to improve the general fluid abilities that support mental competence in most mental tasks?

Because intelligence tests are the best measures of general ability that we currently have, one approach might be to see whether training people to solve intelligence test problems also makes them better on many other different tasks. Many attempts to do this have found that while people trained on solving intelligence test problems always become better at them, this does not help them to learn new or to regain previous skills. Nevertheless, some studies have found that training people on working memory tasks [17] does slightly increase their scores on intelligence tests.

This raises the hope that there are basic, component abilities that are essential for solving all intelligence test problems and that one of these may be working memory – the ability to rapidly sort, hold and re-order information as we process it. In Chapter 16 on fluid intelligence, we noted that solving intelligence test problems requires a working memory system that can hold, sort and re-arrange new information as rapidly as it comes in. John Duncan [18] has shown that general fluid intelligence (gf) depends on working memory and on the executive control that allows plans to be formed, carried out and updated as they are needed. It seems possible that by training people on working memory and frontal executive tasks we may help them to improve on many other different tasks. This has been enthusiastically tested, but with very mixed and, in my view, rather discouraging results. One such study tested whether by training people on some working memory tasks we can also improve their performance on other, different working memory tasks. Young volunteers always improved on the particular tasks on which they were trained, but only became slightly better at tasks on which they had not been trained. This happened even when the change was only in the particular material they had to remember, such as digits or letters or visual as against auditory material. Older volunteers also improved on trained tasks but not at all on other, different tasks. It seems that age reduces even the small amount by which learning a particular skill improves performance on other quite similar skills. The authors suggest that this is due to age-related changes in the striatal area of the brain [19]. In another study, volunteers practised for 45 days on easy and more difficult working memory tasks. They improved on very similar ("near") working memory tasks but not on dissimilar ("far") working memory tasks [20]. The evidence is mixed, and reports of successful and unsuccessful studies seem almost to alternate. In a further study, 80 very elderly people practised a battery of working memory tasks twice a week for three months. The authors report that this improved their performance on other memory tasks for up to one year later [21]. In a large laboratory study, one group of 5487 people aged over 65 was given a computerised training program while another was given no formal training but only general social stimulation and personal attention [22]. It is an essential, but widely neglected, precaution to include an untrained but socially stimulated control group. This is because, as we noticed when discussing the long-term effects of practice on Manchester volunteers, improvements may happen because people get accustomed to the testers, the laboratory and each other rather than because they have learned specific skills. In this large and well-controlled study, generalisation of training to benefit new tasks seems to have been quite small, and to have happened only when the new tasks were very similar to the ones on which volunteers had been trained.

It would be extremely helpful to devise training programmes that improve people's competence across a number of different tasks, so many studies have tried to do this and many careful reviews have weighed their evidence. I have found an analysis of a large number of studies that tried to find a generalisation of working memory in schoolchildren [15]. A review of 300 different studies of training and transfer in older and younger people also concluded that practice on particular working memory tasks does benefit performance on other very similar tasks, but that the evidence that they could also improve performance on rather dissimilar tasks is less convincing [23]. A fair summary seems to be that failures to find a generalisation have been more frequent than successes and that old age reduces the extent to which even limited generalisation occurs.

These failures are very disappointing, but also extremely interesting. They suggest that our brains, like electronic computers, can devise, and run different, highly specialised programs that cope with particular tasks but not general or all-purpose programs that can handle a variety of quite different tasks. Different pathways in our neural circuitry are dedicated to different activities and often do not seem to overlap or to facilitate each other. This remarkable specificity of learning seems to offer more promising clues to how the brain stores and organises new information than the relatively weak evidence for transfer of training across different mental performances.

Once again, we must stress that ambiguous results and disagreements between studies always happen and are very rarely due to carelessness or misinterpretation of data. They are always interesting because they bring to light neglected differences in procedures that, when identified, lead to better experiments and explanations. This is essential for progress and can only happen if it is equally easy to publish not only positive results that agree with the hypotheses that experiments are designed to test and negative results that do not. As things stand, it is much harder to publish studies with negative results, even if they are exceptionally well-conducted and convincing. This is a pity, because successful replication is essential for confidence in experimental results, and failures of replication should be taken as instructive warnings that we do not yet understand what is going on. Another pervasive difficulty is that scientists often seem to suffer from "confirmation bias", both because positive findings encourage further work to explain and extend the results they obtain while negative findings seem to signal dead ends or to be warnings of methodological quagmires in which one may labour throughout a long career for the small satisfaction of getting niggling details right at last.

If we cannot yet devise training programmes that improve a wide range of skills, can we at least devise techniques that make it easier for elderly people to carry out necessary everyday tasks such as efficiently remembering and retrieving information that they need?

Memory improvement systems

The idea that information can be deliberately and actively organised in memory was a staple of courses run by Classical Roman and Greek teachers of rhetoric who drilled their students to construct mental images of locations [24]. These might be elaborate "Palaces of Memory" through which they could take mental strolls placing symbols for the things that they needed to recall in successive locations in the order in which they hoped to remember them. Or recalling familiar walks through city streets or countryside. Using imagined scenarios made familiar by long practice, politicians and lawyers could, without notes, fill even their longest speeches with ordered, detailed and accurate information and arguments. For example a politician who wanted to bring up the Naval Budget in a speech, immediately followed by its consequences for the price of bread, might imagine a golden anchor set at one location and a silver loaf at the next.

One legend of how well such systems can work is of a philosopher, Simonides, who survived when a thronged banquet was interrupted by an earthquake that collapsed the building and killed most of the other guests. He was able to guide identification of crushed corpses by exactly remembering the entire seating plan.

Some readers may be interested to know what they can do to improve their memories. The short answer is that all of many hundreds of different mnemonic systems do work quite well but the serious catch is that they are all tedious to learn and we may need to master inconveniently many of them because each is useful only for a particular, restricted, kind of information such as faces, names or sequences of numbers or playing cards. The classical Greek and Roman device of using memory walks is more flexible and general than most.

Most memory systems can be dramatically successful only with particular restricted kinds of material. George Miller [25] describes the grim virtuosity of a colleague who invented and mastered a system for recoding groups of binary digits into "chunks" of several at a time. He taught himself to do this so well that he could instantly repeat back strings of more than 40 ones and zeros in the exact order in which they had been rapidly spoken to him. This is very impressive but (apart from getting him cited in Miller's extremely famous paper) may have added little to the richness of his life. On the other hand, equally tedious and effective systems for remembering long sequences of playing cards do greatly enrich professional gamblers, entertainers and championship bridge players. Learning routines to remember very long strings of numbers may not be worthwhile for most of us, but forgetting short strings, such as telephone numbers is a daily vexation. One simple device is to practise translating digits, as you hear or read them, into images of everyday objects. To make this easier the name of each digit might rhyme with its object: for example, one is a bun, two is a shoe, three is a tree, four is a door, five is a hive, six is sticks, seven is heaven, eight is a plate, nine is a mine, ten is a hen and nought is a fort – or whatever else works best for you. Those who recommend such systems promise that they work very well and suggest that a good refinement is to make up images of these objects interacting in as entertainingly bizarre a way as possible. So 691480573 might be coded as a bundle of sticks dancing in a mine on the surface of a bun, which is running through a door, to sit on a plate by a model fort next to a hive by the gates of heaven where the tree of life radiantly stands. At which point I, personally, give up. Scores of books on memory improvement describe similar associational systems for remembering people's faces appropriately tagged with their names, or to remember lists of things to do. Some systems are much more pleasant to learn and use than others. In his introduction to an excellent collection of verse, *The Rattle Bag* [26], Ted Hughes describes a delightful way to learn poems by heart by associating successive lines with different, vivid, visual images directly derived from the text. Those who explore this will find that it works well and is much more fun to use and needs far less practice than most others.

There are many published collections of mnemonics for remembering strings of useful information such as the order of the planets from the Sun: My Very Excited Mother Just Served Us Nine Pies (Mercury, Venus, Earth, Mars, Jupiter, Saturn, Uranus, Neptune, and Pluto); the colours of the rainbow: Richard Of York Gave Battle In Vain (Red, Orange, Yellow, Green, Blue, Indigo Violet); the first eight US Presidents: Will A Jolly Man Make A Jolly Visitor? (Washington, Adams, Jefferson, Madison, Monroe, Adams, Jackson, Van Buren); or the families of UK Monarchs: No Plan Like Yours To Study History Wisely (Norman, Plantagenet, Lancaster, York, Tudor, Stuart, Hanover, Windsor). Similar aids are very useful to medical students who have to remember strings of arbitrary names such as for the bones in the hands and feet or the cranial nerves.

The modern curse of PINs and computer passwords has produced an urgent need for mnemonics. For short sequences, such as four-digit PINs, a handy dodge is to label each with the number of its position in the alphabet so that A becomes 1, B becomes 2, C becomes 3, D becomes 4 and so on. Obviously, we run out of tags for digits after I, which is 9. Zero is conveniently O. We can transpose any PIN into letters so that, for example, 4471 becomes DDGA. The next step is to turn this sequence into a memorably silly (or, if you must, a bizarely pornographic) phrase. For 4471 I find that "Dirty Dromedaries Gobble Apples" works very well. The proliferation of the number of different PINs in our lives can lead to occasional confusions but, on the whole, this technique usually sorts things out before a fatal third wrong entry. For the even greater curse of passwords for computer accounts, and for other situations where one can choose one's own identifying sequence of letters and digits, it is easy to find a favourite line of poetry, or an overworked phrase and use the first letter of each word. So "Mary, Mary, quite contrary, how does your garden grow" gives "MMqchdygg", which, especially if sprinkled with a few digits and !s and ?s, will be classified as Very Strong by all but the most fussy sites. Indeed there is a lot to be said for mnemonics and I remember sitting through a long afternoon while a very great deal of this was said by forty distinguished cognitive gerontologists each, in turn, lecturing the others on the advantages that mnemonic systems may bring to elderly people with mild memory impairments. General enthusiasm was sabotaged by an eminent troublemaker, Cameron Camp, who politely asked anybody in the room who, personally, used any mnemonic system for any purpose whatsoever to raise a hand. Nobody did. Of course, this only means that these brilliant colleagues already have infallible memories. Also, that gerontologists are very honest people. Also, that this was before PINs and passwords disrupted our working lives.

Why we can, and should, literally, take heart

At last some clear and positive answers. Those who take exercise in youth retain better cognitive ability in late middle and old age, even if they have since let their fitness slide. Comprehensive reviews conclude that aerobic exercise, at any point of the lifespan and even in late middle or old age improves ability at all mental tasks [27]. Aerobic exercise also benefits our cardiovascular and respiratory systems, improves blood and oxygen supply to the entire brain and is associated with better health, longer life and higher mental ability. Data from the British National Birth cohort, a very large group of people first recruited in 1946, found that those middle-aged volunteers aged from 35 to 50 who still took regular exercise experienced significantly less decline in memory ability as they grew older than more lethargic people of the same age [28]. The other side of this coin was illustrated by self-reports of civil servants in a very large Whitehall study of civil servants headed by Michael Marmot. Low physical activity was a significant risk factor for faster decline for intelligence and general cognitive function in middle age [29]. This raises a crucial chicken and egg question: whether findings that exercise is associated with prolonged mental competence in old age mean that people who are more intelligent tend to have a more active lifestyle and also, in general, to be more prosperous, better cared for and to have better health habits. Or whether, independently of these socio-economic and educational advantages, taking more exercise is the effective factor in preserving our mental abilities. A skilful statistical analysis shows that people stay clever because they take regular exercise rather than vice versa [30].

In summary, there is overwhelming evidence that taking more exercise in youth and middle age improves and maintains memory and intelligence and the ability to learn new things, and that even exercise programmes that are begun late in a lethargic life can improve and preserve our abilities. It is a great pity that sedentary old people like myself are intimidated by conflicting media accounts of the amount of daily exercise that we should take to achieve health benefits. I was stunned into a decade of inertia by being asked by Lynn McInnes in Newcastle and Nuala Bent in Manchester to be a front-man to greet people who had responded to their advertisements for older volunteers who believed that they were still exceptionally fit. Over three hundred remarkable veterans turned up and some of the most embarrassing moments of my career occurred when I was wheeled out to greet groups of these enthusiasts and tell them what we were trying to do and what we would ask of them. This meant confronting scores of astonishing old athletes; bulky weight trainers, tiny gnarled cyclists and stringy runners. They were all very, very, very polite, but the memory of the smiles they could not suppress when I walked into the room still stings.

We measured their aerobic fitness on a stationary bicycle and discovered that nearly all of them were as aerobically fit as they thought they were. As a group, they were also significantly better on all the mental tests that we gave them than the other, more sedentary volunteers in our longitudinal study. We did not publish these data because we had not learned how to take into account the effects of all the confounding socio-economic factors, other than exercise, that might explain the differences we found. A model statistical analysis by Lövdén and Ghisletta [31] showed us how to do this and to test whether exercise improves mental abilities rather than vice versa.

The association of exercise with mental ability in old age gave me pause for self-examination, but I was alarmed and depressed by the remarkable amounts of exercise that these amazing elderly took. Shocked by the contrast with my own lifestyle, I decided that since I could not possibly manage to do nearly as well and so, since I was clearly destined to die soon and stupid, I might at least enjoy the comfort of indolence. This was a very bad decision and I am grateful to better information for putting me right.

Current medical guidelines for improvement hover about the estimate of an average of 30 minutes of moderate aerobic exercise a day but, from time to time, we are challenged by advice that more strenuous commitment is needed. This is scary news for lazy old academics, but a wider survey of the literature is more encouraging. Very modest increases in activity have been shown to have beneficial effects. Even taking long daily walks lasting 20 minutes rather than short walks lasting 10 minutes has a measurable effect on survival and on keeping our wits. Much more may indeed be much better but, as very recent work shows, even moving, preferably briskly, around the house more than we currently do makes a useful difference as an alternative to lethal sitting that shortens life expectancy and so also rapidly dims the minds of those of us who, after a lifetime of inertia continue to crouch over our laptops for eight or more hours a day.

The type of exercise we take is important. Aerobic exercise such as cycling, running, rowing or even brisk walking is best. Any exercise that makes us gasp and markedly raises our heart rate for prolonged periods works very well. In contrast, nearly all studies of the effects of weight training, stretching and exercise to improve balance and posture have found that these are less effective for improving mental abilities. I am surprised, because taking up exercise programmes of this kind results in improvements in mobility, flexibility and motivation that are both encouraging in themselves and allow us to overcome problems of stiffness and muscle weakness and loss of vitality. These difficulties prevent us from improving our aerobic efficiency, even by a little, simply by getting about a little more, and involving ourselves in activities as un-strenuous as light gardening and housework that we shun if we have been weakened and stiffened by years of indolence. It came as a pleasant surprise to find that even a little training in flexibility can make daily life more comfortable, promote a more positive view of life and, most of all, allow us again to do many pleasant things that we have been avoiding, such as going out more, walking for longer, climbing long flights of stairs that had begun to seem daunting and gaining feelings of increased independence and control. Indeed, old age is not for sissies but just a little more physical engagement in life, especially if it involves aerobic activity gets us into better shape to cope with it.

References

[1] Schaie, K. W. (1984). Midlife influences upon intellectual functioning in old age. *International Journal of Behavioral Development*, 7, 463–478.
[2] Lindenberger, U. and Baltes, P. B. (1997). Intellectual functioning in old and very old age: Cross-sectional evidence from the Berlin Aging Study. *Psychology and Aging*, 12, 410–432.

[3] Leggio, M. G., Mandolesi, L., Federico, F., Spirito, F., Ricci, B., Gelfo, F. and Petrosini, L. (2005). Environmental enrichment promotes improved spatial abilities and enhanced dendritic growth in the rat. *Behavioural Brain Research*, 163, 78–90.

[4] Kempermann, G., Gast, D. and Gage, F. H. (2002). Neuroplasticity in old age: Sustained fivefold induction of hippocampal neurogenesis by longterm environmental enrichment. *Annals of Neurology*, 52, 135–143.

[5] Rosenzweig, M. R. and Bennett, E. L. (1996). Psychobiology of plasticity: effects of training and experience on brain and behaviour. *Behavioural Brain Research*, 78, 57–65.

[6] Maguire, E. A., Frackowiak, R. S. and Frith, C. D. (1997). Recalling routes around London: Activation of the right hippocampus in taxi drivers. *The Journal of Neuroscience*, 17, 7103–7110.

[7] Maguire, E. A., Gadian, D. G., Johnsrude, I. S., Good, C. D., Ashburner, J., Frackowiak, R. S. and Frith, C. D. (2000). Navigation-related structural change in the hippocampi of taxi drivers. *Proceedings of the National Academy of Sciences*, 97, 4398–4403.

[8] Maguire, E. A., Woollett, K. and Spiers, H. J. (2006). London taxi drivers and bus drivers: a structural MRI and neuropsychological analysis. *Hippocampus*, 16, 1091–1101.

[9] Boyke, J., Driemeyer, J., Gaser, C., Büchel, C. and May, A. (2008). Training-induced brain structure changes in the elderly. *The Journal of Neuroscience*, 28, 7031–7035.

[10] Lazar, S. W., Bush, G., Gollub, R. L., Fricchione, G. L., Khalsa, G. and Benson, H. (2000). Functional brain mapping of the relaxation response and meditation. *Neuroreport*, 11, 1581–1585.

[11] Rabbitt, P. M. A. (1993). Crystal quest: A search for the maintenance of practised skills into old age. In Baddeley, A. D. and Weiskrantz, L. (Eds), pp. 188–230, *Attention, Selection Awareness and Control. A tribute to Donald Broadbent*. Oxford, Clarendon Press, OUP.

[12] Fuyuno, I. (2007). Brain craze. *Nature*, 447, 18–20.

[13] Owen, A. M., Hampshire, A., Grahn, J. A., Stenton, R., Dajani, S., Burns, A. S., Howard, R. J. and Ballard, C. G. (2010). Putting brain training to the test. *Nature*, 465, 775–778.

[14] Rabbitt, P., Lunn, M., Ibrahim, S. and McInnes, L. (2009). Further analyses of the effects of practice, dropout, sex, socio-economic advantage, and recruitment cohort differences during the University of Manchester longitudinal study of cognitive change in old age. *The Quarterly Journal of Experimental Psychology*, 62, 1859–1872.

[15] Melby-Lervåg, M. and Hulme, C. (2013). Is working memory training effective? A meta-analytic review. *Developmental Psychology*, 49, 270–291.

[16] Hambrick, D. Z., Salthouse, T. A. and Meinz, E. J. (1999). Predictors of crossword puzzle proficiency and moderators of age–cognition relations. *Journal of Experimental Psychology: General*, 128, 131–142.

[17] Jaeggi, S. M., Buschkuehl, M., Jonides, J. and Perrig, W. J. (2008). Improving fluid intelligence with training on working memory. *Proceedings of the National Academy of Sciences*, 105, 6829–6833.

[18] Duncan, J. (2010). *How Intelligence Happens*. New Haven and London, Yale University Press.

[19] Dahlin, E., Neely, A. S., Larsson, A., Bäckman, L. and Nyberg, L. (2008). Transfer of learning after updating training mediated by the striatum. *Science*, 320, 1510–1512.

[20] Li, S. C., Schmiedek, F., Huxhold, O., Röcke, C., Smith, J. and Lindenberger, U. (2008). Working memory plasticity in old age: Practice gain, transfer, and maintenance. *Psychology and Aging*, 23, 731–742.

[21] Buschkuehl, M., Jaeggi, S. M., Hutchison, S., Perrig-Chiello, P., Däpp, C., Müller, M., Breil, F., Hoppeler, H. and Perrig, W. J. (2008). Impact of working memory training on memory performance in old-old adults. *Psychology and Aging*, 23(4), 743–753.

[22] Smith, G. E., Housen, P., Yaffe, K., Ruff, R., Kennison, R. F., Mahncke, H. W. and Zelinski, E. M. (2009). A cognitive training program based on principles of brain plasticity: Results from the improvement in memory with plasticity-based adaptive cognitive training study. *Journal of the American Geriatric Society*, 57, 594–603.

[23] Gross, A. L., Parisi, J. M., Spira, A. P., Kueider, A. M., Ko, J. Y., Saczynski, J. S., Samus, Q. M. and Rebok, G. W. (2012). Memory training interventions for older adults: A meta-analysis. *Aging & Mental Health*, 16, 722–734.

[24] Yates, F. A. (1992). *The Art of Memory (Vol. 64)*. New York, Random House.

[25] Miller, G. A. (1956). The magical number seven, plus or minus two: Some limits on our capacity for processing information. *Psychological Review*, 63, 81–97.

[26] Hughes, T. and Heaney, S. (1984). *The Rattle Bag*. London, Faber and Faber.

[27] Dik, M. G., Deeg, D. J., Visser, M. and Jonker, C. (2003). Early life physical activity and cognition at old age. *Journal of Clinical and Experimental Neuropsychology*, 25, 643–653.

[28] Hillman, C. H., Erickson, K. I. and Kramer, A. F. (2008). Be smart, exercise your heart: Exercise effects on brain and cognition. *Nature Reviews Neuroscience*, 9, 58–65.

[29] Richards, M., Hardy, R. and Wadsworth, M. E. (2003). Does active leisure protect cognition? Evidence from a national birth cohort. *Social Science & Medicine*, 56, 785–792.

[30] Singh-Manoux, A., Hillsdon, M., Brunner, E. and Marmot, M. (2005). Effects of physical activity on cognitive functioning in middle age: Evidence from the Whitehall II prospective cohort study. *American Journal of Public Health*, 95, 2252–2258.

[31] Lövdén, M., Ghisletta, P. and Lindenberger, U. (2005). Social participation attenuates decline in perceptual speed in old and very old age. *Psychology and Aging*, 20, 423–434.

INDEX